The Royal Engineers at Chatham 1750–2012

The Royal Engineers at Chatham 1750–2012

Peter Kendall

ENGLISH HERITAGE

Published by English Heritage, The Engine House, Fire Fly Avenue, Swindon SN2 2EH
www.english-heritage.org.uk
English Heritage is the Government's statutory adviser on all aspects of the historic environment.

The views expressed in this book are those of the author and not necessarily those of English Heritage.

First published 2012

ISBN 978-1-84802-098-6

Product code 51662

British Library Cataloguing in Publication data
A CIP catalogue record for this book is available from the British Library.

The right of Peter Kendall to be identified as author of this work has been asserted by him in accordance with the Copyright, Designs and Patents Act 1988

For more information about images from the English Heritage Archive, contact Archive Services Team, The Engine House, Fire Fly Avenue, Swindon SN2 2EH; telephone (01793) 414600.

Brought to publication by Robin Taylor, Publishing, English Heritage.

Typeset in Charter 9.5 on 11.75

Edited by Lesley Adkins
Indexed by Alan Rutter
Page layout by Hybert Design

Printed in the UK by Butler Tanner & Dennis Ltd

Frontispiece
Aerial view of the garrison area at Chatham, looking north-west towards Upnor, showing the River Medway, the dockyard, the fortifications (now wooded areas) and the open field of fire with the naval war memorial. (© English Heritage, 23188/17 04/08/2003)

CONTENTS

Fortification is the art of enabling a small body of men to resist for a considerable time the attack of a greater number.

Vauban

FOREWORD

Engineer soldiers have trained at a military school in Chatham for at least 200 years, and as part of the bicentenary celebrations for the Royal School of Military Engineering, founded in 1812, the Corps of Royal Engineers has been pleased to co-operate with English Heritage on this book.

If you ask the public about Chatham, they are most likely to describe it as a dockyard town, one that has proud associations with the Royal Navy, rather than as a garrison town for the Army – even though the dockyard closed in 1984. Without the need to defend the dockyard the army might never have come to Chatham, but having done so it became not only a major fortified place, but also a centre for recruits embarking on overseas service in the British Empire and a centre for returning soldiers. Of course, the historic dockyard remains the jewel in the crown of the many heritage assets within the Medway area, but the presence of so many land-based troops has left its own indelible mark on Chatham's character and appearance.

The Royal Engineers moved their headquarters to Chatham from Woolwich in 1856, and ever since it has remained the spiritual home of the Corps. Today, the presence of the Royal Engineers preserves the long and proud tradition of service to the nation exhibited by the Medway towns. The year 1856 was a watershed moment for the British army because the shortcomings exposed in the Crimean War began to be addressed. From then on soldiers were given ever more specialist training in the increasingly technological demands of warfare. The Royal Engineers were leaders in such developments, and at Chatham their school and headquarters were at the leading edge of instruction in military technology and tactics, a role that continues today. Those traditions can still be seen in the historical sites that are described in this book, but they are also a living and developing feature of 21st-century military engineering. With our private sector partners, Holdfast Training Services Ltd, the Corps has embarked on a process of investment that will enable the Royal Engineers to train for the diverse and complex roles demanded of them by present-day military service. The Chatham sites will see further change as part of this process, but as this book demonstrates, this is a continuation of a theme that has been ongoing since 1812 and earlier.

Brompton Barracks is host to a number of memorials commissioned to commemorate the thousands of Royal Engineers who gave their lives in the conflicts of the late 19th and 20th centuries. Their 18th-century forbears who fought in the foreign wars on which the British Empire was founded have no such monuments, though their lives are perpetuated by what they constructed. In England few places can now match the impressive combination of fortifications, the Lines and barracks as seen at Chatham. This is how we should remember their lives and the contribution they made at home and overseas.

This book draws heavily on pictorial information produced by the Royal Engineers, some of it appearing in print for the first time. The quality of the historic maps and plans drawn by military surveyors in an age before computer-aided design is quite simply inspiring. When photography was first introduced, the Royal Engineers as a scientific corps were quick to adopt this new way of recording and studying their own works. This has left us the fantastic resource of historic information on which this book draws so magnificently. As a result, we can see and almost touch the activities of 19th-century sappers as they trained at Chatham. The heritage and tradition which fuel pride and loyalty are tangible within the Chatham area. It is never easy to prepare young men and women for what may require the ultimate sacrifice, but belonging to a longstanding and ongoing tradition of service is part of this. Books such as this one describe those traditions so as to inform serving soldiers, the retired community and the wider public. This is reason enough to commend Peter Kendall's book, but better still it provides a fascinating account of the contribution of the Royal Engineers at Chatham and from there to the wider world.

Colonel Seán Harris, FInstRE
Regimental Colonel Royal Engineers
Brompton Barracks
Chatham

ACKNOWLEDGEMENTS

This book is not all my own work. It has benefited from the advice and information that lots of people have supplied to me, much of it in the course of my work for English Heritage. I hope to thank as many people as possible by name, but to anybody I have overlooked I wish nevertheless to confirm my sincere gratitude.

Colleagues at English Heritage, past and present, have been most helpful. It was Jonathan Coad who first introduced me to Chatham and who has encouraged me to publish my research. Without the support and encouragement of Dr Andy Brown, this would not have been possible. I have discussed Chatham on many occasions with my many colleagues, but chiefly with Magnus Alexander, Wayne Cocroft, Veronica Fiorato, Alan Johnson, Posy Metz, Paul Pattison, Roger J C Thomas and Christopher Young. I thank you all.

My work has also benefited from collaboration with the local authorities who deal with Chatham. Staff from Medway Council have contributed much, including Alice Brockway, Joanne Cable, Stephen Gaimster, Martin McKay, Nicola Moy and Edward Sargent. The Heritage Conservation team at Kent County Council have been my constant partners, first under Dr John Williams and then through Lis Dyson. In particular I wish to thank Dr Paul Cuming, Ben Found and Simon Mason.

Fort Amherst is under the control of an independent trust, and its members have been invaluable to me. I wish particularly to thank Keith Gulvin who has provided me with encouragement and information, as well as Alan Anstee and Bill Fowler. Karyn Wood as a trustee has been of great help through her running of the Kent History Forum website from which several lines of research began. Most recently Martin Rogers has discussed the fort with me and, as a former sapper, has provided new thoughts about it.

Within the military estate I must thank a large number of the Corps of Royal Engineers who have taken time to indulge my interest in them and their predecessors. In particular I thank Tony Purcell, the former property manager at Brompton barracks, for all his information and anecdotes. David Bowen and Paul Fountaine have provided a vital link to the present Chatham garrison. The Royal Engineers Institution has given me its support, and the Regimental Colonel of the Royal Engineers, Seán Harris, has done likewise and provided the foreword to this book. Without the help and generosity of the staff of the Royal Engineers Museum, Library and Archive I could not have completed my work, and I express my thanks to its director, Richard Dunn, to the assistant curator, Amy Adams, and to the other staff there.

Today the Royal Engineers have a private sector partner in the shape of Holdfast Training Services Ltd, and they have generously supported the production of this book through funding, and also with the supply of information and photographs about the 21st-century Royal School of Military Engineering. I wish to thank Nicki Lockhart and Tim Redfern for their assistance.

I have the pleasure of also working in the historic dockyard at Chatham, and there I have drawn on the advice of the staff responsible for that great site. I must thank Bill Ferris, Nigel Howard and Richard Holdsworth for reminding me that without the dockyard, there would have been no army garrison. The dockyard sits at the centre of a proposed world heritage site, and many of the people I have already thanked are also involved in that proposal. I do however wish to thank some additional fellow members of a steering committee. Steve Notley has represented the defence lands organisation and has discussed most of the Medway sites with me. Lindsey Morgan has been of great help, both in her work for Mid Kent College and as the head of the Chatham World Heritage Partnership. Mid Kent College was responsible for an exemplary project at Lower Lines that has been drawn on for this book, and I want to thank Jane Jones and all of the other staff there for their co-operation and support.

So far I have mainly thanked people from organisations who I meet through my official duties. Many other individuals have given equally of their time and knowledge. Victor Smith is an acknowledged expert on the defence history of Kent and fortifications and, with the late Andrew Saunders, has done much to stimulate my interest in the subject. Ben Levick not only assisted me with photography, but has given freely of his ever-growing knowledge about Brompton. David Evans provided a report on the Upnor ordnance depot, which was very useful.

When archaeological services have been required at Chatham, these have most frequently been provided by Canterbury Archaeological Trust, and I have valued my collaboration with their director, Paul Bennett, and his staff members, most particularly Mick Diack and James Holman. Other archaeologists have told me about their work, and Alan Ward has always been ready to help and provide his ideas, as has Graham Keevill.

I have already acknowledged the invaluable assistance from the Royal Engineers library, but many other holders of archive material have also helped me with information. I cannot thank everyone who has assisted me by name, but I would like to single out for special thanks the Medway Archives and Local Studies Centre, then under the overall management of Simon Curtis, and the archivist Alison Cable. The staff at The National Archives and the British Library have helped me with my research, and these organisations have permitted the reproduction of material held by them without which this book would be so impoverished. The National Maritime Museum, the Imperial War Museum and the Royal Collection have also helped in this fashion, for which I am very grateful. For Maidstone Museum & Bentlif Art Gallery, Giles Guthrie has permitted use of some of their images, for which I likewise offer my thanks. The librarian for the Duke of Northumberland's estate at Alnwick castle gave me permission to use an early map of Chatham, for which I am also grateful, and Avondale has kindly allowed the use of the aerial photograph of Fort Horsted.

Some photographs used in this book have been freely provided by individuals, and I must in particular thank Tony Pullen for his underground photography of Fort Amherst. Pictures of re-enactors at Fort Amherst were supplied by the Fort Amherst Heritage Trust.

Not quite finally I must thank those who have worked with me on the production of this book, turning it from a concept to reality. Vince Griffin and Peter Dunn at English Heritage have provided illustrations. Lesley Adkins was my editor and has made a book out of my rough text, and I thank her most sincerely. Last but not least I am very grateful to Robin Taylor for his constant support and advice.

Finally, I wish to thank my family, in particular my parents for always supporting me in pursuing a career in archaeology. To my wife, Jennifer, I owe my very final words of thanks for the way in which she has tolerated my Chatham absences and obsessions.

ABBREVIATIONS

BL	British Library
EH	English Heritage
NCO	non-commissioned officer
NMM	National Maritime Museum
OS	Ordnance Survey
RE	Royal Engineers
RSME	Royal School of Military Engineering
SME	School of Military Engineering
TNA	The National Archives

see also Glossary (p 166)

MEASUREMENTS

Imperial measurements are mostly used in this book, as that was the standard system for much of Chatham's history.

1 inch (in) = 254 millimetres (mm)

1 foot (ft) = 0.30 metres (m)

1 yard (yd) = 0.91 metres

1 mile = 1.609 kilometres (km)

Introduction

Chatham in Kent lies on the River Medway, and for over 400 years the dockyard and fortifications have played a crucial role in the defence of the nation. First came the dockyard, and soon afterwards fortifications were established to defend it, but later these developed to serve much broader military requirements. The term 'Chatham Garrison' describes the fortifications and barracks for the army, and with the dockyard these formed an extensive militarised zone on the east bank of the Medway, north of the present-day town centre of Chatham. Taken together, the dockyard, the Gunwharf, fortifications and barracks make up one of the greatest military complexes anywhere in the world.

To understand the decision to use Chatham for a garrison, it is necessary to consider the strategies for defending south-east England and the impact of topography. The tidal River Medway was well suited for use by the early navy. Its mudflats on which to careen ships were well upstream from the river entrance at Sheerness and beyond threat of enemy attack – or so it was thought. Dockyards were a critical resource for a maritime nation that relied on its naval strength as the main instrument of overseas influence, and it was essential that they were defended.

South-east England presented an obvious target for an enemy state intent on invasion,

Location map showing Chatham in relation to continental Europe. (© English Heritage)

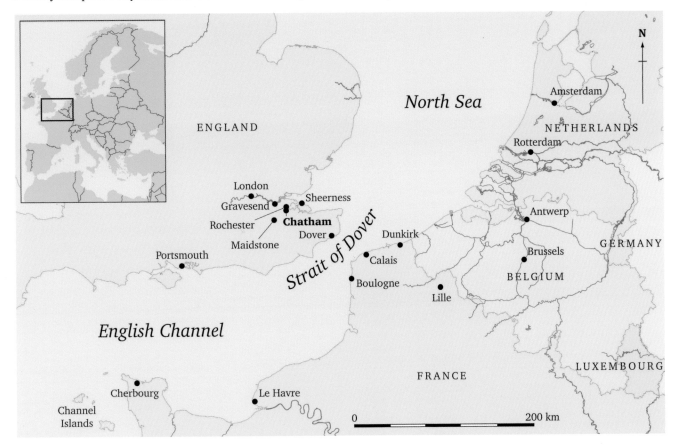

1

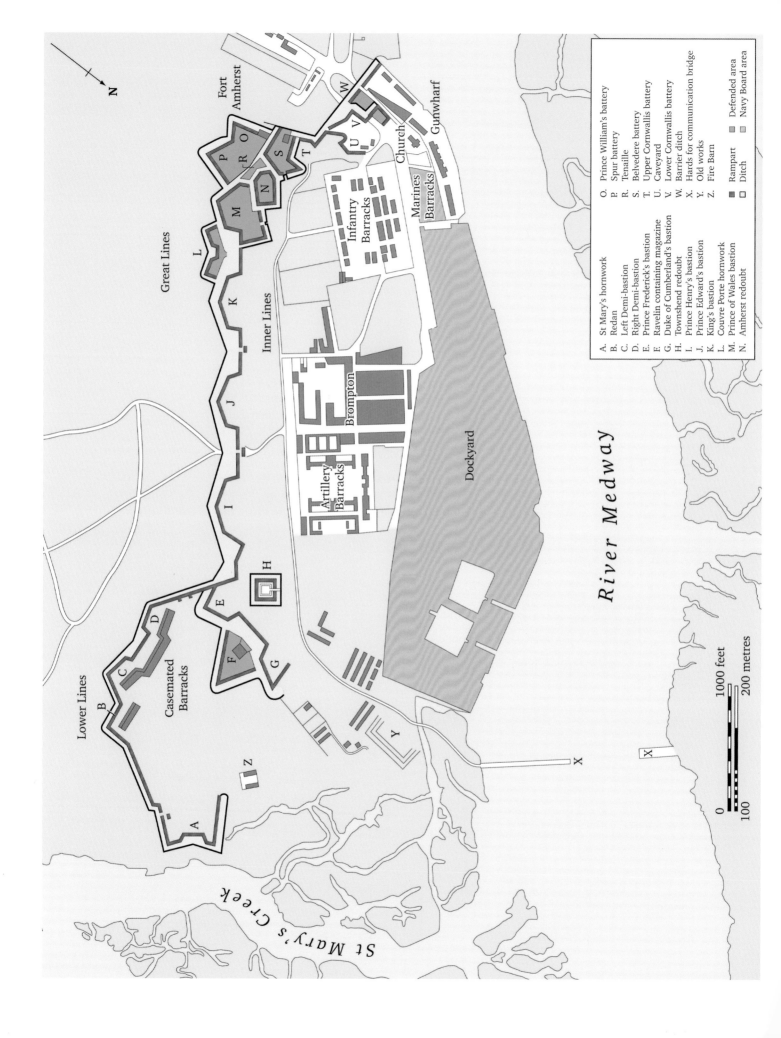

N

Lower Lines

Great Lines

Fort Amherst

Inner Lines

Casemated Barracks

Artillery Barracks

Brompton

Infantry Barracks

Marines Barracks

Church

Gunwharf

Dockyard

River Medway

St Mary's Creek

A. St Mary's hornwork
B. Redan
C. Left Demi-bastion
D. Right Demi-bastion
E. Prince Frederick's bastion
F. Ravelin containing magazine
G. Duke of Cumberland's bastion
H. Townshend redoubt
I. Prince Henry's bastion
J. Prince Edward's bastion
K. King's bastion
L. Couvre Porte hornwork
M. Prince of Wales bastion
N. Amherst redoubt

O. Prince William's battery
P. Spur battery
R. Tenaille
S. Belvedere battery
T. Upper Cornwallis battery
U. Caveyard
V. Lower Cornwallis battery
W. Barrier ditch
X. Hards for communication bridge
Y. Old works
Z. Fire Barn

Rampart   Defended area
Ditch   Navy Board area

1000 feet
0
200 metres
100

with the shortest crossing from continental Europe and several suitable landing beaches. On top of this the capital, London, was vulnerable from an invasion landing here. The dockyards on the River Thames (Woolwich and Deptford) and on the River Medway (Chatham and Sheerness) represented a concentration of military resources that were always liable to be attacked, and the road from Dover to London, a strategic route for any invader, crossed the Medway at Rochester over the lowest bridge on that river.

Invasion was most likely on the coast of Kent or Sussex, from where any invader could have advanced rapidly on London, so the garrison based at Chatham not only defended the dockyard, but also acted as a base from which to react against an enemy force. An invader would therefore need to attack the Chatham garrison or else risk a flanking counterattack on their lines of communication as they advanced towards London.

The winding nature of the tidal River Medway was initially considered to be of great assistance in the defence of Chatham dockyard, and so guns were positioned to fire towards the river to deter any invasion attempt. Events demonstrated that this was a misguided policy. Seizing control of the high ground to the east and south of the dockyard would have enabled invaders to bombard it with impunity. Because the dockyard was vulnerable to assault from its landward side by troops who might come ashore elsewhere, consideration was given to defences against such an attack by land. During the active life of the dockyard, the focus of its defence therefore switched from control of the river to the surrounding high ground and then to a combination of both. Finally, the arrival of aerial attack introduced new vulnerabilities, which required protective measures.

Topography dictated where fortifications were built and how these developed, and within the fortifications, barracks and camps were built to house the soldiers who were responsible for manning the defences and attacking any invaders. This major military presence heavily influenced the development of Chatham, which should be seen as both a dockyard and a garrison town. This area was never exclusively for the military, since the residents of Chatham and Brompton lived and worked alongside them, but the local economy rose and fell with the state of the military activity, and the military quite literally shaped the landscape of the place, right down to where the residents were able to live.

For much of the time from 1750 the army and navy were the responsibility of separate departments of government. The Navy Board built and administered the dockyard at Chatham, while the Ordnance Board constructed fortifications and barracks and supplied guns for both sea and land service from sites known as gunwharves. The aim of this book is an examination of the history of the fortifications, barracks and other facilities in the Chatham area from 1750 to the present day, against a background of the dockyard, the development of the civilian settlements and the life and training of the soldiers. The main focus is the complex development of these sites and the additional roles they came to perform. This book also examines the chronological development of the Ordnance Board sites at Chatham, which were mainly associated with the army, and develops earlier research by the author,[1] as well as including new discoveries and the results of further study.

Technological and strategic advances are reflected in the development of the sites, alongside changes in how the serving soldier was viewed by the public, which led to barracks reform. Although the focus is on Chatham, this narrative also illustrates the rise of Great Britain to a world power through near-constant warfare in the 18th century and colonial expansion in the 19th, and the impact this had upon the army.

Today, many of the original military facilities have been closed, including the naval dockyard. The only major military establishment remaining in Chatham is the prestigious Royal School of Military Engineering, the home of the Corps of Royal Engineers. This was founded in 1812 as the Royal Engineer Establishment, with 2012 being its bicentenary – 200 years of remarkable history.

(opposite) Plan of the fortifications at Chatham to show the component parts in the early 19th century. (© English Heritage)

1

Early Days

Rochester was the major historic settlement on the River Medway. Here the Romans had a defended town at the lowest point where the main road from Dover to London could be carried over the river by a bridge. Subsequently the great medieval castle was built to control this bridging point. Although the naval anchorage associated with Chatham dockyard ran from downstream of Rochester bridge, the castle could not defend the dockyard, and it was derelict before the main period of Chatham's garrison.

At Chatham, evidence for an Iron Age arable landscape comes from late Iron Age pottery recovered during recent archaeological excavation of ditches within the dockyard, the alignment of which corresponds to field boundaries on early 18th-century maps.[1] A Roman

Fig 1.1
A map of the Medway area showing the position of forts and other defences.
(© English Heritage)

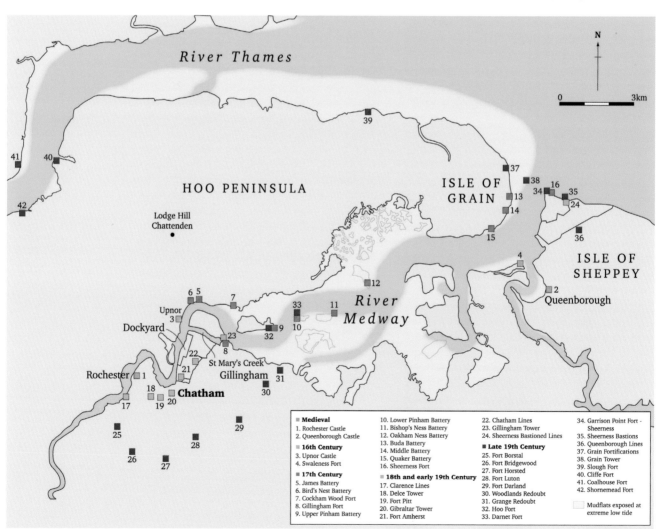

Medieval
1. Rochester Castle
2. Queenborough Castle

16th Century
3. Upnor Castle
4. Swaleness Fort

17th Century
5. James Battery
6. Bird's Nest Battery
7. Cockham Wood Fort
8. Gillingham Fort
9. Upper Pinham Battery

10. Lower Pinham Battery
11. Bishop's Ness Battery
12. Oakham Ness Battery
13. Buda Battery
14. Middle Battery
15. Quaker Battery
16. Sheerness Fort

18th and early 19th Century
17. Clarence Lines
18. Delce Tower
19. Fort Pitt
20. Gibraltar Tower
21. Fort Amherst

22. Chatham Lines
23. Gillingham Tower
24. Sheerness Bastioned Lines

Late 19th Century
25. Fort Borstal
26. Fort Bridgewood
27. Fort Horsted
28. Fort Luton
29. Fort Darland
30. Grange Redoubt
31. Hoo Fort
33. Darnet Fort

34. Garrison Point Fort - Sheerness
35. Sheerness Bastions
36. Queenborough Lines
37. Grain Fortifications
38. Grain Tower
39. Slough Fort
40. Cliffe Fort
41. Coalhouse Fort
42. Shornemead Fort

Mudflats exposed at extreme low tide

building is known from Fort Amherst, with archaeological discoveries elsewhere pointing to further Roman and Saxon occupation. It is only with 1066 and the Domesday survey that a clearer idea of the nature of early Chatham is possible, comprising a small settlement with a church and mill and an economy based on agriculture (16 ploughs) and fishing (6 fisheries).[2] The Domesday valuation included woodland, but archaeological evidence shows that much of the escarpment east of the river had been cleared for agriculture, and its slopes had numerous Saxon burial mounds.[3] Though very much rebuilt, the parish church of St Mary's retains some early medieval fabric and marks the heart of old Chatham. The watermill and millpond shown on later maps close to the church also confirm that this was the nucleus of the settlement.

The Roman road left Rochester in the direction of Canterbury and hugged the edge of the River Medway before turning up the south side of the major river valley (now known as The Brook) to connect with Chatham Hill. This alignment is today followed by Chatham High Street and takes in the area known as Chatham Intra. It is probable that there was always some linear settlement along this road from the Roman period. Development between Chatham and Rochester was not continuous as it is today, and indeed in 1078 Bishop Gundulph of Rochester founded the hospital of St Bartholomew for the treatment of lepers. The hospital, which still survives, would have been placed away from the centres of population.

Philip MacDougall (1999) has covered the early history of Chatham, though a detailed study of the town in the medieval period has yet to be done. After the Norman Conquest, the manor of Chatham passed to Bishop Odo, but on his disgrace the king gave it with that of Leeds in Kent to Hamon de Crevecoeur. Chatham was the main residence of this family until the building of Leeds castle. The same family endowed Leeds priory and transferred to it 30 acres of land from the Chatham manor, including the parish church. When the church was destroyed by fire, the Prior of Leeds chose not to fund its rebuilding. This task fell to the villagers who could ill afford it, and in 1352 there was a papal indulgence remitting penance for anyone willing to make a financial contribution to the rebuild.

It can be conjectured that by the late medieval period Chatham had obtained the character

Fig 1.2
Part of a 1633 map of the Medway.
(Collection of the Duke of Northumberland)

that is depicted on the earliest known map of 1633 (Fig 1.2).[4] Houses around the church formed one focus, while linear development along what became the High Street formed another. In between lay the marshy ground of the valley bottom, and a roadway must have linked the two parts of Chatham. The marshy ground, which was not occupied save for the large millpond, may have acted as a flood defence, and from this we can see the origin of the causeway that would later be called the Land Wall (Fig 1.3).[5]

Before the arrival of the navy around 1550, the economy of Chatham appears to have been mainly agricultural, supplemented by fishing and other river activities. MacDougall has estimated that as few as 200 people might have lived at Chatham at this time.[6] Chatham was a small place under the jurisdiction of the ancient city of Rochester, where the more wealthy members of local society were likely to reside.[7] Throughout the period covered by this book, Rochester was always a better-quality settlement.

The early dockyard

At what point Chatham first participated in mercantile trade making use of the river is unclear. It is probable that some form of wharfage existed at Chatham by the 13th century and that this later formed the basis for the first naval use of the river. The earliest reference to the use of the River Medway by the English navy is for *c* 1547 when storehouses were

Fig 1.3
Detail of the 1633 map
illustrating 'The Old Dock'
and the form of late
medieval Chatham.
(Collection of the Duke of
Northumberland)

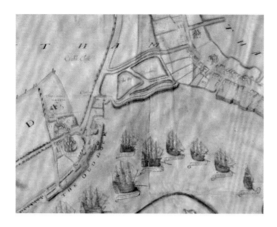

rented, which implies that some members of the local population were already engaged in river-related commercial activities. In 1550 orders-in-council mentioned that 'the kinges shippes shulde be harborowed in Jilyngham Water'.[8] This marks the start of the first dockyard at Chatham, though it would be some time before it was truly worthy of such a name. The first naval use of the Medway was as a safe anchorage – the construction of ships in purpose-built facilities came later.

Sir William Monson in the 17th century showed why the Medway at Chatham was so appealing as an anchorage:

Chatham is so safe and secure a port for the ships to ride in that his Majesty's navy may better ride with a hawser at Chatham than with a cable at Portsmouth. The reason for the long continuance of the navy at Chatham is the convenience of the docks and all other places for the commodity of ships. Chatham is near to London and may be supplied thence with all things necessary for the ships. The water at Chatham flows sufficiently every spring tide for even the greatest ships to be graved. No wind or weather can endanger the coming home of an anchor at Chatham and the river affords sufficient space for every ship to ride without overcrowding.[9]

The use of Chatham as a principal anchorage for the overwintering of the fleet led to the development of fortifications to defend it against attack. There were then no meaningful fortifications on the Medway. Henry VIII had used blockhouses to make the Thames impassable and had fortified the south coast with artillery castles, but the entrance to the Medway was guarded by only a single small blockhouse at Sheerness. In 1559 Elizabeth I ordered the construction of a castle at Upnor

as a specific defence for the anchorage at Chatham.[10] This took until 1564, using stone dismantled from Rochester castle, and the work was supervised by Richard Watts, a prominent citizen of Rochester. Later works have obscured the original form of the fortification, but from the start it had a great water bastion so that guns could fire across and along the river. A residential block was built against the river bank, and there was some form of tower at either end of the walled river frontage.

It is not clear when the first purpose-built structures for naval use were erected at Chatham, but their location is beyond dispute, because the site of the old dockyard is indicated on many maps (such as Fig 1.3) below the parish church and north of Chatham mill, at the place that is today part of the Gunwharf. Here the repair of ships began, which needed facilities like forges, saw pits and a mast pond, but could make use of stranding vessels on the tidal mudflats. In 1580 a long wharf was provided, and the following year the first known dock at Chatham was built. The first recorded Chatham-built ship was the *Merlin,* a pinnace of 10 guns built in 1579.[11] In 1588 much of the English fleet to counter the Armada was prepared at Chatham.

Improving the defences

Antagonism with Spain made the English fearful that a raid might be mounted on the Medway using the Spanish-controlled ports of the Netherlands. In 1575 a review of the Medway defences concluded that they needed to be strengthened. A new fort was required at Swaleness, close to the medieval castle of Queenborough, in order to deprive an attacker of the option of using the Swale to avoid the guns in the rebuilt blockhouse at Sheerness. This fort was started but not completed.

When war commenced with Spain a chain was stretched across the River Medway below Upnor castle as a barrier to enemy ships (Fig 1.4). In 1588 the costs of this chain are given as £250 for a 'great chayne' brought from London and £360 for its installation, with timber works on either side of the river, a house, two great wheels for raising the chain and lighters, cables and anchors to keep it in position. A further £100 was spent in blocking up St Mary's creek, £240 on the repair of Upnor castle and £420 for the employment of men to keep watch and man beacons. The captains and officers on ships at

Fig 1.4
The chain at Upnor as
depicted in 1633.
(Collection of the Duke of
Northumberland)

Chatham were paid £100.[12] By 1595 additional gun batteries were added to the Medway defences, and two of these (Bay and Warham sconces) were downstream of Upnor castle.[13] At this date the emphasis for defence was on the river itself.

The instructions to be followed in the event of an enemy attack survive for the year 1596.[14] They record that on identifying an attack, the guardship at Sheerness would have a message carried upstream by boat to Chatham, while gunfire would signal the alarm to the dockyard, Upnor castle, the riverside sconces and the beacons on Chatham and Barrow Hills. The alarm having been raised, the inhabitants were to rally for defence at Chatham church and at Upnor castle to receive instruction from the Deputy Lieutenant of the county. Five captains with 1,080 men were to take their ships to Upnor and four captains with 540 men to Chatham church.

Although Spain did not attack the Medway, work continued on strengthening the defences, with a major modification of Upnor castle starting in 1599, when the castle took on much of its present appearance (Fig 1.5). A timber palisade was erected in front of the bastion, which was itself raised in height and made suitable for use by 'great ordnance'. The landward ditch was dug and new flanking towers provided to cover it. The gatehouse and drawbridge also belong to this major revision of the castle. In the late 16th century the castle at Upnor stood on its own. In 1603 Upnor was described in a survey of ordnance: 'The castle of Upnor and two sconces there situate for the guarding and defence of the same your most Royall Navy; wherein I dare averre that no Kinge in Europe is able to equall your excellent Majeste.'[15] At this date Upnor village did not exist, but only grew up where the ferry from the other side of the river landed after the castle had found a new function.

The new dockyard

By the close of the 16th century Chatham was the main fleet base of the English navy, and Deptford on the River Thames was the main shipbuilding centre. The site of the Tudor-period dockyard below the parish church was from the start constrained in terms of its possible expansion by the topography and by the presence of the church, mill and many privately owned houses. In 1618 the decision was

taken to move the dockyard operation to a new and much larger site downstream of the existing dockyard. It is this site that forms the core of the present-day historic dockyard. As first conceived, it continued to rely on Upnor castle and its chain as the main means of defence, but ultimately major new fortifications were required.

Some 80 acres of new land were taken by lease on which to build the new Stuart-period dockyard (Fig 1.6). The form of this is well known from several later plans, not least the description in Edward Dummer's great survey of Chatham for the Navy Board in 1698.[16] Three ranges of buildings were constructed, forming an approximate square, with the river as the fourth side. Within this a double dock was constructed. There was also a ropehouse in approximately the same location as the present day ropery, and the old and new sites were linked by a roadway that is now part of Dock Road.

Fig 1.5
Upnor castle and barracks.
(Gentleman's Monthly Intelligencer *1753, 104*)

Fig 1.6
The early 17th-century new dockyard.
(Collection of the Duke of Northumberland)

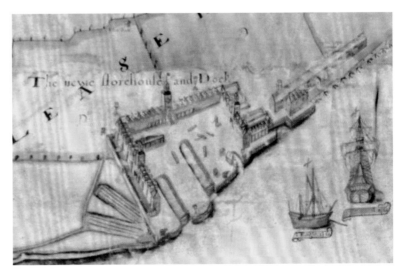

The old dockyard was leased to Richard Isaacson in 1649, and there are references to a great storehouse, a barge house and a dock near the watermill. In 1656 the Government bought out the remainder of the lease so that the site could be returned to state use, this time as the Ordnance or Gunwharf. In 1665 a new wharf was made as 'the ordnance lies ready to fall into the river'.[17] In 1670 Commissioner John Box of the navy wrote that the four watchmen at the old dock could be taken off and the expenses saved, because there was nothing belonging to the navy but a few guns and anchors. From this date it seems that the navy was completely finished with the old dockyard and that it now belonged to the Ordnance Board,[18] who would build new facilities upon the site. Dating to 1685 is a naïve map of the dockyard area by James Almond. It includes the site of the former dockyard, which is shown with small structures of a non-military character, but this is probably inaccurate at this date.

In the late 16th century, Chatham was changing fast from a small settlement to a dockyard town. Shipwrights were brought in when the demands of the fleet required them. This was seasonal work, but they gradually began to reside at Chatham, increasing the size of the local population and causing overcrowding. Naval officers were spared some of this inconvenience, because in 1567 an already standing dwelling had been rented for their use. This was Hill House, which stood in its own grounds on what is now Dock Road, slightly north of the parish church. Amongst the visitors to Hill House must have been Sir John Hawkins,

Treasurer to the Navy, who played a major role in the development of the fleet and its defeat of the Armada in 1588. When he saw how seamen and shipwrights were distressed in the aftermath of that victory, he founded two charitable institutions at Chatham to ease their plight. The Chatham Chest was an early pension scheme for seamen and dockyard workers by which contributions made by men employed all over England were used to fund assistance in the event of their incapacity. The second institution was the almshouses for poor mariners and shipwrights in Chatham High Street, opposite St Bartholomews hospital. These almshouses still bear the Hawkins name.

As first the dockyard and then the army garrison were put in place, the attraction of people to work in the government establishments or to otherwise earn a living from them caused the population of Chatham to grow rapidly. MacDougall has used the increased burial rates at the parish church to demonstrate the influx of shipwrights in the 17th century, and the expansion of the population must have placed a great strain on the local resources. During the period of the plague he refers to 534 burials in one year (March 1666 to February 1667) as indicative of the numbers of people living at Chatham. The expansion of the dockyard created problems for the accommodation of the labour force, and landowners were able to benefit from the lack of housing by building for rent many small one-roomed dwellings. This inevitably led to Chatham having a reputation as one of the most overcrowded and unhygienic towns of the 17th century, with a high death rate.

The Medway Raid

By the mid-17th century Chatham was firmly established as a major dockyard and as the principal anchorage for the fleet in home waters. The Anglo-Dutch wars were trade wars between two competing naval powers for control of maritime commerce. The theatre of operations was the North Sea and Channel, for which Chatham was geographically well placed. In 1666 during the Second Dutch War, England faced a financial crisis, made worse by the plague and the Great Fire of London, and peace negotiations were opened. As an economy measure in 1667 the fleet of larger warships was kept at anchor at Chatham. In June of that year, against all expectations, the Dutch mobilised their fleet and appeared in the Thames at

Fig 1.7
The Dutch fleet in the Medway attacking English warships, depicted in a painting by Willem Schellinks (1627–78). (Maidstone Museum & Bentlif Art Gallery)

Gravesend, where the defences forced them to withdraw. The Dutch commander, De Ruyter, decided instead to attack Chatham in what is termed the 'Medway Raid' and what the Dutch know as the 'Battle of Chatham'.

On 10 June De Ruyter attacked and burnt the unfinished fort at Sheerness and started to probe his way up the difficult navigation of the Medway. At Upnor the chain was in position, and field batteries were hastily improvised at either end of it. The Dutch advanced on the 12th and succeeded in breaking the chain with their ships. Because the chain was far downstream of Upnor Castle, the guns mounted at the castle could not defend the entire anchorage. Three ships had been placed at the chain by the English as guardships, and the Dutch used fireships to sink these. Battle was rejoined the next day, by which time the Earl of Albermarle had reorganised the English defences by mounting more guns at Upnor. The Dutch fleet received heavy fire and withdrew down river to Queenborough and then to sea.

The Dutch came very close to sacking the dockyard at Chatham. Six ships were burnt and sank, and two were taken away – the flagship *Royal Charles* and the *Unity*. In addition, the English had sunk eight of their own ships to try to impede the progress of the Dutch. Three more were sunk near their moorings at the dockyard, ropeyard and church but were later salvaged, and seven others were left intact.[19] The fort at Sheerness was entirely destroyed. John Evelyn described the sight of the burnt-out English ships as 'a dreadful spectacle as ever any Englishmen saw and a dishonour never to be wiped off'.[20] This was the only serious assault ever undertaken upon Chatham as a dockyard and it was a major naval setback for the English.

The hospital that never was

The Dutch Wars were very nearly responsible for what would have then been a unique building in Chatham. John Evelyn served on the Government's Sick and Hurt Board that was responsible for the supervision of sick and wounded seamen. Such was the pressure on the Chatham area as a result of the conflict that Evelyn proposed the construction of a large hospital for 400 patients in place of the more costly alternative of paying for them to be looked after at inns and alehouses. A description of the proposed building and even a ground plan survive in Evelyn's published letters.[21] From this and from the evidence of contemporary maps, it is possible to suggest that the hospital was planned for the Warren. A place of similar name on the 1633 map of Chatham (*see* Fig 1.3) means that the hospital would have been where the upper parts of Fort Amherst are today. If built, it would have predated the great hospitals of Greenwich and Chelsea, Les Invalides in Paris or Kilmainham in Dublin. As it was, funds could not be spared for its construction.

2

On the Defensive

The events of 1667 were a major warning to the English about what a determined attacker could achieve. It did not end the concentration on the defence of Chatham's dockyard through control of the River Medway, but as the Dutch had landed troops to capture both Sheerness and Queenborough, it set in train a significant change in England's defences. As long as fortifications have been built, military minds have examined how to make them invulnerable to attack and how to overcome them. The introduction of gunpowder changed the form of defences. By 1500 permanent fortifications based on the use of guns were starting to take on wholly new designs in parts of Europe. Masonry walls now had to be backed with earthworks to create ramparts capable of absorbing shot. Towers were no longer essential. Instead of masonry wall walks, broader earth ramparts to resist artillery allowed the defenders to concentrate their forces at the point of attack.

Most attention was paid to the elimination of dead ground in which attackers could gather and undermine defences. Bastions therefore became ubiquitous as outward projections from the main circuit of the defences, so that enfilading fire could be brought to bear in all directions and one bastion could support the next. This resulted in highly geometric and regular shapes of fortification, which was a radical departure from previous designs. It forms part of what has been termed the 16th-century 'Military Revolution', which also saw the rise in importance of military specialists skilled in the use of artillery and other siege tactics and in the design of defended places. This was the birth of the military engineer.

During the Renaissance, new designs of fortifications were developed and built in Italy (*trace italienne*), but they soon spread throughout Europe, and the Dutch were responsible for a refinement of the bastion system. Warfare in Europe became less about pitched massed battles and much more a matter of war by attrition through the defence of strategic locations against siege. Britain was slow to adopt the new forms of fortification, perhaps as a result of complacency through being an island nation and regarding the sea as a first line of defence. In continental Europe, where the need to defend against land armies was greater, many places were soon defended by highly geometric fortifications laid out on mathematical principles so as to best resist artillery bombardment and siege warfare. The most famous designer of such fortifications was Sébastien de Vauban, known for his late 17th-century work for Louis XIV of France. The theoretical basis of both artillery and fortification design could be transmitted by textbook, which allowed military engineers to study the works of others, and consideration of the various historic systems of defence would be a mainstream of a Royal Engineer officer's education well into the 19th century.

In England the bastioned system of fortifications was not used until improvements at places such as Carisbrooke Castle and Berwick-upon-Tweed were carried out for Elizabeth I, often by Italian engineers. Such fortifications were most commonly employed during the English Civil War (1640–9). At the Restoration, Sir Bernard de Gomme (a Dutchman by birth) was more responsible than anyone for the adoption of the European fortification designs using linked bastions to create a defensive circuit. He became Charles II's chief military engineer, and the best surviving examples of his work are at Tilbury Fort in Essex and the Royal Citadel in Plymouth.

New Medway fortifications

Following the Medway Raid of June 1667, there was a complete revision of England's coastal defences, and colossal sums of money were spent on new works, particularly to defend naval dockyards like Chatham. Much of this work was designed by de Gomme. The major fort at Sheerness was incomplete at the time of the raid, but it was now finished and was designed to control the entrance to the River Medway. The fort is known largely from engravings and plans, but limited fabric of this date does survive, incorporated into the 18th-century and later fortifications. Most of the fort was destroyed by the early-19th-century re-planning of Sheerness as a dockyard and by the construction of the present Garrison Point fort.

On the Medway near Chatham, de Gomme's refortification works survive to a better extent. They are shown in a detailed survey of 1669, which depicts the revised river defences of the dockyard. From this survey, it is evident that the fleet at its moorings was now intended to be entirely upstream of Upnor Castle (unlike at the time of the Dutch attack). The survey also shows that in the aftermath of the attack, batteries had been improvised north of the dockyard (8 guns at the mast dock and another 20 guns below the dockyard).

The chain across the Medway remained as a defence, but was moved further downstream, so that if it was breached, any attacker would come under crossing fire from two new major forts designed by de Gomme to control the pas-sage up Gillingham Reach – Cockham Wood Fort on the Upnor side and Gillingham Fort on the dockyard side (Fig 2.1). Gillingham Fort was a diamond-shaped battery with guns located to engage ships downstream as they broke through the chain and then upstream as they moved up Gillingham Reach. Cockham Wood Fort had a double tier of 30 guns in total, aimed for broadside effect into the river. If a ship did manage to get past Gillingham Fort, it would be engaged from Cockham Wood Fort as it turned to make the bend towards Upnor Castle.

These two new forts were aligned on the river, and they also had tower-like redoubts for close defence to prevent them being taken by a landing party. Cockham Wood Fort still exists, but in a ruinous condition,[1] while Gillingham Fort survived until the later 19th century when it disappeared during the Victorian dockyard extension. It may yet await rediscovery, since it is unlikely that it was totally destroyed.[2]

Downstream of Upnor Castle, de Gomme retained two intermediate batteries, one of 10 guns (James battery) and the other of 18 guns (Bird's Nest battery). Upnor Castle itself had fired its last shot in anger, because despite the resistance offered to the Dutch, it was considered redundant by virtue of the new defences. From 1668 the castle was instead converted from a fort into a gunpowder magazine. For

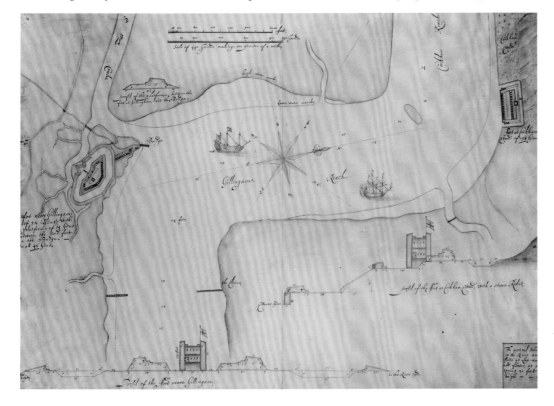

Fig 2.1
De Gomme's scheme for the defence of the Medway following the Dutch raid in 1667.
(© National Maritime Museum, Greenwich, UK, GOM/218: 8/31)

Fig 2.2
The late 17th-century
batteries of Hooness and
Lower Pinam on the
Medway.
(TNA MR 1/503)

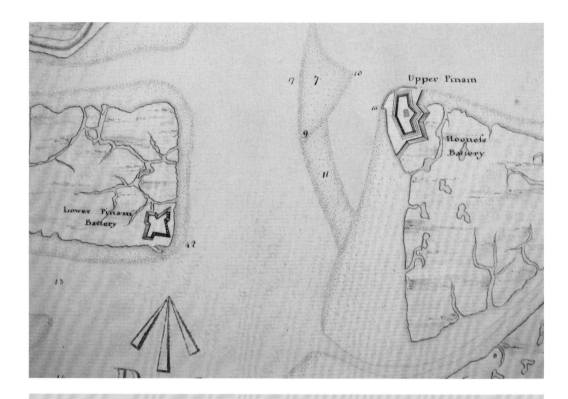

Fig 2.2
The late 17th-century batteries of Hooness and Lower Pinam on the Medway.
(TNA MR 1/503)

The Ordnance Board

The Ordnance Board can be traced back to 1414, but it was not constituted as a full board until 1597. It was the oldest permanent military department and grew out of the need to provide equipment and goods for military campaigns and sieges. One of its tasks was to supply artillery and the experienced gunners. At this date there was no regular army and navy as we understand them today. Instead, forces were raised when necessary. The supply of war material required a standing organisation and stores.

The Ordnance Board came to have two main responsibilities. First of all, it supplied all arms and munitions, from hand weapons to great guns, for the use of government forces both on land and at sea. Secondly, it was responsible for the construction of fortifications and barracks. The board had an existence that was separate from the army and the navy, but came to be most closely identified with the army. There were civil and military branches, and the Tower of London was its headquarters. The senior officer was the Master General of Ordnance. As a cabinet member, this was a political appointment, and one that was highly influential.

His deputy was the Lieutenant-General of Ordnance, and there were four heads of separate departments (Surveyor-General, Clerk of the Ordnance, Principal Storekeeper and Clerk of the Deliveries). These six men made up the Board.

Reporting to the Master General, the military branch of the Ordnance Board was headed by the Master Gunner and had a limited number of salaried gunners and initially a few engineers. After 1683 it developed its own artillery and engineer specialists. While the infantry and cavalry regiments were controlled by the Commander-in-Chief from Horseguards in London, these specialist branches of the British army were commanded separately by the Ordnance Board. In the late 17th century, as the army grew in size, and then during the sustained periods of warfare in the 18th century, the Ordnance Board came to control hundreds of troops at home and abroad in what would become the Royal Artillery and the Royal Engineers. The Ordnance Board kept its separate identity until 1855 when, in the context of the major shortcomings exposed in the British army during the Crimean War, it was abolished and its responsibilities were transferred to the War Office.

this, the castle was altered in appearance one more time, including the removal of gun platforms from the tops of the towers. A storekeeper's house was also constructed.

Storage of gunpowder was a matter of great concern to a fortification and to a naval anchorage. Magazines in which the powder was stored had to be made safe from accidental explosion, and keeping powder at Upnor on the opposite bank to the dockyard limited the chance of damage to the dockyard or its ships in the event of a catastrophe. In 1691 Upnor held 5,206 barrels of powder, more than any other ordnance site, including the Tower of London which held 3,692 barrels.[3] Upnor would retain this ordnance storage and manufacturing role until after World War II.

Riverside batteries along the Medway between Sheerness and Chatham continued to be added in the late 17th century,[4] including a pair of batteries to increase control of the navigable channel between Hoo and Darnet islands (Fig 2.2). Hooness battery was at Upper Pinam on Hoo island, and Lower Pinam battery was on Darnet island. James II (brother of Charles II) was Lord High Admiral of the navy and familiar with the defence of Chatham. In 1688, faced with the threat of invasion by his Protestant son-in-law William of Orange, James wrote to William. Perhaps to deter a repeat of the successful attack on the Medway some two decades earlier, James made a deliberate reference to these new defences: 'I intend to go tomorrow to London and the next day to Chatham to see the new batteries I have made in the Medway and my ships which are there'.[5] William of Orange chose not to invade at any of the well-defended locations and landed instead at Torbay in Devon.

Invasion fears

The Glorious Revolution of 1688 forced the Catholic James II into exile and replaced him as monarch with his daughter Mary and her husband William of Orange, both Protestants. This was resented and opposed by the Jacobites, who regarded James II and his successors as the true ruling dynasty. France was willing to support plans for a Jacobite invasion of Britain, and this threat dictated the defensive policies of William and Mary and subsequently Queen Anne. By the 1707 Act of Union, the kingdoms of England and Scotland were joined and ruled by a single Parliament. The same Act guaranteed a Protestant succession by stating that if Anne

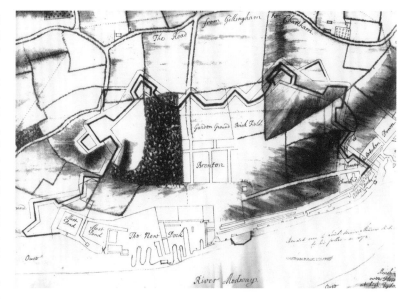

died without an heir, the succession should pass to Princess Sophia, the Electress of Hanover, who had a distant claim to the throne as the granddaughter of James I. The Act of Union stirred up nationalist and Jacobite feelings in Scotland, and in February 1708 news reached the English Court that the French were assembling a fleet at Dunkirk in readiness for an invasion to support the cause of James Edward Stuart (the 'Old Pretender'), the son of James II who had died in 1701.

As this invasion fleet could have headed for either Scotland or England, preparations were deemed necessary at Scottish castles and English dockyards. On 29 March 1708 Queen Anne was asked to authorise new works at various locations, based on a report prepared by the Duke of Marlborough, who was Master General of the Ordnance. He recommended for Chatham that 'there be a fortification erected upon the rising ground behind the dock to prevent an insult upon it by land'.[6] At that time, nothing came of his proposal.

The start of the 18th century saw major changes to the dockyard at Chatham, and consideration was given on how to best defend this facility. Responsibility for new defences fell to the Royal Engineer Talbot Edwards, and in 1708 he prepared a proposal for bastioned linear fortifications on the high ground on top of the escarpment to the east of the dockyard. Edwards's design (Fig 2.3) was labelled 'A Plan for Fortifying Chatham Docks and Storehouses from any Suddaine Attempt by Land without Great Artillery but not against a siege', which reveals its intended purpose.

Fig 2.3
The first proposal for land defences as designed by Talbot Edwards in 1708. (Royal Engineers Museum, Library and Archives)

Fig 2.4
A painting of Chatham by an unknown artist, possibly dating to the late 17th century, showing in the foreground houses that formed the town of Chatham, clustered around the medieval parish church. The site of the first dockyard at Chatham is out of view below the church, but warships ride at anchor on the River Medway. In the distance is Rochester, with its bridge, cathedral and castle.
(© National Maritime Museum, Greenwich, UK, BHC0832)

Fig 2.5
Plan of Chatham for the 1708 commission into the purchase of land for new fortifications. The site of the church (bottom left) is not depicted as it was not subject to purchase. The many houses and tightly packed building plots illustrate how Chatham had grown in size after 1550, following the founding of the first dockyard. None of the buildings survive, as they were swept away by the construction of fortifications in 1756. The site is now occupied by Fort Amherst.
(TNA MFC 1/85)

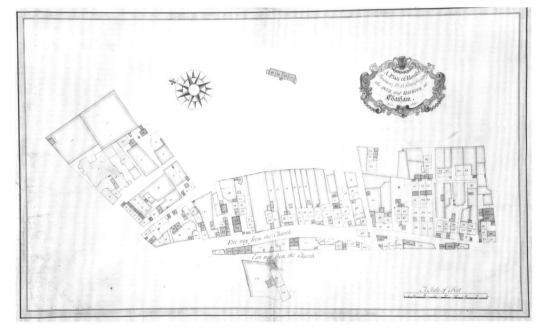

In other words, these were field defences to hold back an enemy's troops from the dock-yard and to prevent bombardment by the type of light artillery that an invading army on the march could transport. The defences were not designed to withstand heavy guns with greater range and power, or to delay a conventional siege for a long period. Elements of earlier river-dominated defence thinking creep into his plans, with a water bastion projecting into the river in the dockyard at what is now Anchor Wharf. Edwards's planned fortifications were never built, but they were similar to the later Chatham Lines.

A late 17th-century painting (Fig 2.4) gives the appearance of the buildings around Chatham parish church, while Edwards's 1708 plan depicts how the proposed fortifications would have sliced through this area of Chatham. Although it simply refers to 'houses to be taken down', the plan relates to a series of documents that record the 1708 Government commission which was held in the Guildhall at Rochester.[7] This was an enquiry into the land that was required to build new fortifications, to find out who owned it and how much the land was worth, in order to pay compensation.

Two maps provide a picture of this part of Chatham in 1708. A general map[8] shows who owned land around the dockyard, and a coloured plan (Fig 2.5) depicts the multiple tenements that needed to be acquired and demolished to build the fortifications. Such a detailed picture of property ownerships at this date is unusual and highlights the very cramped nature of the houses lived in by the labour force of the early 18th-century dockyard. An Act of Parliament in 1710 authorised the purchase of land, but no land acquisition took place.

The heir to the throne, Sophia of Hanover, died in June 1714, and Queen Anne died two months later, leaving Sophia's son to succeed to the British throne as King George I. The Treaty of Utrecht of 1713 had included recognition of Queen Anne as the true queen of England and the expulsion from France of the Jacobite pretender. The new Hanoverian dynasty in Britain that began with George I was the excuse for France to break this treaty and prepare to support a new invasion by the Jacobites. This resulted in the first Jacobite rebellion in Scotland in 1715. The fear of invasion led to the reconsideration of the 1708 Commission and 1710 Act of Parliament, and the Government

Fig 2.6
Clement Lempriere's plan of Chatham in 1719 (drawn for the Ordnance Board at a scale of 1in to 200ft) showing the major expansion of the dockyard in the period before the building of the key fortifications. The houses depicted in Fig 2.5 are shown, with the church on the right-hand side of the plan.
(TNA MPH 1/247)

used a further Act of Parliament of 1714 to authorise the acquisition of land needed for the fortifications at Chatham, although no fortifications were actually built.

Expansion of the dockyard and Gunwharf

Although the early 18th century was not considered the right time to build new fortifications at Chatham, elsewhere the Government was making a very major investment in the dockyard and gunwharf facilities. Chatham remained an important fleet base in the first half of the 18th century, but by now the dockyard had outgrown its 17th-century boundaries, despite expansion to the north to create additional docks and mast ponds. Captain Clement Lempriere of the Ordnance Board drew up a plan of Chatham in 1719 (*see* Fig 2.6). This shows the new boundary to the dockyard that was formed by means of a high wall and a castellated gatehouse and tower houses. The dockyard wall

was intended less as a fortification proper but rather a defence against espionage and a means of controlling theft by the workforce. The new wall took in an expanded area for the dockyard and ropeyard, within which were built several new and impressive buildings such as the Officers Terrace (1722–33) and the Sail and Colour Loft (1723).

Meanwhile, significant investment was also taking place at the Ordnance Board's Gunwharf, on the site of the old dockyard. Preparatory surveys for Lempriere's 1719 plan[9] show three large storehouses on the southern end of the Gunwharf and also the civilian-owned watermill. The Storekeeper's House[10] of the early 18th century is also shown. At the northern end of the Gunwharf a Grand Storehouse was built in 1719 (Fig 2.7) to a design attributed to Hawksmoor, replacing an earlier structure of comparable size that dated to around the very end of the 17th century.[11] It is not clear why two such large buildings were provided in short succession, but the first one may have

Fig 2.7
The Grand Storehouse of 1719 (since demolished) on the Gunwharf.
(© English Heritage AA44-01481)

been destroyed by fire. The Grand Storehouse of 1719 was not demolished until after World War II.

With such major investment in the dockyard and Gunwharf, it is easy to see why Daniel Defoe described the place as he did at this time:

The buildings here are indeed like the ships themselves, surprisingly large, and in their several kinds beautiful. The ware-houses, or rather streets of ware-houses, and store-houses for laying up the naval treasure, are the largest in dimension, and the most in number that are any where to be seen in the world: The rope-walk for making cables, and the forges for anchors and other iron-work, bear a proportion to the rest; as also the wet-dock for keeping masts, and yards of the greatest size, where they lye sunk in the water to preserve them, the boat-yard, the anchor-yard; all like the whole monstrously great and extensive, and are not easily described.

We come next to the stores themselves, for which all this provision is made; and *first,* to begin with the ships that are laid up there: The sails, the rigging, the ammunition, guns, great and small-shot, small-arms, swords, cutlasses, half-pikes, with all the other furniture belonging to the ships that ride at their moorings in the River *Medway* ... The building-yards, docks, timber-yard, deal-yard, mast-yard, gun-yard, rope-walks; and all the other yards and places, set apart for the works belonging to the navy, are like a well ordered city.[12]

Foundation of Brompton

Threat of invasion was not removed by the defeat of the Jacobites, particularly as England found herself at war with Spain, a long-term enemy. Although land had been acquired at Chatham from a diverse number of people at a cost of £16,734.16s.4d, it was still not consid-ered appropriate to go ahead and fortify the dockyard. Instead, the land was leased to Charles Goatley Esq (Serjeant at Arms under Queen Anne) at a rent of £330 per annum. By now, Chatham no longer looked like the view in the late-17th-century painting (*see* Fig 2.4). In 1719 Mr Goatley petitioned the Treasury to renegotiate the lease on the grounds that it had cost him £1,000 to repair the houses, because half were empty and building materials had been 'run away with', and most were inhabited by poor people. This was an early example of planning blight, as the estate had lain waste for a considerable time, ever since Queen Anne had first authorised its purchase for possible fortifications. One river wall was described as having 'broken in' and another was in danger of doing so. The lease required that the land be given up immediately if fortifications were required by the Government, and since there were constant rumours that a garrison was about to be formed, the affected houses could only be sublet at low rents.

Goatley's petition was unsuccessful, and in 1725 the Government resumed control of the land leased to him on the grounds that he had ignored his covenants. Instead, a new lease was granted to a Sir Edmond Bacon of Gillingham, but he is described as paying as little attention to the property as Goatley. Without proper authority, he sublet the open land on which fortifications would need to be built to James Hicks, who used it to make several million bricks. Earlier brickearth excavations and kilns are depicted on the 1719 Lempriere plan (*see* Fig 2.6).

The Tudor-period dockyard had been served by the labour force living in the old settlement at Chatham, but the expansion of the dockyard

Fig 2.8
Brompton on the hill behind Chatham dockyard in an engraving of 1756.
(Royal Engineers Museum, Library and Archives)

Fig 2.9
The surviving 1719
barracks at Upnor Castle.
(Author)

The blight suffered by so many of the houses at Chatham that were under threat of demolition to make way for fortifications must also help explain the founding of Brompton. The site of Brompton was part of the historic manor of Westcourt, and it appears that an entrepreneur called Thomas Rogers bought the latter in 1697 and took the opportunity to create a new town before 1700. His actions would allow property owners dispossessed by forced acquisition of their buildings in Chatham somewhere to reinvest and or move to.[14]

Another stimulus to the creation of Brompton may have been errors made in the acquisition of the land on which the new dockyard at Chatham had been built in the early 17th century. This land also came from the Westcourt manor but was never properly conveyed to the Crown. The owners of Westcourt manor pursued a 40-year claim with the Treasury for compensation, which was finally settled in 1707 for a sum of £4,000. This money may also have been used to help finance the new town of Brompton.

The first barracks

Across the Medway at Upnor, map evidence shows that by 1724 the development of the High Street was well underway.[15] The use of the castle as a gunpowder magazine had prompted the Ordnance Board in 1719 to build a barracks block to house the soldiers who guarded the powder stored there. These were the first purpose-built barracks provided at Chatham,[16] and the building is amongst the oldest surviving barracks in the United Kingdom. Built to hold 2 officers and 64 men, the design follows the Ordnance Board model of the day as seen at barracks like Berwick-upon-Tweed. Barracks at this time consisted of rooms stacked around a central staircase but with no interconnection between the rooms. The officers enjoyed far superior accommodation to the men who were crowded into single rooms, which they sometimes also shared with the families of married soldiers.

in the early 18th century created new demands for labour. This was one reason why Brompton was founded as a new and planned settlement in the first decade of the 18th century, as it was better located for the dockard (*see* Fig 2.8). The precise date and mechanism by which this town was created are not yet understood. The first building in Brompton is thought to have been 'a house of public entertainment, distinguished by the sign of the Sun in the wood, built about 1699'.[13] Edwards's 1708 plan (*see* Fig 2.3) shows the grid of three streets (Wood, Middle and West Court Streets) set out off the High Street. Garden Street and Prospect Row followed on afterwards.

3

The First Chatham Lines

In 1744 the French prepared to invade in support of the Jacobite cause, and only the wrecking of the invasion fleet by a storm at Dunkirk prevented this. Britain's first line of defence remained her navy, but new preparations were needed to defend the strategically important dockyards. Attention was turning yet again to strengthening the Chatham defences, as seen in a plan of 1742 that depicts a square redoubt by Upnor Castle with associated batteries (Fig 3.1), but none of this seems ever to have been built.

The Seven Years' War of 1755 to 1763 was essentially a continuation of the War of Austrian Succession (1740–8), and it was fought in two main arenas. In continental Europe the old powers sought to resolve longstanding disputes. In North America and India, Britain and France fought for control of the lucrative colonial trade as much as for territory. In this sense, the Seven Years' War can be thought of as a world war, contested on a global scale both on land and at sea. As ever, Britain was afraid of an invasion by France. By 1759 France had assembled sufficient troops to land a force 15,000 to 20,000 strong in Scotland and a further 48,000 in southern England. Such a force could have overrun the British home forces, and France at this date also had a fleet capable of dispersing the Royal Navy and thus securing the sea route for invasion.

At the start of the Seven Years' War, the defences at Chatham were inadequate. Gillingham Fort was occupied by a garrison with a gunner, housed in new barracks, and there was also a gunner, but no guns mounted, at Hooness Fort. Otherwise there were no other guns mounted at Upnor castle or at Cockham Wood Fort, where the 42-pounder guns were lying disused and a retired gunner was living in the house.[1] In April 1756 the Duke of Marlborough, Master General of the Ordnance, received royal approval for plans to defend Chatham,

Portsmouth and Plymouth with lines of defences,[2] and by Act of Parliament in 1757 authority was given for the compulsory acquisition of land.

Work at Chatham had actually been underway since late 1755, which would create the system of fortifications known as the Chatham Lines – lines of fortifications. The initial words of the 1757 Act show that work had already started here and elsewhere:

Whereas by the unjust and hostile invasion lately made on his Majesty's dominions in America and the Mediterranean and by great preparations made in France for invading these realms, it became absolutely necessary for the security of his Majesty's docks, ships of war and stores to erect and raise fortifications and intrenchments near the docks of Portsmouth, Chatham and Plymouth.

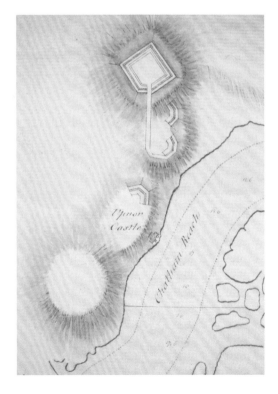

Fig 3.1
A plan of 1742 showing a proposed square redoubt and batteries next to Upnor Castle.
(TNA MR 1/959)

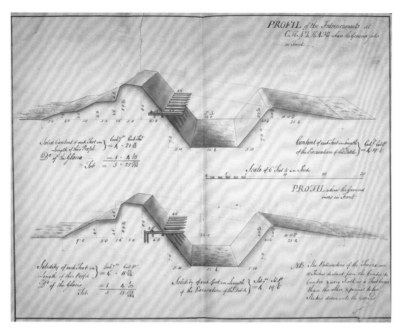

The Chatham Lines principles

When permanent fortifications were conceived for Chatham in the early 18th century, these inevitably exploited the bastion system of design that had by then become the orthodoxy for the construction of defences. To understand how the Chatham Lines were intended to work, their design should be considered from the point of view of both an attacker and a defender. The lines were made up of a continuous earth rampart formed from the material obtained by the excavation of a broad ditch. The rampart was raised up so as to provide the defenders with a commanding view of the land before them, and it was shaped to provide gun positions and a firestep over which the defenders could fire from cover. To impede any attackers who reached the ditch and prepared to mount the rampart, stout timbers sharpened to points were used to create obstacles.

The rampart was carefully placed to command the ground being defended, taking advantage of the topography so that where possible there was a steep natural slope to the front. Bastions provided enfilading fire covering all the ground. The earliest fortification designs at Chatham (*see* Figs 3.5 and 3.6) have projecting bastions at the northern and southern ends of the lines, but more significantly they have four broad (but shallow in depth) bastions, placed one after another in the central section where a frontal assault was felt most likely.

Ramparts made solely of timber and earth were only temporary and suffered from erosion. To withstand bombardment by artillery and to decrease the likelihood of successful siege works, the earthen rampart and ditch could be revetted, and at Chatham brick was used for this purpose. The first fortifications at Chatham had some features built of brick, such as the gun emplacements and the firestep, and in time both sides of the ditch would be faced entirely in brickwork.

The design of the defences extended beyond the ditch. The ground just outside the external edge of the ditch was carefully formed into an earthwork known as the glacis. This created sloping ground rising in the direction of the rampart and had two main functions. Sculpting the approach to the fortifications made it easier for the defenders to see and fire on their enemy, and it prevented the attackers from obtaining a clear view of the ramparts and of the ditch that was a final major obstacle to an assault. Also,

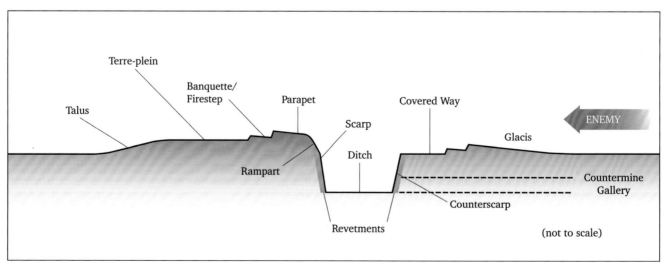

the glacis prevented the guns of the attackers being trained on the rampart to form a breach. In order to move the guns close enough to be effective, the attackers had to dig an approach trench through the field of fire and the glacis.

The land in front of the fortifications within view of the defenders was known as the 'field of fire', and this was levelled and cleared of obstructions, such as trees, hedges and ditches, so denying attackers any shelter from fire directed off the ramparts. It was the height of the ramparts that gave the defenders an advantage. Solid cannonballs would remain deadly in the field of fire after their first bounce (termed the 'first graze') and would continue to bounce through the ranks of attackers. Anti-personnel forms of shot and shells could also send lethal fragments amongst any attacking force, alongside volleys of musketry from infantry drawn up on the ramparts.

Bastioned lines were not just for static defence. The defenders could emerge onto the field of fire via sallyports to engage an enemy directly, supported by the guns on the ramparts. They might use a covered way formed in the uppermost part of the glacis as a line behind which to mass troops unseen by the enemy and from which to fire from cover at the besieging force.

Military engineers perfected fortifications such as the Chatham Lines by using mathematical calculations and by observing the range, accuracy and power of artillery, as well as the ability of fortifications to withstand siege tactics, such as by mining. At Chatham, fortifications were designed to prevent an enemy from taking control of ground from which the dockyard could be bombarded, but increasingly they came to serve another purpose. By forcing an invader to try to take the defences by siege or else risk a counterattack on his lines of communication, they could delay an invading army so that the defence of the rest of the country, and London in particular, could be organised.

Engineers and artificers

The Board of Ordnance retained a Chief Engineer to head its engineer committee (a post that was replaced in 1802 by the Inspector-General of Fortifications). In 1716 the creation of the Royal Regiment of Artillery left the engineers as a separate entity, though one that was always closely linked with the gunners. Military rank was granted to the Corps of Engineers in 1757, from which time the regiment dates it full existence. It was made up of officers only, and the number of these professional military engineers was very low for the service required of them. The title Royal Engineers was granted to these officers in 1787.

Non-commissioned engineer soldiers first appeared in the context of the fortification of Gibraltar (c 1772), giving recognition to the value of such permanent specialist craftsmen under military discipline. They had the title artificers, and in July 1779 Hugh Debbieg, faced with the defence of south-east England, wrote to Lord Amherst about the benefits of having a corps of artificers to assist him. The Royal Military Artificers was formed in 1787, by a warrant approved by Parliament and issued to the Duke of Richmond as Master General. They were craftsman soldiers commanded by Royal Engineer officers. Six companies each of 100 men (4 sergeants, 4 corporals, 2 drummers, 60 artificers and 30 labourers) were formed at Chatham, Gosport, Portsmouth, Plymouth, Woolwich and Guernsey-Jersey. The skills covered were masons, smiths, miners, bricklayers, sawyers, painters, coopers and collar makers. A 5-guinea bounty was paid to each recruit, and it was instructed that all the miners were to be obtained from Cornwall.

In 1792, throughout the stations at home and abroad, there were only 72 Royal Engineer officers and 952 artificers. Several years later, during the Peninsular War, their shortcomings in terms of both numbers and the skills required for siege warfare were exposed. In 1812 Charles William Pasley founded a training establishment at Chatham to address this weakness, and in 1813 the artificers were renamed the Royal Sappers and Miners. Both officers and enlisted men were trained at Chatham alongside their equivalents for the East India Company's forces destined for service in India. In 1828 there were 250 Royal Engineers and 1,095 Royal Sappers and Miners. Men and officers were not united as a single corps made up of all ranks and known as the Royal Engineers until 1855 and the post-Crimean reforms.

Fig 3.4
The Royal Engineer monogram: Everywhere, where right and glory lead. (Royal Engineers)

Fig 3.5
A plan and sections of Desmaretz's proposed new fortifications (the Chatham Lines) dating to 1755, prepared to illustrate his estimate of the cost of the design options. Drawn at a scale of 1in to 200ft, with the sections at 1in to 20ft. (TNA MR 1/358)

Fig 3.6 (opposite)
Hugh Debbieg's 1756 survey, showing the newly constructed Chatham Lines, the yellow boundary of the land that was purchased and the troop encampments (the five grey rectangles). (© The British Library Maps Kings Topographical 16.40)

The fortifications of Desmaretz

The superintendent appointed to oversee the new fortifications from 1755 at Chatham was the Royal Engineer, Captain John Peter Desmaretz. Since he also held responsibility for much of the south of England, the work was under the direct control of Hugh Debbieg. In November 1755 Desmaretz supplied proposal drawings and an estimate of costs,[3] which illustrate various schemes with different projected costs. The plan shows a line of fortifications similar to the 1708 proposal of Talbot Edwards (*see* Fig 2.3). Desmaretz proposed either a simple line of ditch and rampart with V-shaped projections known as 'redans', or else a line made up of broad bastions. His plan (Fig 3.5) depicted various sections that corresponded with profiles to show how the fortifications might be constructed at different parts of the site and the possible methods of construction.

The construction of the lines with simple redans (shown as a solid outline) made of earthworks but with limited areas built in brick was estimated to cost more than £15,000. The use of broad bastions (shown with a yellow line) was estimated to cost a similar amount. The inclusion of a brick revetment would have increased either of these options by between £26,000 and £27,000. The cheapest option given by Desmaretz was for a simple earthwork series of bastions with minimal use of brickwork revetment and the work to be carried out by military labour. This was estimated at only £4,757, and on 20 January 1756 the Treasury approved this option.

Work on building the first stage of the Chatham Lines lasted from 1755 until late 1757, creating a system of ramparts, ditches and bastions. Land first identified as required for fortifications by the 1708 commission was now taken over, and around the Gunwharf many houses and the watermill were demolished. In the oldest part of Chatham nearest the parish church, notice-to-terminate leases were served on residents on Christmas Day 1755, and their houses were then demolished in two phases.[4] In 1756 Debbieg did a survey of the land that was purchased and of the newly constructed defences, and on this survey the yellow boundary round the purchased land excludes the settlement of Brompton (*see* Fig 3.6). This new town was to be a civilian enclave surrounded by the Chatham garrison. The areas marked out for the encampments of the troops within the new lines are shown on Debbieg's survey as five grey rectangles, each with the number of a regiment.[5] These were the troops who were responsible for the bulk earthmoving to create the lines under the supervision of the Royal Engineer officers led by Debbieg.

An account of the construction of the Chatham Lines is found in the journal of Corporal William Todd of the 30th regiment.[6] Todd records the formation of working parties consisting of 200 men from each of 5 regiments. The payment to each man was 8d per day instead of the standard 6d paid to a soldier. Subsequently they became the force needed to man the new defences, and camp accommodation was all that was available to them until

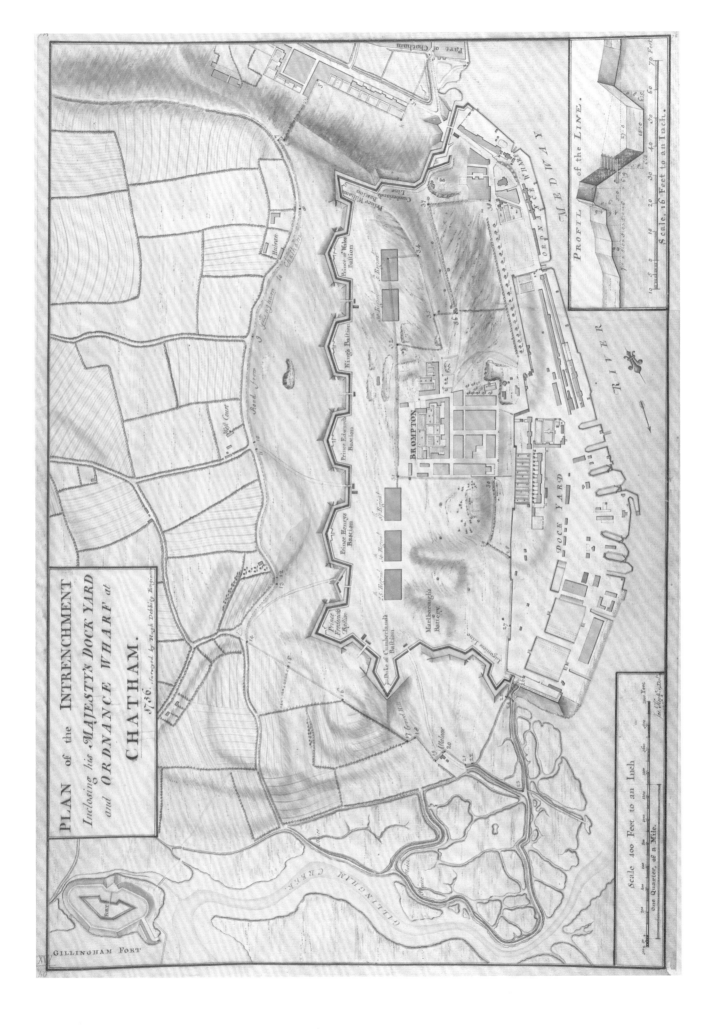

PLAN of the INTRENCHMENT
Inclosing his MAJESTY'S DOCK YARD
and ORDNANCE WHARF at
CHATHAM.
N.º 56. Surveyed by Hugh Debbig Engineer.

GILLINGHAM FORT

PROFIL of the LINE.

Scale, 16 Feet to an Inch.

MEDWAY

ORDNANCE WHARF

RIVER

DOCK YARD

BROMPTON

Marlborough Bastion

Duke of Cumberland Bastion

Prince Frederick Bastion

Prince Henry's Bastion

Prince Edward's Bastion

King's Bastion

Prince of Wales Bastion

Prince William Bastion

Cumberland Line

Legionise Line

Part of Chatham

Road from Gillingham to Chatham

Well Court

Hulton

GILLINGHAM CREEK

Scale 400 Feet to an Inch.

One Quarter, of a Mile.

completion of barracks at Chatham. Even then, during the summer months, when invasion was thought most probable, the field force to counterattack any invader lived under canvas within the lines.

The Surveyor to the Ordnance Board's minutes[7] allow the progress of Debbieg's work on the lines to be followed in detail. It is clear that various issues combined to make the £4,757 estimate for the cost of the work hopelessly optimistic. In December 1756 the cost was stated as being £14,647,[8] but writing in 1780 Debbieg increased this to £17,000. The Ordnance Board records provide a very human insight into this major construction project, such as in 1755 when Debbieg was instructed to keep the valuable intrenching tools in a guarded shed at night. Yet in October 1757 we learn that the tool store had been broken into and the contents stolen. Debbieg admitted that stores were kept at the Gunwharf as there was no suitable building for them on the lines. He refers to a 'subterraneous cavity' at the chalk pit, which at a cost of £120 could be fitted up to hold 260 barrels (of gunpowder). This is the first known reference to the underground works at what is now Fort Amherst and points to the non-military origins of the tunnels as caves or dene holes. Debbieg borrowed bricklayers from the dockyard in order to complete his project, and a Mr Morris supplied the 'sentinel' boxes.

The completed defences

In the summer of 1757 construction of the first Chatham Lines was nearly complete. What was actually built is revealed in Debbieg's 1756 survey (Fig 3.6), which includes a profile through the ditch and rampart of the new fortification, and a more detailed pair of similar sections by an unnamed hand also exists (see Fig 3.2). At the Gunwharf, a wet ditch connected the defences to the river. The road from Chatham entered the newly defended area through a major outwork and a set of gates that are seen in profile no. 1 of Desmaretz's proposal (see Fig 3.5). The fortification then rose up the high ground (where Fort Amherst now stands), making use of the steepness of the slope to create two ramparts, such that the inner could safely fire over the top of the outer, according to profile no. 2 of Desmaretz's proposal. On top

of the high ground the fortifications turned sharply to the north, creating a spur (Prince William's bastion), which was profile no. 3 in the Desmaretz proposal, to take maximum advantage of the escarpment.

The central section of the new Chatham Lines is best seen in Debbieg's survey. Four broad bastions were constructed to close off an attack from the east. These were named, from south to north, the Prince of Wales bastion, King's bastion, Prince Edward's bastion and Prince Henry's bastion. These four bastions created the shape of the central section of the Chatham Lines that remains to the present day. The northern end of the lines was formed by two large bastions (Prince Frederick's and Duke of Cumberland's) and a line of entrenchment (Ligonier line) that connected to the corner of the dockyard wall. The southern end had the Prince William's bastion and the Cumberland Lines. The names of parts of the lines probably result from a 1756 royal inspection by HRH Duke of Cumberland, accompanied by the Duke of Marlborough as Master General of the Ordnance and Lord Ligonier as head of the army.

In November 1757 the Ordnance Board ordered that all guns for the lines at Portsmouth, Plymouth and Chatham be despatched as quickly as possible. A sketch by the antiquary Francis Grose dated 1759 captures much of what the first Chatham Lines looked like. His view over the river towards Upnor Castle depicts the dockyard wall, as well as the earthwork rampart of the new lines, complete with sentry box, tents and soldiers.[9] Outside the new lines, the newly acquired land was needed to create a field of fire or open ground that an attacker would have to cross under assault by the defenders. The new land extended as far as the existing Gillingham–Chatham road, leaving only two farms, Westcourt and Upberry, both of which were most probably medieval in origin. These farms did lose many of their fields to the west of the road, because hedges were uprooted, ditches were filled in and the ground was levelled so that it was commanded from the bastions and could not offer any cover for an attacker. It was here that an attack would have been broken up by infantry emerging from within the lines and supported by the guns on the bastions. The lines offered a place of retreat and a line of defence should the enemy continue to press home an assault.

Barracks and Billeting, 1756–1801

Chatham was not unique in having newly constructed fortifications, as the defences of the other principal dockyards were also being strengthened, but a unique project was about to commence – the construction of barracks. Barracks were unpopular with Parliament, who preferred to see troops billeted amongst the general population on the grounds that they were less likely to rebel against the elected government. Billeting was the system by which the holding of a licence as an innkeeper obliged the licensee to accommodate a number of soldiers in return for payment of a fixed fee. At locations such as dockyard towns, where the military were concentrated, and with the creation of the marines as a separate force making a bad situation worse, it was impossible for the billeting system to meet the demands imposed upon it.[1]

Chatham Infantry Barracks

In the summer troops could sleep under canvas, but without barracks they had to be dispersed to winter quarters. The solution was permanent and purpose-built barracks, and in 1757 the Ordnance Board sought royal approval for the construction of such barracks at Chatham.[2] Assent was given in February 1758: 'Our will and pleasure is that you do forthwith cause barracks to be erected within the lines at Chatham (to contain two battalions of 900 men each).'[3] These were to be the Chatham Infantry Barracks (now known as the Kitchener Barracks), some of the largest purpose-built barracks yet constructed in the country. The barracks were intended to hold 1,800 men, roughly the equivalent of two regiments.

Desmaretz provided an estimated cost of £39,664,[4] though Debbieg probably had day-to-day responsibility for the works. Four unsigned drawings dating to 1757 show what was originally intended, but they bear little resemblance to what was actually built.[5] Draw-

ing no. 2 is a plan of the proposed barracks and is most similar to what was built, with the officers' quarters occupying the higher land to the east of a parade ground. No. 3 is a section through the site showing how the sloping site was to be exploited to create rows of barrack blocks running north–south.[6] No. 4 (Fig 4.1) is a plan and elevation of a proposed barracks for 'private men', which can be compared with no. 5 (Fig 4.2), the barracks for officers.

Although these were unimplemented proposals, they show the conditions under which men and officers were expected to be housed in barracks. Rooms for ordinary soldiers were grouped round a single staircase, and each room had three windows, one fireplace and nine beds. Two men shared a bed, so a room was designed for 18 men.[7] The quarters for officers were of a much better standard, with

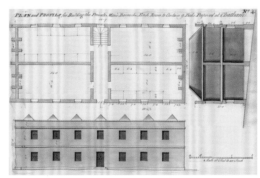

Fig 4.1
Drawing no. 4 of Chatham Infantry Barracks, giving a plan, elevation and section for the accommodation for private men.
(TNA MPF 1/349)

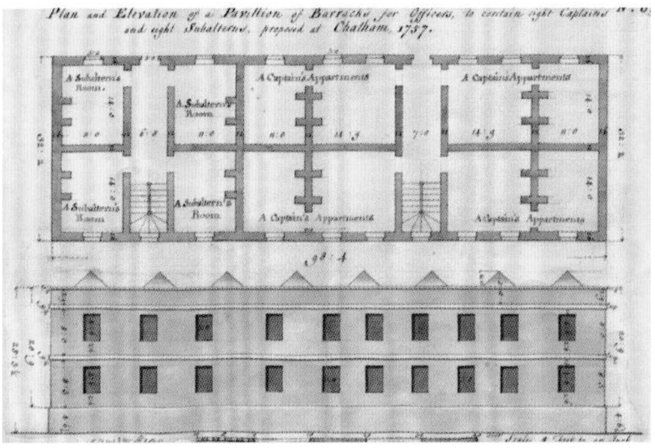

Fig 4.2
Drawing no. 5 of Chatham Infantry Barracks, giving a plan, elevation and section for the accommodation for officers.
(TNA MPF 1/349)

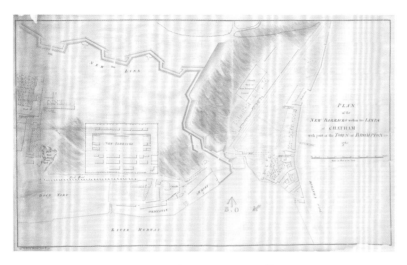

Fig 4.3
A 1763 plan of the new infantry barracks at the south end of the Chatham Lines.
(TNA MPHH 1/23)

Fig 4.4
Chatham dockyard as painted by Joseph Farington in the late 18th century, showing the strategically vital place that had to be defended and which gave rise to the garrison.
(© National Maritime Museum, Greenwich, UK, BHC1782)

even the most junior officers having individual rooms, and higher ranks having several rooms each. The design chosen for the barrack blocks did not follow these 1757 proposals, but had more in common with the earlier design at Upnor (*see* Fig 2.9).[8]

The site selected for the new barracks was between what is now Dock Road and a rope-walk in the area now known as Amherst Hill. A 1763 plan (Fig 4.3) shows the rectangular walled site, with six blocks of accommodation for the officers built on a higher terrace that was connected to the parade ground by a double ramp and with further ramps in the corners. On the lower ground stood the barracks for the rank and file. The plan was symmetrical around a central axis, with two of each type of facility.

As constructed, this symmetry was largely achieved and most probably reflects the fact that the barracks were built to hold two battalions that required separate but matching buildings.

There were gates in the centre of each side of the rectangular enclosure, with a road running from Brompton High Street through the barracks site and on to Chatham. Guardhouses at either end of the central route were referred to as the Brompton and Chatham guardhouses. Two buildings stood north of the parade ground and another two on its south side. These were not for accommodation but appear always to have been offices or canteens. Four hand pumps served by cisterns provided the water supply on the west side of the parade ground. Initially, there was no garrison commander's house in the south-east corner of the barracks, but there was a house in the south-west corner that may have originally served this purpose. Adjacent to it were coal yards, which were walled to prevent pilfering.[9] Despite variations in size, each barrack block shared an identical architectural treatment of two floors standing over cellars and garret accommodation in the roof space, with dormer windows behind a solid parapet.

The appearance of the barracks as a whole is best judged from its inclusion in the painting of Chatham dockyard by Joseph Farington (Figs 4.4 and 4.5). Farington was

commissioned in 1785 to do four paintings, including one of Chatham. It was apparently done using perspective drawings of Mr White, the Chatham draughtsman, and Farington may never have actually visited the site. Completed between 1785 and 1794, this painting is significant because it is extremely accurate and depicts not just the detail of the dockyard but also the fortifications, the infantry barracks and the settlement of Brompton. Although painted some 30 years after their construction, little had been done to alter the site of the barracks. The rigid apportionment of space and symmetry is evident, but the solid appearance of the individual barracks belies their actual crowded and unhealthy character. Only one of the original 18th-century barrack buildings survives, though many more were intact until major redevelopment in the late 1960s.

Construction of purpose-built barracks should not lead to the assumption that the common soldiers housed there lived under good conditions. From the outset the barrack rooms were crowded and poorly lit, ventilated and heated. Soldiers slept two to a bed. Rations for which deductions were made from the daily pay were often of low quality and insufficient. The radical MP William Cobbett wrote about his early experiences as a soldier at Chatham, living in these infantry barracks in 1784:

I remember well what sixpence a day was, recollecting the pangs of hunger felt by me, during the thirteen months that I was a private soldier at Chatham, previous to my embarkation for Nova Scotia. Of my sixpence, nothing like fivepence was left to purchase food for the day. Indeed not fourpence. For there was washing, mending, soap, flour for hair-powder, shoes, stockings, shirts, stocks and gaiters, pipe-clay and several other things to come out of the miserable sixpence! Judge then the quantity of food to sustain life in a lad of sixteen, and to enable him to exercise with a musket (weighing fourteen pounds) six to eight hours every day.[10]

On the conditions in the barracks, Cobbett wrote:

The edge of my berth, or that of the guard-bed, was my seat to study in; my knapsack was my bookcase; a bit of board, lying on my lap, was my writing-table; and the task did not demand any thing like a year of my life. I had no money to purchase candle or oil; in winter-time it was rarely that I could get any evening-light but that of *the fire*, and only my *turn* even of that … To buy a pen or a sheet of paper I was compelled to forego some portion of food, though in a state of half-

Fig 4.5
Part of Farington's late 18th-century painting of Chatham, showing the 1757 infantry barracks.
(© National Maritime Museum, Greenwich, UK, BHC1782)

starvation; I had no moment of time that I could call my own; and I had to read and to write amidst the talking, laughing, singing, whistling and brawling of at least half a score of the most thoughtless of men, and that, too, in the hours of their freedom from all control. Think not lightly of the *farthing* that I had to give, now and then, for ink, pen, or paper! That farthing was, alas! a *great sum* to me! I was as tall as I am now; I had great health and great exercise … I remember, and well I may! that, upon one occasion I, after all absolutely necessary expenses, had, on a Friday, made shift to have a half-penny in reserve, which I had destined for the purchase of a *red-herring* in the morning; but, when I pulled off my clothes at night, so hungry then as to be hardly able to endure life, I found that I had *lost my half-penny*! I buried my head under the miserable sheet and rug, and cried like a child![11]

Concentrations of troops were a draw to those wishing to sell them alcohol, food or other comforts. At military camps, booths were set up on their periphery so that those soldiers with money could spend their time eating, drinking, gambling and whoring. Sutling was a permitted activity by which troops could purchase provisions and alcohol from recognised individuals, some of whom could be soldiers' wives. For 1762 the notebook of one officer refers to a number of booths built in the rear of the camp of the Cornish and Dorset regiments at Chatham by persons not entitled to erect them and who have 'occasioned very great disorder by admitting common strumpets and other irregular persons. A grievance prejudicial both to the service in general and to the health of the men has thus arisen.'[12] The booths were taken down and their occupants turned out of the camp.

Though not encouraged to do so, some

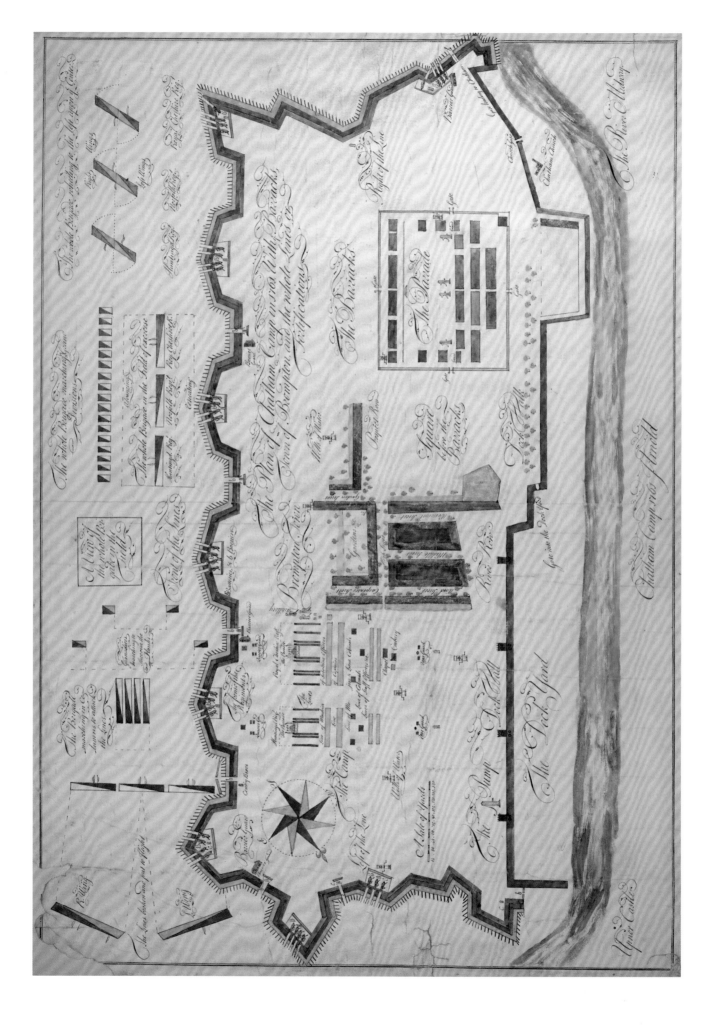

soldiers did marry, and they often had their wives and children with them when in barracks or in camp. There were no separate married quarters, and the wives and children had to live alongside the unmarried men. The quantity and quality of rations were poor, with only two meals (breakfast and lunch) provided, for which deductions were made from a soldier's pay. The daily pay of a soldier (6d) was insufficient to feed himself, let alone his family, after deductions for these rations and other necessities. Complaints of soldiers faced with starvation are common, which would account for entries in the notebook of one officer for 1761 and 1762 that mentioned 'soldiers and women of the regiment' going into farmers' fields and orchards around the lines to steal produce. Sentries were posted to try to prevent this.

The women of the regiment were essential to daily barrack life and were responsible for much of the cooking, washing and mending for each barrack room. They also ensured that their men were well turned out in the complicated uniform of the day. Some officers saw soldiers' wives as a cause of vice and indecency amongst the men. An 1816 instruction gave a clear idea how the army viewed women and their value to life in barracks:

The comptroller of the barrack department may, if he sees fit, and when it in no shape interferes with, or straitens, the accommodation of the Men, permit (as an occasional indulgence, and as tending to promote cleanliness, and the convenience of the soldier) four married women per troop or company of sixty men, and six per troop or company of a hundred men, to be resident within the barracks; but no one article shall on this account be furnished by the barrack-masters, upon any consideration whatever. And if the barrack-masters perceive that any mischief, or damage, arises from such indulgence, the commanding officer shall, on their representation, displace such women. Nor shall any dogs be suffered to be kept in the rooms of any barrack or hospital.[13]

Some decades later, in 1843, women were still poorly regarded, as Major-General Arthur Hill Trevor demonstrated: 'Soldiers' wives in Barracks, poor things! ... Soldier's wives, are generally the greatest nuisances, and I have had more trouble to control their conduct & behavior than I can describe; altogether the system of admitting them into the men's rooms is revolting to decency and certainly demoralizing.'[14]

Troop encampments

During the Seven Years' War, the Chatham Lines acted as a troop concentration from which to mount a counterattack against any invader. When called upon for military service, county-based militia regiments were sent in summer to Chatham to camp within the lines and so be ready for service.[15] These camps continued in use, because the new barracks were not sufficiently large to hold all the troops. A naïve plan of the Chatham Lines and barracks was produced in 1761 by J Arnold (Fig 4.6). It shows the troops encamped within the lines, with the military encampment precisely laid out with the tents, each containing six men, set out in companies so as to form streets. The drums and colours were placed together to identify the regiment, and sentries were posted as a quarter and rear guard. Sergeants and corporals each had their own groups of tents, and then came the lines of marquees for the officers – first the subalterns, then the captains, lieutenant colonels and colonels and finally the staff officers. There were also separate field kitchens and a chapel. To one side of the camp, field artillery pieces are shown. These were not guns supplied for the Chatham Lines defences, but would have been for the use of troops in the field.

In addition to showing where guns were actually mounted on the lines, Arnold's plan shows the Norfolk, Huntingdonshire and Royal Cheshire regiments engaged in drill on the field of fire. From the beginning, the field of fire was also regarded as an exercise ground, and it was to retain this purpose throughout its ownership by the military. The main infantry weapon of the mid-18th century was the flintlock musket. This was a notoriously inaccurate weapon, but this did not matter as infantry tactics relied on combining many soldiers together in well-drilled formations so as achieve an impact by volleys of collective fire at short range. Troops were required to perform a series of movements (known as the manual exercise), to load and fire their muskets and to move about the battlefield by well-drilled formations, thinking and acting as a body of men in response to orders signalled by drum beat. Perfecting these tactics took long hours of drill and constant practice. Arnold's plan shows one example of the three regiments that formed a brigade wheeling to get into position without breaking step.[16]

This picture of the military encampment at Chatham during the Seven Years' War is made

Fig 4.6 (opposite)
J Arnold's plan of 1761 with encampments and training exercises.
(© The British Library Add MS 34814)

all the more real by an officer's notebook for 1761 and 1762, in which he records the minutiae of the routine in the Chatham camp, such as the parole or password to be given to the sentries each day. One description is of the constant exercises needed to perfect the military drill:

The Lt Gen recommends to the Commanding Officer to accustom their men to fire with ball as frequently as possible and to march in front by platoons and form as battalions so that officers know the distances that ought to be preserved to perform this in a regular manner. 18 men from each battalion are to be appointed to the field pieces for instruction by the Officers of Artillery.[17]

He also records how time was devoted to ceremonial duties, with the troops made ready to be reviewed by their royal highnesses the Dukes of Cumberland and York or to fire a salute in recognition of British victories achieved, such as that at Pondicherry in India for 1761.

Another officer based at the Chatham camp in 1762 also kept a handwritten notebook. Although it contains little that is specific to Chatham, its description of military tactics helps to understand what the soldiers were practising, both at home and in service abroad. Instructions included:

In all evolutions officers to be particularly careful in keeping their divisions in proper distance that the lines may be always properly formed and dressed under the above wheelings. No new evolutions to be begun before the battalions are completely dressed and steady. In performing of which it is best to accustom the soldiers to do it themselves in order to ground them in so essential as well as graceful part of the exercise.[18]

He added: 'Intrenchments or redoubts are to be defended obstinately. The fire is to begin in a regular manner when the enemy is within shot at about 200 yards and to continue till they approach very near. When the troops perceive that they endeavour to get over the parapet they are to fix bayonets and make a bloody resistance.'[19]

A renewed fear of invasion from 1779 saw the reinstatement (until 1782) of military camps by troops in the summer months. The *Lady's Magazine* in 1781 referred to a 'Grand Camp' of 10,000 soldiers and artillery at Chatham. These troops were intended to man the Chatham Lines and to act as a field force against any attackers.

Changes in Chatham town

With the construction of the Chatham Lines and the infantry barracks, Chatham as a town was undergoing massive change. The 1763 plan (Fig 4.3) shows something of what was happening. All the houses identified for compulsory purchase by the 1708 commission had been demolished and much of old Chatham swept away. The parish church remained in use, but was within the militarised area. A new burying ground was provided at what is now Town Hall Gardens, presumably because the old churchyard was full, with no room for expansion. Near the church, privately owned buildings remained on the west side of Dock Road, and Hill House was still standing.[20] In 1762 it was leased out as an inn that doubtless did good business from the proximity of so many soldiers in the new barracks.

By 1763 development was starting to take place along the eastern slopes of what is today The Brook. Properties were also built north of the High Street, which, with the demolition of the houses around the church, was now the main nucleus of Chatham. In this way the town began to spread into the less suitable low marshy ground of the valley bottom. Due to the loss of so many houses to the military for fortifications and the constraints of topography, there was little alternative. The watermill and millpond had also been lost to the fortifications. The 1763 plan shows a small creek where the stream of The Brook ran out to the River Medway as a drain. It did so under a roadway that connected the militarised area to the rest of Chatham and which still carried the name Land Wall.[21] The poor rate assessments of 1767 have been by used by MacDougall to give an indication of the size of the local population, which he estimates as numbering 5,600.

On the Gunwharf the increased presence of so many more soldiers must have placed new demands on the site, and a range of new storehouses (since demolished) was built against the eastern side of the site where the road from Chatham rises up towards the church. Brompton appears to have prospered at this time, and an engraving of the dockyard in 1756 (Fig 2.8) shows the neat terraces of the planned streets of Brompton in the background.

Chatham had a reputation as a dirty, ill-planned town where the concentration of soldiers, sailors and marines attracted various aspects of criminality, including prostitution.

Efforts were nevertheless underway to make the town more pleasant for its citizens. By Act of Parliament in 1772 two types of highway improvements were permitted. Construction of the New Road was authorised so that the poorly maintained High Street closest to the river could be avoided by travellers leaving Rochester for the road towards the coast. To avoid Chatham being altogether bypassed, the Act also permitted the main streets of Chatham to be paved, cleaned, lighted with oil lamps and guarded by nightwatchmen, all at the expense of the ratepayers.

The New Road should have made more pleasant land available for speculative residential development, and some such development did take place along its length, but the 1782 purchase of the south hill for fortifications seriously constrained the ability of Chatham to grow in this direction. The town therefore remained concentrated on the low-lying ground nearest the river and on the slopes of the rising ground.

Marines barracks

A further major investment in barracks at Chatham was made by the Admiralty. Marines were soldiers carried aboard naval ships who were under the command of the Admiralty, with the Navy Board responsible for their accommodation on shore. The Corps was made permanent in 1755, and divisions at each of the main dockyards of Portsmouth, Plymouth, Chatham and Woolwich were established. Marines thus swelled the military presence in 18th-century Chatham. Initially they had no purpose-built barracks and were instead billeted upon local innkeepers. The Navy Board tackled this problem by building barracks for the marines, starting in 1777 with the selection of a site. This was opposite the infantry barracks on the west side of Dock Road.[22] An area of private houses and inns in Cat Lane remained between the new barracks and the parish church.[23]

The design of the new barracks (Fig 4.7) was a stage on from that adopted in 1757 by the Ordnance Board for the infantry barracks.[24] Internally the barrack rooms were of a similar size and quality to the army design, but they were grouped around staircases on four floors in order to create a single monumental block on the west side of the central parade ground. The officers were housed in their own blocks on the north and south sides of the parade ground, with an infirmary and a sutling house (canteen) completing the buildings. The east side of the parade ground looked on to Dock Road and was open to view through railings and gate piers. The 18th-century marines barracks were significantly altered in the 19th century and

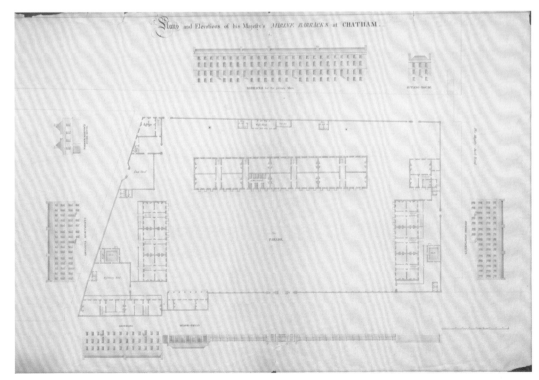

Fig 4.7
Plan and elevations of the marines barracks at Chatham.
(TNA ADM 140/120)

were then demolished after World War II. Today the site is occupied by the offices of Medway Council.

Recruiting

Periods of war created major challenges for the recruitment of sufficient soldiers. During the American war an Inspector-General of Recruiting was established to oversee recruitment to the main army, and his headquarters were at Chatham. Disease more than wounds of war created high mortality amongst the British troops, and so it was necessary to keep a steady stream of new recruits to the regiments to make good the losses. Regimental recruiting parties sent their recruits to Chatham from all over Great Britain and Ireland. They were delivered to the infantry barracks to receive their basic training before despatch to regiments, most of which were on overseas service. The infantry barracks in effect acted as the depot for these regiments. This began a national role for Chatham that it would retain into the late 19th century.

The muster rolls dating to after the end of the war with America show who was at Chatham barracks and when.[25] Other records describe the recruiting role of Chatham and can also be used to understand what must have happened in the period of the American war and beyond. A complete and detailed example of a muster roll for 1786 gives 51 officers, 66 sergeants, 69 corporals, 43 drummers and 1,201 private soldiers belonging to 25 different regiments. The largest numbers of recruits belonged to the 36th, 52nd and 73rd regiments. These three regiments fought in India in the Second Mysore War (1780–4) and were still in India in 1786. The muster rolls also show that a few recruits were claimed back from the army as runaway apprentices, some deserted, others were recognised as previous deserters,[26] and a few were dismissed as unfit for service.

The radical MP William Cobbett observed the recruiting process at Chatham, in the infantry barracks:

I enlisted in 1784, and, as peace had then taken place, no great haste was made to send recruits off to their regiments ... The best battalion I ever saw in my life was composed of men, the far greater part of whom were enlisted before they were sixteen, and who, when they were first brought up to the regiment, were clothed in coats much too long and too large, in order to leave room for growing. We had several recruits from Norfolk (our regiment was the West Norfolk); and many of them deserted from sheer hunger. They were lads from the plough-tail. I remember two that went into a decline and died during the year, though when they joined us, they were fine hearty young men. I have seen them lay in their berths, many and many a time, actually crying on account of hunger. The whole week's food was not a bit too much for one day.[27]

Many recruits (some from prisons) arrived in a dirty and diseased state and could not be allowed to associate with the existing soldiers in the overcrowded rooms until they had been washed and clothed and inspected by the surgeon. A 1795 plan (*see* Fig 4.8) shows the 'cleaning house for recruits'. Individual drafts of men sent abroad can be identified, such as that in 1799 when 100 men were despatched from Chatham aboard the *Woodford* for general service.[28] The record contains the age and height of each man and shows what uniform he had been issued with. It also reveals that the men were paid before they departed, receiving 8½d for every day of the anticipated 92-day voyage to India, from which deductions were made for provisions while at sea. Poignantly, the back of the return lists the names of six wives (one of whom had a child) permitted to accompany their husbands. This does not mean that the other 94 soldiers were unmarried. Six out of 100 was the most commonly used official quota for women to accompany their men overseas. Lots might be drawn to decide who the six wives should be, and the unsuccessful women were left behind.

The same records also contain a pay list from 1801 for the staff of the recruiting depot. These include 15 staff sergeants who must have taken the lead role in training the men, as well as 3 boatswains and 6 boatmen. The latter probably manned the boats that brought recruits from London to Gravesend and Woolwich, from where they were marched to Chatham.

Overcrowding

Overcrowding in the infantry barracks was a big problem. They were designed to hold 1,800 men. A muster roll for 1789, five years after Cobbett's experience, records 2,305 men at Chatham, and these were not the only troops at the barracks since the Ordnance Board was also responsible for housing its Royal Engineer officers and its own soldiers (the Royal Military

Artificers), to say nothing of the artillery. The barrack blocks must have been filled to bursting, and the situation was made worse by the presence of soldiers' wives and children who lived alongside the men.

How the existing infantry barracks were divided between the regiments of the line and the engineer and artillery troops of the Ordnance Board is revealed in a plan drawn up in 1795 (Fig 4.8) and by statements of the resident Commanding Engineer, William Spry. All of the officers' terrace, both guardhouses and most of the men's block were given over to the infantry. The artificer and artillery soldiers had separate parts of the blocks assigned to them, while whole blocks were assigned to the artillery officers and the commanding Royal Engineer and his department. There were separate canteens and separate infirmaries for the infantry and ordnance troops. The plan also shows that by 1795 the garrison commander had a substantial house for him and his household in the south-east corner of the barracks.

A crisis in army barrack accommodation led to Oliver Delancey being appointed Barrack Master General in 1794 to head a new Barracks Department to build new barracks across the

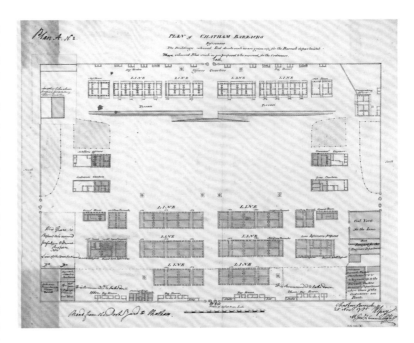

United Kingdom, though nothing new was then built at Chatham. The Ordnance Board had been responsible for barracks through a barrack master, but this role was transferred to the new department.

Fig 4.8
The site of the Chatham Infantry Barracks as depicted in 1795 with the green coloured buildings for the Ordnance Board troops, but the majority, coloured pink, for the infantry regiments.
(TNA MPI 1/203)

Reinforcing the Chatham Lines

The cost of the Seven Years' War had been massive, and to meet the debt the British Government looked to taxation, including revenue from the colonists in North America. By 1775 the American colonies were in open revolt in what they term the American Revolutionary War. The French and Spanish navies had been rebuilt after the reverses of the Seven Years' War, and both countries, working as allies, started to challenge Britain. Initial French support for the American rebels by providing war supplies became open warfare in 1778, once more raising the threat of invasion and spreading the American war to Europe. In June 1779 Spain joined the war, and this was a moment of considerable danger to Britain since the combined French and Spanish fleet outnumbered the ships available to the British for defence. The combined enemy fleet was, however, poorly supplied and was unable to force a decisive engagement with the Royal Navy. In August 1779 Britain had perhaps only 20,000 effective regulars at home to meet the French invasion force of 31,000 assembled at Le Havre. Only French naval mismanagement prevented an invasion attempt. The crisis passed, but the invasion threat continued until the end of the war in 1783.

Dockyard investment

The Ordnance Board had invested heavily at Chatham in new facilities that were to remain in use for centuries. The fortifications were not unusual in design, and similar ones were built elsewhere, but the infantry barracks were a new departure. By contrast, at the dockyard there had been little major investment in new buildings since the early 18th-century expansion of the site. Priority for investment had switched to the dockyards at Portsmouth and Plymouth, partly because of their better strategic location for access to the Atlantic and routes to far-off colonies, but also because larger ships had problems reaching Chatham up the tidal Medway, so limiting its suitability as a fleet base. However, in 1773 the Admiralty Board under the Earl of Sandwich announced a new purpose for Chatham dockyard, for building and repairing ships:

I am now more and more convinced that if it is kept to its proper use as a building yard, possibly more useful service may be obtained from it than from any other dockyard in His Majesty's Dominions; the great extent of the yard which faces the river and the great length of the harbour which has room to moor half of the fleet of England of a moderate draught of water, are conveniences that are not to be found elsewhere; and it will appear that by the repairs that have been carried on during the visitations I have lately made that more business in the way of building and repairs has been done here than in any one, possibly more than in any two of the other yards … The best use to be made of this port now is to build or repair ships sent from Portsmouth and Plymouth; therefore all improvements at this yard should be for that end.[1]

Soon after, work was started to rebuild the southern end of the dockyard with a new ropery and the first of the massive Anchor Wharf storehouses. The defence of the dockyard was as important as ever.

Strengthening the defences

The French did not invade Britain during the Seven Years' War, and the defences at Chatham were not put to the test, which was probably just as well, because they were not as strong as they might have been. A revised version of Daniel Defoe's earlier account of Chatham incorporated a reference to the new Chatham Lines: 'they are near three miles in circumference, fenced with a strong barricado of very stout timbers, and a deep dry ditch; and at proper distances are bastions, faced with stone and sods, and are well fortified with heavy cannon'.[2] The truth was very different.

The 1756 decision to build the cheapest form of fortifications made mostly of earthworks had caused problems. The defences were easily eroded by stray animals, by spectators who came to see the military encampments and by the troops themselves. A 1757 proposal to fence the ramparts was never carried out,[3] and in the final years of the war the lines had been neglected. In October 1761, even before the war ended, land was let for pasture, most probably in the field of fire,[4] and the Master Gunner impounded cattle belonging to Farmer Dann of Gillingham that had strayed onto the lines. After the Seven Years' War, in 1766, the Ordnance Board reported that the mainly earthwork fortifications were in a poor state: 'The Lines and new works are greatly destroyed and rendered almost defenceless by cattle grazing thereon, which the Ordnance have endeavoured but cannot prevent. The barracks are in very good condition. There is a scarcity of water but directions will be given to remedy if possible. 35 guns.'[5]

The engineer Hugh Debbieg had supervised the initial construction of the Chatham Lines and had subsequently seen active service as an engineer in North America at the siege of Louisberg (1758) and the taking of Quebec (1759). He returned to Chatham as a more experienced soldier and military engineer. Continued Anglo-French antagonism meant that each power carried out covert reconnaissance of the other's dockyards and fortifications, and in 1767 Debbieg was sent to the dockyards of France and Spain on such a mission. A French Colonel of Dragoons who toured England for the same purpose produced from memory a series of maps. The one for Chatham drawn in September 1768 (Fig 5.1) lacks accurate details, but records the essential military character of the place.

A renewed threat of invasion from 1779 prompted the Ordnance Board to substantially rebuild and reinforce the Chatham Lines. The engineer given responsibility for the new works was once again Debbieg, assisted by Gother Mann, a future Inspector-General of Fortifications but at that time a Royal Engineer captain.[6] Royal approval for new works at Chatham was given in December 1779,[7] by which time Debbieg was already designing new fortifications and suggesting that 7,000 soldiers were needed to hold the re-formed lines and a further 2,000

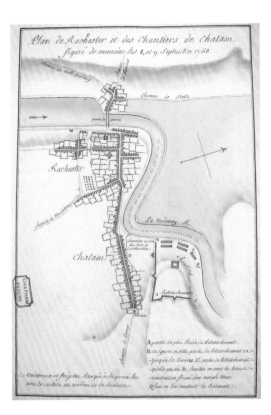

Fig 5.1

A French map of Rochester and Chatham drawn in September 1768.
(TNA MF 1/54)

if land to the south of Chatham was also occupied.

A drawing by Debbieg dating to 1779 (Fig 5.2) reveals what he had in mind for the revised fortifications. He was planning works to the north of the dockyard, including at St Mary's marsh, a new redoubt and a series of bastions close to Gillingham (where the Lower Lines would later be built), a couvre porte (a defended gate) to provide access onto the field of fire between the Prince of Wales and King's bastions, works to Prince William's bastion, two redoubts within the defended area of the lines, and a detached fort to occupy the high ground south of Chatham.[8] Debbieg's drawing also included sections through the rampart to show how they would be substantially stronger than those built in 1756.

Only some of these proposed improvements were carried out to the Chatham Lines, but preparations were made for them all, including the acquisition of more land by Act of Parliament in 1782.[9] Debbieg wrote to the Ordnance Board in 1780 to report how much better the fortifications were:

You will be pleased to observe that you now have a line round Chatham dock containing near twice as much earth as the old one and together with the new works about three times the quantity, a powder magazine and a great mass of brickwork and more-

Fig 5.2
Hugh Debbieg's 1779
proposal to rebuild the
Chatham Lines.
(TNA MPH 1/358)

Fig 5.3
A plan of the Chatham Lines
in 1786 showing the extent
of the remodelling of the
fortifications.
(Royal Engineers Museum,
Library and Archives)

over (if I may be allowed to pronounce upon the advantages of the whole reformation) you have a line of quadruple the strength and ten times the durability of the former one.[10]

He also gave information about the scale of the new work and its cost:

The whole amount of the part of the Line now reforming of the same length and contour as that constructed in 1756 but now erected with a profile more suited to the situation as a proper cover for the commanding grounds with the addition of near twice the depth of ditch and a larger glacis in front which greatly adds to the strength of the whole contains 147,250 solid yards of earth. The content of the addi-

tional new works contains 42,465 solid yards and the content of the earth removed at the powder magazine and behind the retaining wall amounts to 8,333 solid yards. These three sums together make 218,048 solid yards of earth for the present line and new works when completed. All incidental charges included. Therefore by analogy if 80,000 solid yards in the line constructed in 1756 cost £17,000 218,048 solid yards of earth in the new line will cost £45,600.[11]

The Royal Engineer letter books for 1781 also contain details about the re-formation of the parapet in sod work, the use of masonry to revet some of the existing bastions, the making of 8 sallyports as ways through to the field of fire, the construction of 30 gun platforms and the completion of a new powder magazine. The extent of the new works is clearly seen in a plan done in 1786 (Fig 5.3).

Major additions within the defended area were Townshend's redoubt in the north and Amherst redoubt to the south. New works associated with the Amherst redoubt saw the start of what would later be Fort Amherst. Prince William's bastion was pushed out into the field of fire to create the Spur battery, and what is today known as Belvedere battery was built. A magazine to hold 1,000 barrels of powder was constructed in 1783, which survives at Fort Amherst.[12] The couvre porte between the Prince of Wales and King's bastions was also constructed. Other works were carried out to modify the northern end of the lines at the

Duke of Cumberland's bastion and near the dockyard.[13]

No works were built in the newly acquired land near Gillingham, but Debbieg did propose major works for the newly acquired land south of Chatham. One of his letters to the Ordnance Board explains why this was necessary:

The new works south of Chatham are intended as the main support of Chatham Lines; the spot whereon they are to stand commands a view of the whole dock and the line in flank within reach of cannon shot so that Chatham lines become untenable till this ground is occupied with works of some strength. It is properly the key to Chatham.[14]

This land is today the site of Fort Pitt, and the panoramic view from there shows why this high land had to be defended. Debbieg made a design for a fort at this location, and preparations were made to start the building work. In 1783 Debbieg advised the Ordnance Board that 4½ million bricks had been delivered to the site for the building work.[15]

Opposing views

The Master General of the Ordnance at this time was the Duke of Richmond. He made no secret of his opinion of the Chatham Lines. In 1781, speaking in the House of Lords, he criticised their original construction:

He particularly instanced the lines at Chatham, which he declared, as a military man, were the most absurd and ineffectual that could possibly be devised, and yet they were erected at an immense expense. The thickness of the parapet was no more than seven feet whereas every person at all used to fortifications knew that the proper thickness of a parapet, cannon proof was 18 feet. Such mere paper works would be knocked to pieces at the first fire were guns brought to bear on them.[16]

The Duke was no doubt correct in his views that the earthen ramparts were totally insufficient. As the engineer responsible for building the first lines and designing the reinforced version of them, Debbieg must have felt slighted.[17] The Duke was happy to spend much larger sums on the two major dockyards of Portsmouth and Plymouth. Between 1 January 1770 and 31 December 1783, £297,903 was spent at Portsmouth on fortifications and £128,178 at Plymouth. At Chatham in this period, £144,009

was spent on the fortifications, and a further £68,000 was estimated as necessary to complete the process. It was judged that another £183,000 was needed to complete the work at Portsmouth and Plymouth, and by 1783 the Duke of Richmond was even proposing a programme of works at these two sites estimated at between £400,000 and £500,000.[18] As far as he was concerned, Chatham was a much lower priority.

With the ending of the American war, it is not surprising that a halt was called to new work on the defences of Chatham in the autumn of 1783. In a letter dated 13 October Debbieg refers to 'when the general order was issued for stopping the works'. He also refers to an inspection that took place in August by the two most senior army officers of the day, Viscount Townshend, the Master General of the Ordnance, and Lord Amherst, the Commander-in-Chief. The visit of these two men may well have led to the suspension of work. During their visit, Debbieg had urged both men to send a committee of the most eminent military engineers to Chatham to provide their opinion on how best to defend it.[19] His request was granted, and a committee composed of Major-General Bramham, Major-General William Roy, Colonel James Moncrieff and Colonel John Brewse spent two days of inspection at Chatham, from 5 November.

Debbieg's preparations for this meeting included a plan that still survives (Fig 5.4). He proposed enormously increased defences, with new fortifications on both sides of the Medway that took in all the high points from which the dockyard could be bombarded. Radial lines were centred on the dockyard and set at half-mile intervals. The outermost fortifications would have been 2 miles from the dockyard. No fewer than eight bastioned forts were proposed as an outer line of defence, with the land in between controlled by lines of bastions and detached redoubts.

Debbieg's design was wholly impractical. The cost of the works and the numbers of soldiers required to man the defences would have been prohibitive. Debbieg was devastated to learn that he had not even been made a member of the committee of inspection, and so in order to make them understand his vision for the defence of Chatham, he sent them a series of questions.[20] On 10 November he followed this up with his own opinions, based upon the plan he had done. Debbieg need not have worried, because the official report of the committee of inspection agreed with him on nearly all points.

The report of the committee was submitted as a letter to the Master General of the Ordnance on 12 November[21] and looked at how Chatham might be attacked by three routes – up the River Medway, by land along the Kentish road after making a landing elsewhere in east Kent, and by land across the Hoo peninsula after making a landing from the Thames. The first route was quickly dismissed, since by the 1780s works were planned to strengthen the fortifications around Sheerness dockyard,

which would control the entrance to the Medway, described as 'that winding intricate river of very difficult navigation'.[22] The second mode of attack by land was the reason why the Chatham Lines had originally been built. The committee thought that such an attack was unlikely, because after they had landed, an enemy force would be engaged by a defensive field force in open country. They did, however, concede that the dockyard should be defended against an enemy who managed to penetrate that far.[23] For this, the outer ring of forts proposed by Debbieg was supported, and the committee even said that were it not for the

Fig 5.4
Debbieg's extravagant
proposal of 1783 for the new
Chatham defences.
(TNA MPHH 1/296)

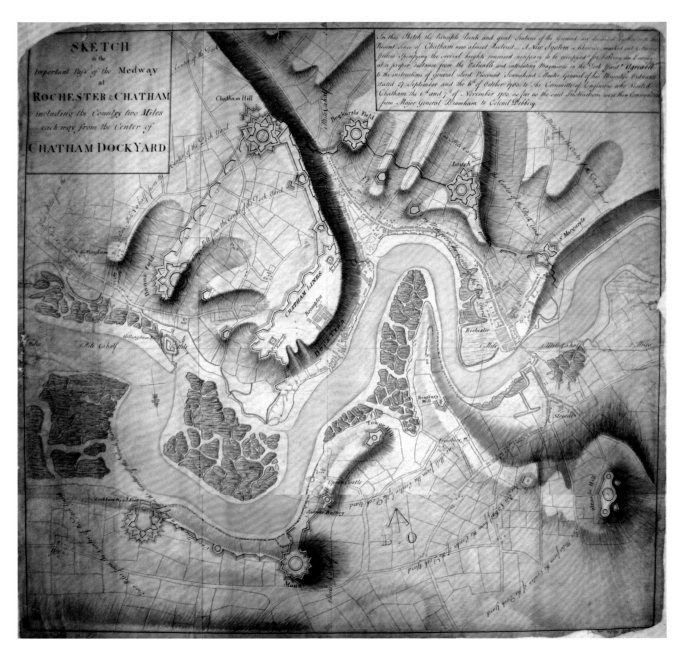

cost of acquiring the land, the village of Gillingham might have been purchased so that fortifications could be built there. The committee did not agree that the expense of linking the proposed forts by continuous bastioned lines was justified. Instead, it was thought that correctly positioned forts could control the land between them, a recommendation that foreshadowed the defensive solution adopted in the late 19th century by the concrete ring forts.

The committee thought that the dockyard was most vulnerable to the third method of attack, from the direction of the Thames, and that the Chatham Lines provided no defence against an assault from the west which might bombard the dockyard across the river. To counter this threat, the committee agreed that new forts were justified. In order to move defending troops over the Medway, the committee relied on the existing bridge at Rochester, which they considered would be protected by the works proposed at St Margarets. An army of 8,000 to 10,000 men was judged necessary to defend Chatham properly.

The report acknowledged that the cost of the proposed new works would be very great:

it is sufficiently obvious that the proposed works being numerous and some of them considerable the expence as well as the body of troops absolutely necessary for their defence must be very great independent of the army acting in the field. We therefore submit whether it will not be advisable to limit the execution for the present at least to three of the most essential posts, namely Four Elms Hill, Gillingham and Chatham Hill. The other posts ... we think might be left to be executed by the troops as field works only on the commencement of any future war.[24]

The three sites identified for immediate works were broadly in accord with Debbieg's earlier 1779 proposal for strengthening the Chatham Lines. A fort at Four Elms Hill on the Hoo side of the River Medway was a new concept, though it was never built, while the need for works near Gillingham and south of Chatham was well known.

The committee reported to Viscount Townshend who was then temporarily in charge at the Ordnance Board. When the Duke of Richmond resumed control as Master General, he still considered that Portsmouth and Plymouth were the most important dockyards to defend, not Chatham, and so he did not accept the rec-

ommendations of the 1783 report. Debbieg seems to have felt insulted and began to champion the cause of Chatham. In 1784 he wrote to Richmond in an insulting manner for which he was court-martialled, escaping with minor punishment. In 1789 he repeated his criticism of Richmond and his zeal for erecting military works, saying that he was 'like the architect who built an elegant town hall and forgot a staircase to ascend to it.'[25] Another court martial saw Debbieg tried for insult and disrespect. He was suspended for 6 months, and this once eminent military engineer spent the last 20 years of his life in retirement, until his death in 1810.

The Duke of Richmond did not get his own way over the defence of the other dockyards. In 1785 some of the same engineers who had visited Chatham now offered their expertise with reference to Portsmouth and Plymouth. Armed with their advice, Richmond proposed major works at both places estimated to cost £760,079 in total – a colossal sum for the late 18th century and requiring 22,000 troops to man the defences. The proposal was debated in the House of Commons in 1786, and when the House divided it was exactly split, 169 votes in favour of the new fortifications and 169 against. The speaker used his casting vote, and by coming down on the side of the *noes* he ensured that Richmond's grand scheme was voted down.[26]

Debbieg was replaced as commanding Royal Engineer for Chatham by Andrew Durnford, who was responsible for completing work on parts of the lines started by Debbieg, including the couvre porte with its casemated guardhouse. In 1786 Durnford advertised the sale of up to 7 million bricks from the south hill at Chatham that Debbieg had intended for a new fort there.[27] The same year also saw works at the Amherst redoubt, the main magazine and Belvedere battery, indicating that Fort Amherst had come into existence by this date. In May 1787 Durnford was replaced at Chatham by William Spry, but little work was done under his command, though he did sign an unimplemented 1796 proposal to extend the Gunwharf, which would have required a new barrier ditch. Spry was at Chatham for 10 years, until 1797. Despite the recommendations of the 1783 committee, no new works would be built at Chatham until after 1803. Thomas Nepean took over from Spry, and he was the Royal Engineer who would be responsible for starting the next major construction phase of the Chatham Lines.

Napoleonic Wars and the Threat of Invasion

French support in 1778 for the rebellious American colonists had unforeseen consequences for France. The subsequent importation of American ideals was a contributory factor to the 1789 revolution that deposed Louis XVI and plunged Europe into crisis. For almost the next 25 years there was war, as the old monarchies opposed the new order established in France. This war spread throughout Europe and to the overseas colonies, and it was fought at a scale and ferocity that presaged the great wars of the 20th century.

Britain stood against France in all of this great period of destruction. As a maritime nation with only a small army, Britain looked to the navy as its traditional line of both defence and attack. The French fleet was blockaded in its ports and attacked when it put to sea. Naval victories confirmed British superiority at sea, but on land the French dominated Europe. One

by one French armies neutralised the countries of the alliances ranged against them. By 1802 Britain stood alone, with Napoleon preparing for invasion, and with the resumption of war in 1803, France once more threatened invasion.

The outbreak of the Revolutionary Wars with France in 1793, unlike other wars, did not prompt immediate investment at Chatham to defend the dockyard. To judge by the expenditure on the fortifications (Fig 6.1), little work was carried out before 1803.[1] For 10 years expenditure on the lines appears to have been less than was needed for their upkeep, and it can be assumed that they were once more neglected and unserviceable. Indeed, in 1798 the general commanding the southern district of England described the Chatham Lines as 'not tenable in their present state'. From 1803 the renewed threat from France brought about the largest programme of homeland fortification

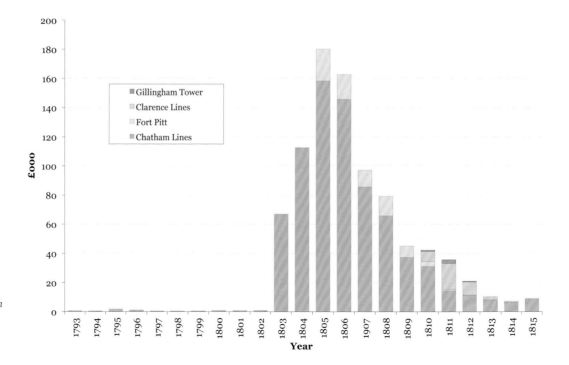

Fig 6.1
Expenditure at Chatham in the years 1793–1815 (calculated from various sources).

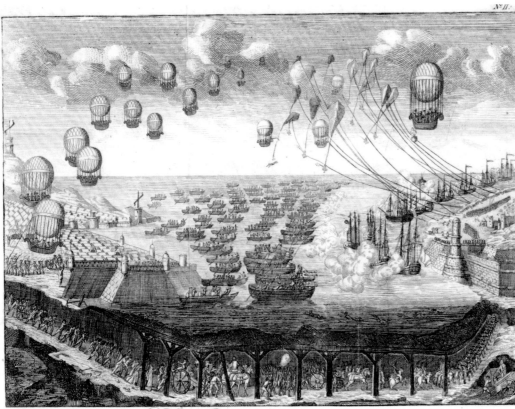

Fig 6.2
A French print of the early
19th century showing
fantastic plans for invading
England, with a tunnel
under the Channel, balloons
dropping bombs and a
flotilla of boats.
(Author)

that had yet been seen in the United Kingdom, and it included major works at Chatham. The period of greatest construction activity at Chatham and the majority of the surviving military sites, including the third and final phase of the lines, belong to the period 1803–15.

Invasion threats

New works in Kent to counter an invasion were concentrated on the coast, but French intentions for an invasion did not focus on England, but rather on Ireland, which they considered to be in a condition more susceptible to revolution and an uprising against the British. Between 1796 and 1798 six invasion schemes were planned for Ireland, with differing degrees of seriousness of intent. The 1796 attempt was the only one to actually land significant numbers of troops ashore. This was at Bantry Bay, but most of the attacking force was prevented from landing by bad weather. A better opportunity for an invasion occurred in 1797 with the paralysis of the naval defences caused by the naval mutinies, but the French failed to take advantage of this.

In 1798 Napoleon, then a general in the army, was called on to assess the opportunity to invade England. He concluded that such a project was doomed to failure, stating 'To undertake an invasion of England without being masters of the sea would be the boldest and most difficult operation ever carried out'. A war-weary Britain made peace with France in March 1802 with the Treaty of Amiens, but what followed was more a period of armed truce than a real peace, because the causes of the conflict remained. While the British nobility flocked to fashionable Paris once more, neither side disarmed, and indeed Napoleon used the short period of peace to build up his army and navy and to try to repair the French finances.

Resumption of open warfare was inevitable, and it came in May 1803, leaving thousands of British nationals trapped in France. As soon as war was resumed, Britain re-imposed the blockade of the enemy harbours. Despite later naval victories for the Royal Navy, it was this relentless year-on-year blockade that provided the key to success, while British dominance at sea also facilitated attacks on France's commercial shipping.

FRENCH INVASION _or_ BUONAPARTÉ Landing in Great Britain.

Fig 6.3
A cartoon by James Gillray
published in June 1803
showing the valiant British
fighting the French invaders
on the landing beaches and
forcing them to retreat in
disarray.
(© National Maritime
Museum, Greenwich, UK,
PAH7338)

Napoleon prepared to invade. If the French could have avoided the Royal Navy, they might have made a successful landing in 1803, because the major coastal defences were not yet underway. Had they done so, it would have meant tackling the fortress at Dover on their flank and the lines of Chatham that lay on their line of advance from east Kent to London. If they had marched around Chatham via Maidstone, the Chatham force could have mounted a counterattack. Both Chatham and Dover might have had to be taken by siege, which required heavy artillery, not the lighter field pieces that accompanied mobile infantry and cavalry. Heavy artillery could not be landed until a port was under French control, and even then it would take some time to move a siege train into position.

The French not only had to land where there were sufficient resources to support their forces,[2] but they also needed a harbour to land heavy equipment such as large guns and the siege train. They therefore looked to the shortest crossing in the Dover straits, although years later in exile on St Helena, Napoleon told his physician Barry O'Meara that 'I would have hastened over my flotilla with two hundred thousand men, landed as near as Chatham as possible, and proceeded direct to London'.[3] He possibly intended to land at Pegwell Bay, which suggests that the less than well-defended harbours on Thanet were his target, with an arrival timed for the harvest period when agricultural produce would be readily available to support his force.[4]

By 1804 Napoleon had a force of 120,000 men to land in Britain, and with these he might

have achieved local superiority over the defending forces, as they had to cover all possible invasion points. On land in 1805 the British regular army numbered 20,316 cavalry, 17,109 artillery and 124,521 infantry, making a total force of 161,946, supplemented by a militia of 89,809 men.[5] This was a considerable home defence force and made Napoleon plan for a much larger landing force than that envisaged in 1759 or 1779. To transport these men, specialised invasion craft were built. To embark an invasion force required major construction projects on the French side of the Channel. Four new harbours were constructed, of which Boulogne was the largest, with smaller ones at Étaples, Wimereux and Ambleteuse. This was a massive construction programme of new basins and improved access to the sea to enable rapid embarkation. In addition, forts and batteries were built to defend the French harbours in case of a pre-emptive British strike.

In Britain, new defensive fortifications were likewise judged necessary, as the threat of French invasion persisted. Up to 1805, it was a very real threat, as seen in June of that year when Napoleon outlined his thoughts on invasion to Marshal Berthier:

Master all the details as to provisions, brandy, shoes and everything concerning the landing. Put on board a great quantity of artillery tools. You know there is always a deficiency in campaigning. I shall have to lay siege to Dover castle, Chatham and perhaps Portsmouth. Talk it over with Marescol, General of Engineers. It is possible to land troops enough perhaps to besiege the three places at the same time. We must have no ifs or buts or fors. All my chances are calculated beforehand. Let tools of every sort be shipped and take care that nothing is wanted.[6]

By August 1805 an invasion flotilla had been assembled that was capable of transporting 167,000 men, and 93,000 men were encamped, ready to embark. Much speculation is possible about what would have happened if the French had attempted to invade. The purpose-built invasion craft were actually unstable in rough seas, as a disastrous drowning of many troops during an exercise proved. If not first destroyed by the Royal Navy, the invasion force would have been vulnerable to gunfire from coastal batteries that mounted heavy guns firing anti-personnel munitions. Carnage would have awaited the first troops to land on a defended beach, particularly as they would have been largely defenceless until damp weapons were dried out.

The moment of most danger for Britain was from the end of 1804 when a declaration of war by Spain increased the number of ships with which Napoleon could confront the Royal Navy, but the combined French and Spanish fleet was destroyed by Nelson at Trafalgar in October 1805. The loss of the warships removed the ability to protect an invasion force and did much to postpone the threat of invasion. The moment of crisis had passed, but there were more significant reasons why invasion did not come. In the summer of 1805 the chances of a French invasion were ebbing away as Pitt's diplomacy was gaining ground and the Third Coalition of Britain, Russia, Austria and Naples was formed to oppose Napoleon. Before Trafalgar, Napoleon had in fact already diverted his invasion force to march against Austria, subsequently winning the stunning victory at Austerlitz. With his army still intact, he regarded the invasion as postponed rather than cancelled and never fully abandoned his aspiration to attack Great Britain.

France had theoretical control of much of Europe, frequently through puppet monarchs, and despite the defeat at Trafalgar, Napoleon continued to build up his fleet and constructed dockyards in conquered territories. Completion of the defences of the south coast of England and the close blockade of the available embarkation ports made it unlikely that a surprise invasion could be made. Numerical superiority had to be achieved by neutralising the Royal Navy beforehand. Countering this threat lay behind much of British policy for the remainder of the war. The pre-emptive assault on Copenhagen in 1807 was to prevent the Danish navy from falling into French hands and to prevent French control of the Baltic and the shipbuilding materials that it provided. In 1809 the disastrous Walcheren campaign by the British was intended to prevent the use of the Scheldt as a base for invasion and shipbuilding.

Even by 1812 the threat of invasion had not lifted. Napoleon considered that war in the Iberian peninsula had so denuded troops available to the British at home that an attack could not be resisted. He said that 'nothing can stop 25,000 men from going and burning Chatham'.[7] He contemplated either a quick raid or a larger-scale expedition to Ireland, and in autumn 1812 he spent time at Boulogne. Naval superiority could not be secured, and instead he invaded Russia, but to keep Britain in a state of permanent alarm, a considerable flotilla was maintained at Boulogne.

The 1803 analysis of the defences

The French did not of course invade, but the British felt under constant threat, and so investment in defences at Chatham and elsewhere continued well beyond the period of greatest danger in 1803–5, as the details of fortification expenditure show (Fig 6.1). Expenditure on new works at Chatham did tail off from 1812 and almost ceased by 1813, which is not surprising as the threat of invasion was considered to have passed and the war was being fought out in Europe. The situation might have been very different at Chatham, because the abandonment of its dockyard and those on the Thames was considered in favour of a huge new naval arsenal at Northfleet.[8] Instead, work was undertaken to better equip the dockyard for its role as a major building and repair yard for the Royal Navy.

In early 1803 the coastal defences along the south coast of England were considered inadequate, which led to a very large programme of new fortifications, and the rebuilding of the Chatham Lines to protect the dockyard and the wider area formed part of this programme. Command of the vulnerable southern army district was given to General Sir David Dundas, and he analysed the strategic situation for south-east England

and its defence. His 1803 report explains the work that subsequently took place not just at Chatham but throughout Kent and Sussex:

London may be regarded as a centre to the whole of the coast of Kent and Sussex no part being less than 56 miles from it and no part exceeding 70. An enemy landing on the coast of Sussex has a very difficult intricate and defensible country to pass through and no material object to attain till he arrives in the neighbourhood of London but an enemy landing on the east or south coast of Kent has a short passage to make and a short communication to establish with his own coast and may probably gain such a position as will enable him to receive reinforcements. He will have in view the possession of the coast at Deal and perhaps be enabled to render the anchorage of the Downs very precarious. Canterbury and east Kent would afford him a strong situation and great resources. If his superiority enables him to advance with success his right flank will be covered. In gaining the establishment of Faversham, Chatham and Sheerness he will possess a fine and productive country where from its local situation it will be very difficult afterwards to approach him covered as he will be by the Medway and by the range of chalk hills from Maidstone to Folkestone.[9]

Dundas went on to give his ideas on the defences of Chatham:

In this point of view the substantial repair of the old lines that cover Chatham Dock and holding them and the high ground of Brompton as a tête de pont communicating with and supported by an army then supposed behind the Medway would not only delay but make it impossible for an enemy however in numbers (though necessarily ill provided with artillery and the means of attack) to force a passage ... The situation of the lines is favourable. They so effectually cover the approach in sight of the dock. Shipping in the river could be placed to flank them so effectually and their remains are so considerable that it is thought they could be re-established at an expence moderate for the object proposed. A secure communication with Upnor ensured to the troops and an enemy unprovided with heavy artillery would be obliged to retire before them ... On the whole east Kent may be considered as the first and most desirable object an enemy can have in view on attempting an invasion of this country as from thence alone he can hope to establish a communication with France however precarious and at leisure pursue his further projects.[10]

The Commander-in-Chief was HRH the Duke of York, and his response to the invasion threat was revealed in a letter of 25 August 1803 to Lord Hobart, Secretary of State for War:

The works proposed at Chatham are intended to place an army in his front, on the right bank of the Medway; those upon the Western Heights *(Dover)* another body in his rear ... In regards to the works at Chatham I should deem it sufficient reason for their construction that they offered a reasonable prospect of preventing the naval arsenal which they cover from falling into the hands of an enemy. But this is not their only advantage. As a Tete de Pont on the right bank of the Medway they place an entrenched army in the front of the enemy which cannot be neglected with impunity or reduced without siege.[11]

The 1803 programme of work

Napoleon boasted that he would be in London within four days of an invasion. The purpose of Chatham was to hold up his advance long enough for troops to be massed for the defence of London and for field fortifications of entrenchments and palisades to be dug to protect the capital. Even after clearing Chatham, the French could not directly assault London, because advanced works were prepared on Shooters Hill to further delay them.

From the summer of 1803 Chatham was reinforced as a fortress capable of withstanding a siege and capable of defending the dockyard. In the 10-year period until 1813, the appearance of Chatham was transformed by a programme of construction that included additional fortifications and also two new sets of barracks, two military hospitals, two new magazines, an extension to the Gunwharf and various lesser projects. All this work was supervised by a small team of Royal Engineer officers, initially under Thomas Nepean, and from March 1804 by his successor, Robert D'Arcy.

The major changes to the defences included a new magazine within a ravelin between Prince Frederick's bastion and the Duke of Cumberland's bastion, the revetment in brick of all the scarps, counterscarps and parapets of the bastions, a hornwork at the site of the couvre porte, the completion of Fort Amherst as a major citadel and a new barrier ditch above the Gunwharf. An entirely new fortification near Gillingham was known as the Lower Lines.

Other work was also carried out to guarantee the security of the dockyard, picking up on the recommendations of the 1783 committee. This work included the construction of Fort Pitt on the south hill above Chatham, with two detached towers, Delce and Gibraltar, and the construction of the Clarence Lines on land at St Margarets, near Rochester. Strangely, no significant steps were taken to fortify the Hoo side of the river, even though a successful landing from the River Thames could have compromised the Chatham defences. Some redundant fortifications such as Cockham Wood Fort ceased to have any real military purpose. Gillingham Fort was largely given up, but a new gun tower was built adjacent to it.

A military road network was created through the town of Chatham to connect Fort Amherst to Fort Pitt, and a communication in the form of a pontoon bridge was placed across the River Medway at a point just north of the dockyard over to the Upnor shore. For the Ordnance Board, expanded facilities included a large new magazine downstream of Upnor Castle and new buildings at the Gunwharf, along with an extension known as the New Gunwharf.

At the existing infantry barracks, a military hospital was added, and the Brompton barracks were constructed for the artillery and casemated barracks were built within the Lower Lines.

The men responsible for the remodelling of the Chatham Lines and returning them rapidly to use were the Duke of York, who was the commander-in-chief, General Sir David Dundas, the commander of the southern army district, William Twiss, the senior engineer advising him, and the Earl of Chatham, who was Master General of the Ordnance. Below the Earl of Chatham was the Inspector-General of Fortifications. This post, created in 1802 to replace the Board of Ordnance's Chief Engineer, was held by Robert Morse. The commanding Royal Engineer for Chatham was Thomas Nepean. The correspondence between these men in the anxious days of summer 1803, when invasion was anticipated at any time, provides an interesting and all-too-human insight into events.[12]

The Ordnance Board took charge of upgrading the Chatham fortifications, but the Royal Staff Corps started the work, not troops of the Ordnance Board. On 2 July the Duke of York instructed the construction of 'fieldworks' to form a tête de pont, and under instruction from Dundas, the commander of the Royal Staff Corps, Lieutenant-Colonel Brown (Assistant Quartermaster General), put 200 soldiers of the guards and 100 of his own corps to work, clearing the ditches and preparing to palisade

them. The involvement of the Royal Staff Corps did not go down well with the Royal Engineers, who thought that their seniority and responsibility for garrisons and for permanent fortifications had been usurped.

Nepean was clearly of the view that the work should have fallen to the engineers of the Board of Ordnance, and he reported to his superior, Robert Morse, that he was being requested to assist the Royal Staff Corps with the supply of intrenching tools and timber. On 9 July Morse suggested in strong terms to Horseguards that the building of fortifications should be the work of his Royal Engineer department. Two days later, in a private letter to Morse, Nepean gave his low opinion of the Royal Staff Corps:

> the Staff Corps will soon be tired of what they have undertaken. They have certainly very bad materials to work with, loose gravel and sand to be supported by sod that blows off in dust as it dries which has been found by way of experiment that have been made of it here to be totally useless so that the work that is done today they will have to do again so soon as the sod dries, after having expended a large sum of money it will be found necessary to consider by what means the works are to be made secure from an assault.[13]

The work continues

On 16 July 1803, Morse wrote to Nepean indicating that the re-formation of the Chatham Lines would be accepted as a project by the Ordnance Board, under Nepean's direction, and that he should expect military working parties. Captains Gravatt and Handfield were ordered to Chatham to assist Nepean. Two days later Morse confrmed this officially and relieved Nepean of his Sheerness work so that he might concentrate on Chatham. Meanwhile, William Twiss visited Chatham and reported to Dundas on the 17th that for a cost of between £20,000 and £30,000 and a garrison of 6,000 soldiers, the existing Chatham Lines could be made tenable by the following works:

> In obedience to your orders I have considered the very important objects, you mentioned to me of affording some security to the dockyard at Chatham, and proposing at the same time a force on each side of the river Medway so near to the Thames. I entirely agree with you that these general objects can only be obtained by a very commodious communication across the Medway and fortifying Chatham Lines as

Royal Staff Corps

The first training establishment for military engineers at Chatham was not for the Royal Engineers, but for the Royal Staff Corps. The depot of the Royal Engineers was at Woolwich, and the Royal Engineers as an officer-only corps under the control of the Master General of the Ordnance was very small in numbers. The army, commanded from Horseguards, was frequently short of trained engineers to use on campaign, and so in 1799, in the context of the Duke of York's expedition to Holland, the solution was to create the Royal Staff Corps. This was a body of military engineers composed of officers and men who reported not to the Ordnance Board, but to the Quartermaster General of the army.

The Royal Staff Corps was established as 4 companies, each consisting of 2 sergeant overseers, a drummer or bugler, 14 carpenters, sawyers or others capable of working in wood, 4 shipwrights, 4 stonemasons, 2 blacksmiths, 2 bricklayers, 4 miners or quarrymen and 20 labourers composed of woodsmen, ditchers, basketmakers and so on. It was proposed that the depot of the Royal Staff Corps should be at Chatham:

It is obvious that nothing can be done until such a depot is permanently established and ground provided as will afford the requisites and opportunities of practical instruction. No place can be more eligible than Chatham should His Royal Highness think it proper to apply to the Master General of the Ordnance for the ground adjoining to the barracks originally taken by the public for the purposes of defence for a plan since abandoned and which has occasioned the ground to be applied for private use.

The depot once fixed a general system of instruction ought to be established by which every individual ought to be employed in the construction of field works to be taught the different modes of applying the materials generally found in a country to the purposes of bridges, repair of roads also making of wickerwork construction gabions, fascines, preparing and planting palisadoes, cheveaux de frise etc. It is also highly necessary that the practice of pontooning should be generally taught a duty however essential in itself which has hitherto been little attended to in the British Army.[14]

In 1803 the duties of the staff corps were amended, with a clear emphasis on support of troops when on campaign:

Services unprovided for are those of the pontooneer and pioneer, when it is intended to fortify a village or secure the avenues of a position, to direct the profile and ensure the solidity of fieldworks and also to prepare materials for their construction, at other times to facilitate the movement of an army over enclosed or intersected ground using the materials at hand for the purpose of bridges, to repair roads, passage of swamps or when it becomes necessary to impede the progress of an enemy by the felling of timber, destruction of roads and bridges.[15]

After only two years, the Royal Staff Corps moved their depot to Hythe from where they were responsible for the construction of the Royal Military Canal, their greatest legacy, creating a water-filled defensive gun line to isolate the rear of Romney Marsh and try to stop an advancing invasion force. The Royal Staff Corps would also provide particularly valuable service in the Peninsular campaign of Wellington, where their numbers increased the available trained engineers. The separate existence of a pioneer corps under command of the army lasted until the 1830s when the Royal Staff Corps was absorbed into the Ordnance Board troops.

a Tete de Pont. To carry such a system into effect it seems essential ... to be certain that the communication across the Medway can be made commodious and secure, and at present I see no very great difficulty in accomplishing this, providing we are assisted by the great resources of men, vessels and materials with which the Dockyard abounds.

The most commodious passage ... is from the upper end of the mast houses across the opposite marsh to the nearest chalk pit, the total distance between which we judged to be about 1000 yards.

The commanding post of Chatham Lines is on the right where Fort Amherst with its dependencies (being reveted) may be considered secure against a coup de main; between this and the Gun Wharf may I also conceive be rendered unassailable in two months supposing it defended by a good garrison.

Some of the fronts of the Lines which join Fort Amherst on the left are on a soil mixed with chalk, and may be considered nearly in the same predicament, but a general extent of the lines on the high ground on the left are in a sandy loose soil which appears to be unfavourable for field works that I should doubt the possibility of constructing any in this front which can be deemed unassailable even when strengthened by palisades; however to obtain great objects some risks must be run. A square redoubt called Fort Townsend offers here many advantages: I think that in three months by using the old bricks on the spot it might be renewed and strengthened by loop holed guard houses in the counterscarp constructed under the opposite angles so as to maintain itself even after the lines were forced. I should also strongly recommend that the wall which surrounds the dock should be occupied and considered as an entrenchment ...

It is impossible to speak with any certainty either of the time or expence of such works, but I should suppose they might be in a tolerable state of defence at the close of the present summer, provided the means were liberally granted, and an efficient system adopted.[16]

Though incapacitated with gout, such that he found it difficult to walk or ride, Nepean lost no time in forming his own opinion of what had to be done, and on 22 July he reported to Dundas:

The lines on the left of Prince of Wales bastion I propose to palisade in every part where the ground will admit of fixing them securely at the foot of the scarp and its tenacity such that the scarp will stand in such a direction as to make it difficult for a man to ascend if the pallisades were destroyed. The remaining part where the soil is composed of sand with a very small mixture of other matter must be revetted with brick of a slight profile and fraised as they contribute more to defences than palisades.

On that part of the lines between the wall of the dock yard and nearly to the scarp wall below Townsend redoubt a wet ditch may be obtained by forming a sluice at the entrance to the pond at the north end of the dockyard (now used to receive old masts) and a dam to prevent the water passing off by the creek which will save the expense of palisades or fraise and the parapet may be formed at pleasure. By the same sluice the marshes and low ground in front of this work may be flooded if necessary. The whole of the counterscarp of the front of the lines will be formed with the least slope from a perpendicular as the different qualities of the ground will allow.

Townshend's redoubt to be revetted both the scarp and counterscarp with loopholed casemates for the defence of the ditch and fraise upon the berm. The space between the magazine and Gunwharf to be occupied by a line of good profile and fraised keeping on the commanding ground where its natural foundation will permit, the old trace being too low and exposed to enfilade. Different landing places must be prepared opposite the dockyard and causeways across the marsh. Barges with boats to tow them ... should be employed to transport troops and keep the communication open between the two shores.[17]

On the 24th Nepean informed Morse that he would have preferred time in which to prepare proper sections and estimates for the works, but that the presence of military working parties requiring his immediate direction prevented this. These working parties came from regiments at or near Chatham and undertook much of the early labour. Nepean asked for more assistance to be sent to him in the form of junior officers, a draughtsman, a master mason and an overseer. Morse replied the same day, pointing out the scarcity of trained engineer officers and suggesting that in view of the urgency, work parties could be overseen by NCOs and steady privates of the Royal Military Artificers, adding: 'As Capt Gravatt and Capt Handfield have joined you, who are both active and able officers, I trust your progress will be rapid and I will send you some subalterns the first moment it shall be in my power, perhaps you are not aware that we have not at this time a second lieutenant in the corps.'[18]

The next day Nepean privately voiced his opinion of Dundas to Morse:

Sir David Dundas has taken it into his head that he is a great engineer. He calls once or twice a day with something to propose or talk about. At first he wished to have deep ditches, now he is sorry that the ditches have been formed before the curtain but recommends that the counterscarp should be fraised. And abbatis, trou de loups, cheveaux de fries should be made use of. Since Twiss has made his report the wall of the dockyard has become a favourite object tho only musket proof and completely commanded at less than a hundred yards distance which with a six pounder might be beat down in four minutes. The troops are to embark (if obliged to retire) from the ships in the dockyard so that a considerable part of this famous wall must be broken down for the troops to pass through. He came to me last night to tell me that the Duke of York was to be here Wednesday next and that he wished that something might be done to make some show. Luckily enough the foundation of the scarp wall of Townshend's redoubt was laid this morning and by Wednesday will be far advanced so that his Royal Highness will be able to guess as what is intended to be done.[19]

On 1 August, and perhaps as a result of the royal inspection, Morse wrote to Nepean urging him on:

an observation among the great men whilst at Chatham that the repairs are not carrying on with vigour, not a gun mounted and a working party of 600 men only whereas when the Staff Corps was employed they had a party of 2,000 men. Now my dear Nepean as you, I and Lord Chatham are all pledged for the due and explicit execution of this work I must exhort you to strain every nerve for its completion. Although I have no subaltern engineers to send you I will order Major D'Arcy from Gravesend if you think you can employ him to advantage. I wish to have all the different parts of the works going on at the same time. I believe an order has gone for the Staff Corps to work under your direction. This corps will furnish officers to answer the purpose of subaltern engineers. If bricklayers are to be had in the country and a master or foreman to conduct the work engage them so that the revetments and field works may be going on together whilst embrasures are opening and platforms laying. Do not be limited either by forms or fear of expense.[20]

An affronted Nepean responded in private to Morse on 3 August to assert that the Royal Staff Corps had never had 2,000 men engaged on the project and to welcome the offer of assistance from Major Robert D'Arcy, then based at Gravesend. D'Arcy would continue to reside at Gravesend and make the short journey to Chatham to assist Nepean. Thus another of the Royal Engineer officers, who like Debbieg and Nepean would have such influence on the fortifications, was introduced to Chatham. On the same day Nepean wrote again to Morse to explain his proposals for the new works near Gillingham, known now as the Lower Lines. Pressure on the Royal Engineer officers must have been great, for Morse responded on the 4th:

I am so anxious about the progress of the works at Chatham that I answer both your letters by return of post. As upon this occasion we have not only to fortify but if we can to please and make a show. I think some guns upon the right in Fort Amherst or where you may find more further might be mounted ... Sir Thomas Hyde Page having offered his service and who is certainly a very capable man I propose sending him to you and would recommend your employing him in forming the communication across the river in which sort of work he is particularly conversant. I also think you might employ him with advantage upon the works on the opposite side to Chatham.[21]

Thomas Hyde Page was a member of the Corps of Invalid Engineers, having lost a leg at

the battle of Bunker Hill during the American war. A highly experienced Royal Engineer, he was therefore volunteering to come off the inactive list at this time of national crisis, and this letter confirms his role in the construction of hards to enable a pontoon bridge to be thrown over the Medway.

The next letter from Nepean to Morse on 13 August reveals that after an intense period of activity lasting just six weeks, the Chatham Lines were approaching a viable state, as he was able to request that guns be supplied from the Gunwharf and elsewhere. This letter also reveals the design to be adopted at the Lower Lines. From a sketch attached to the letter, it is clear that the works as built did not follow the 1779 design of Debbieg but were designed by the officers headed by Nepean:

I enclose a sketch of alterations it has been necessary to make from the plan I sent you. I was unwilling to do it or to mention it to you until I had taken the opinion of Twiss who was here on his way to Woolwich and D'Arcy who has given me so much of his time as he could spare from his duty at Gravesend. There happened to be here at the same time six engineers, Twiss, D'Arcy, Ford, Gravatt, Handfield and myself and ... we all agreed that the sketch I now send should be adopted ... Platforms are in part laid and other laying on such part of the works as are in a state to receive them and matters appear to give satisfaction to Sir David as he has been unusually quiet for some time. I send a request for more tools (those I have are very bad) and shall be very glad to be furnished with horses for the carts. I send likewise a list of such guns as will be required for the works. The 2 ten pounders and 30 nine pounders mentioned in the return that are now upon the Gunwharf should be proved before they are mounted. If only 8 nine pounders the number required for the lines are proved it will be all that is necessary. I am very glad that Sir T H Page is likely to be with me. He will be of great use in establishing the communication across the river which I mean to give to him entirely. I am of opinion that bridges can be formed notwithstanding the tides by means of a floating raft to low water mark and boats or barges. At the bottom of this is a sketch of the raft I propose.[22]

On 15 August Morse wrote to Nepean and promised him the services of two subalterns: 'The alteration you have proposed having been considered upon the ground by so many engineers I must conclude is for the better so that I have only to impress upon you the necessity of speedy execution.' On the 21st Nepean was once more reporting good progress to Morse:

I have got 200 more men for the works and a strong regiment will be here tomorrow from which I hope to get 500 more. The West Middlesex from which I got 200 the whole they could furnish the rest being recruits was sent for from Coxheath and the Darby which will be here tomorrow were sent upon my application to Sir David Dundas for more men. I can employ more men than they are able to give me which I have told Sir David so that there can be no occasion to complain of the small number employed in future.

Sir T Page joined me the 17th inst and is perfectly satisfied with his situation. He has begun about the communication and will take any other duty that may be necessary. The parish officers of Gillingham have complained of the paths through the lines being stopped. They are to state their complaints in writing which I will transmit to the Board.

We go on very well for our numbers, very quietly and without any ill natured remarks from any person and as our means are increased the more rapidly we move. I hope Mrs Morse and young ladies are well.[23]

On 7 September Nepean reported further good progress to Morse:

The works are going on very well but we shall in a day or two want very much of wheelbarrows and other articles I wrote for some time since. Some tents are very much wanted for the men as it has become necessary to place guards over the tools and materials for we are surrounded with thieves. General Dundas left us last Saturday and we expect Lord Chatham every day.[24]

The Earl of Chatham reportedly inspected the works on 19 September. In October Colonel Whitworth, the commanding officer of the Royal Artillery at Chatham, asked the Ordnance Board for munitions and tools so that the guns mounted on the remodelled Chatham Lines could be fired.[25] In the Royal Engineers letter books at the RE Museum and Library, there is a schedule of guns to be supplied to Chatham that Nepean requested in August 1803, with 140 separate pieces of artillery (Table 6.1).[26] While it is not easy to relate these guns precisely to the works described by Nepean in his letters, there is no doubt that he and his small group of Royal Engineer officers had restored the Chatham fortifications to fighting capacity in less than four months. To have done so in such short order means that the fortifications must have consisted largely of hastily dug new fieldworks and the remodelling of the existing 1783 lines – work that was a remarkable achievement.

Table 6.1 The 140 guns requested by Thomas Nepean for Chatham in August 1803.

	Guns			Carronades				
Where mounted	24lb	18lb	12lb	9lb	24lb	18lb	10in mortar	8in howitzer
Amherst redoubt	14		6		5	14		
Front of lines	2	8		5		18		
New works on left	1	17				8		
Battery in creek				4				
Ravelin	1	7						
Advanced work on left		1					4	4
New works on right	3	7	5	3	3			
Total	**21**	**40**	**11**	**12**	**8**	**40**	**4**	**4**

The New Fortifications

In March 1804 Robert D'Arcy took over from Nepean as the senior resident engineer at Chatham. Work now concentrated on making Nepean's refurbished Chatham Lines permanent by using brick to fully revet the ditches, parapets and gun platforms. Many other projects were also undertaken, all depicted on an 1819 map (Fig 7.1), which provides the clearest idea of the scale and complexity of the changes at Chatham during the Napoleonic Wars, particularly when compared with the situation in 1786 at the end of the American war (*see* Fig 5.3). Robert D'Arcy supervised the majority of the new works, but combined this role with other duties, because the Royal Engineers in the Medway district were also responsible for the dockyard defences and barracks at Sheerness, as well as the gunpowder mills at Faversham. In addition, D'Arcy was a serving soldier, available for overseas duty.

The engineers established a base (an engineers' park) in Prince Edward's bastion on the Chatham Lines.[1] The infrastructure for such a major construction programme was itself significant. The Board of Ordnance had its own brickfields at Upnor, from where bricks could be exported from a brick wharf downstream of the castle.[2] Bricks could be landed at the Gunwharf, and there is map evidence for a wharf that could deliver material straight to the works. Timber purchased by contract was also delivered here and stored in a timber pound.

Fig 7.1
A plan of the Chatham Lines, signed by D'Arcy on 1 February 1819, showing the state of the defences at the end of the Napoleonic Wars. (TNA MR 1/553)

The 1806 survey and other map evidence show that works depots were established close to the ongoing projects. The land now behind Chatham Town Hall was used for temporary sawpits and workshops and at least three lime-kilns. From 1804 mills with rollers were adopted on a model perfected at Woolwich to mechanise the production of mortar, and examples of these mills appear on various maps. The movement of materials was done by horse, and the Ordnance Board contracted for horses and civilian drivers.[3] The 1806 survey shows 2 mortar mills and stables for 200 contract horses in the land north of Brompton barracks.

Military working parties continued to be used as a source of labour in the subsequent works, though not exclusively so. A large amount of the new construction was carried out by private contractors, who bid for Ordnance Board commissions, or by contract civilian labourers working under the Royal Engineers' supervision. An 1805 statement of those employed at Chatham reveals over 1,800 individuals in 19 trades working under the supervision of 5 officers, 8 subalterns and 13 sergeant overseers.[4] Not surprisingly, bricklayers and their labourers formed a large proportion of the workforce, with a further 785 general labourers. There were also 90 miners. A further statement for military dispositions in 1805 mentions 528 men of the Cambridgeshire regiment and 387 of the Denbighshire available as military working parties and a further 286 Cornish miners and the men of the Royal Staff Corps.[5] It is fair to assume that the miners worked on the underground elements of the new fortifications, such as enlarging the tunnels of Fort Amherst.

The Lower Lines

The Lower Lines formed an extension to the revamped Chatham Lines. Back in 1779 Hugh Debbieg had identified the need for this ground to be fortified, but until 1803 the obsolete fort at Gillingham was the only defence against an attack coming from the River Medway or exploiting St Mary's creek. An entirely new and substantial line of rampart and ditch was connected to Prince Frederick's bastion and was carried by a pair of demi-bastions and a redan to end in a hornwork at the creek edge (Fig 7.2).[6] A casemated guardhouse (St Mary's) gave access to the hornwork. The creek was seen as a point of weakness, and in 1810 a gun

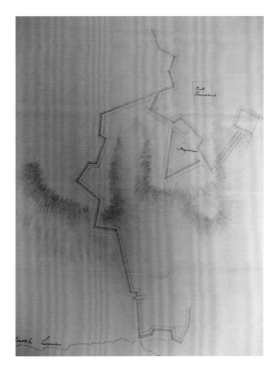

Fig 7.2
A sketch of the Lower Lines built in 1803.
(TNA WO 55/767)

tower was constructed on the mudflats adjacent to Gillingham Fort at the location of an existing barbette battery. This tower was situated to command the creek and provide fire southwards back to the Lower Lines to control a valley that leads up from the waterside.

The Lower Lines ramparts had guns positioned to fire down into the ditch bases for close defence, and others were aimed out over the glacis into the field of fire so as to keep attackers at a distance. Guns mounted on top of and inside the new barracks within the Lower Lines would have increased the available amount of fire. During recent construction works at the Lower Lines site, an entirely unsuspected element of the fortification not described in any known written record was discovered – countermine galleries (Figs 7.3 and 7.4). These were underground works planned as part of the construction of a fortification so that the defenders had a network of brick-lined tunnels from which to listen for the approach of an attacker's mining parties and to act as a starting point for their own digging of tunnels (mines) to intercept and destroy them. Such features were well known to early 19th-century engineers from military textbooks,[7] but this is the only location in Britain where prepared countermine galleries have so far been identified in Napoleonic-period fortifications. A 'magistral' gallery ran behind the counterscarp wall of the ditch, beneath the covered way, and was entered from

Fig 7.3
The domed brick structure marks the intersection of brick tunnels with examples lined in timber. (Canterbury Archaeological Trust)

Fig 7.4
An air photo of Mid Kent College under construction with the network of countermine galleries marked on it. Red line indicates brick countermine galleries; green line indicates timber shored countermine galleries. (Canterbury Archaeological Trust)

the ditch base. From this, radial tunnels or 'galleries of communication' were pushed forward under the glacis and were then linked together by an 'envelope gallery'. The ends of the radial galleries were called 'listening galleries'.

Where tunnels intersected, underground domed chambers could be formed so as to allow men to pass each other and to create places for storing tools and so on. One example is at the

Lower Lines (*see* Fig 7.3), though it appears to be later in date from the time of the later 19th-century Royal Engineers' siege training. The main galleries are red brick, corresponding with the ditch walls. The logical time to construct countermine galleries was when the ditches were dug and the glacis was formed, and so it appears that countermine measures were an original feature of the Lower Lines,

Fig 7.5
The brick-lined ditches of the Lower Lines are a patchwork of different bricks as a result of the repair of major damage to the walls caused by 19th-century siege training. (Author)

dating to around 1803. Similar works should not be discounted elsewhere on the Chatham Lines.

Today, the survival of the Lower Lines is partial but still impressive. The demi-bastions and redan remain, with the deep brick-lined ditch to the front (Fig 7.5), but the fortifications to the north were destroyed in the late 19th century for works associated with the naval barracks.

The central section of the Chatham Lines

Three of the broad bastions from the initial 1756 construction of the Chatham Lines were retained as part of the post-1803 scheme of fortification. It remains to be established whether or not their solidity was improved after the criticism voiced by the Duke of Richmond in 1781, but the ditches and parapet were now fully formed in brick. Ways through the lines on to the field of fire were needed for military purposes[8] and also to allow civilians, including workers in the dockyard, to go about their business. The main road to Gillingham from Brompton passed through the lines and over the ditch at the Brompton Barrier. The precise nature of this road is not clear as few elements of the original scheme now remain. Twin drawbridges carried the road over the ditch, and inside the rampart there was a guardhouse (since demolished) on the north side of the road. The bridge crossing was covered by guns on top of the fortification.[9]

The couvre porte–defended gateway through the lines, built as part of the 1779–86 works, was converted into a hornwork with guns to provide additional enfilade fire onto the field of fire along the length of the lines (Fig 7.6). In order to further strengthen this possible weak point in the defences, buried gun chambers under the rampart, entered from the former casemated gatehouse, were sited to fire along the ditches of the hornwork. Such buried, concealed guns behind the walls of the ditches were a feature of the re-formed Chatham Lines after 1803.[10] Today it is difficult to appreciate the form and purpose of the hornwork, because the southern half was excavated in the late 19th century to form a reservoir. A substantial casemated guardhouse (since demolished) at what is now called Sallyport Gardens seems to be of later construction.

An Act of Parliament in 1804 allowed additional land to be purchased, including an extension to the field of fire in the central section known as the Great Lines. This probably resulted from better-quality powder for use in artillery, much of it produced in the state-owned powder mills such as Faversham. The guns mounted on the defences therefore had a greater range, and so Westcourt and Upberry Farms, which pre-dated the fortifications (*see* Fig 3.5), were now taken over and demolished (*see* Fig 7.1).

Southern defences: Fort Amherst

The new Napoleonic-period fortifications at Chatham were concentrated at the northern and southern ends of the existing lines. The southern part was formed by Fort Amherst, Fort Pitt and the Clarence Lines (Fig 7.7).

Fort Amherst is acknowledged as one of the best-preserved fortifications of the early 19th century. It provided the southern termination to the Chatham Lines and was located to control the approach from the town of Chatham, including along the river, and also to support Fort Pitt. It had taken on much of its present form by 1786, but the post-1803 works saw it transformed into a citadel, dominating the surrounding land and capable of holding out even if the main fortifications were breached. Spur bastion and Prince William's bastion controlled the southern field of fire. Along with Amherst redoubt, the Prince of Wales bastion and Belvedere battery, these two bastions meant that Fort Amherst was formed of four 'defensive cells' (Fig 7.8) intended for all-round defence, unlike the older bastions on the Chatham Lines that had open backs and so could only be defended in the direction they faced. Ramparts and ditches completed the northern side of the

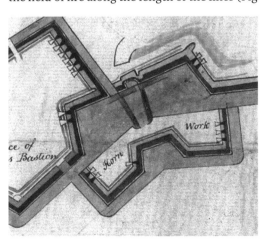

Fig 7.6
The couvre porte of 1779–86 rebuilt by D'Arcy to create a hornwork, depicted on a plan dated November 1813. (TNA MPH 1/209)

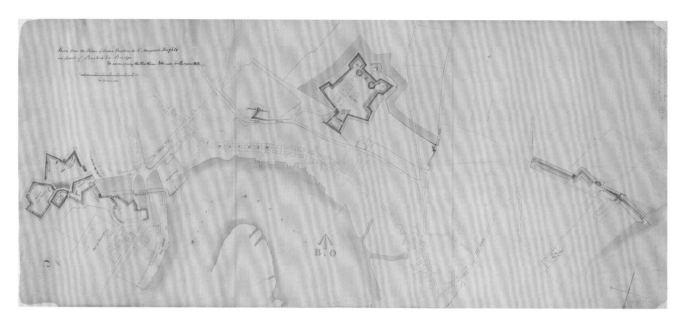

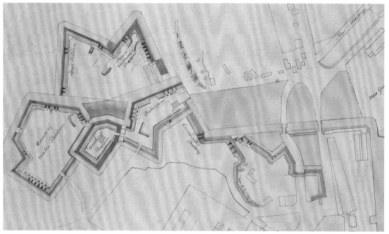

Fig 7.7 (top)
A sketch dating to 1813 from the Prince of Wales bastion to St Margaret's Heights in front of Rochester Bridge. (TNA MPHH 1/585)

Fig 7.8 (middle)
Fort Amherst in 1813. (Detail taken from TNA MPHH 1/585)

Fig 7.9 (right)
Replica gun carriages on the Upper Cornwallis battery at Fort Amherst. (Author)

fort, so that even if an enemy had forced his way through the main lines, Fort Amherst would not be compromised.

Guns were sited within the remodelled Prince of Wales bastion and in Belvedere battery, and these could fire northwards across fields of fire that were internal to the Chatham

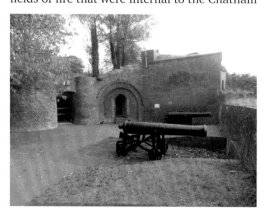

Lines. The resulting open land was a deliberate part of the military planning for the Chatham fortifications at the sites known as the Inner Lines and on Amherst Hill behind the infantry barracks.[11] The upper part of Fort Amherst was completed by the Cornwallis batteries, which had guns located to fire over the town of Chatham so as to control the newly refined road network and the broad bend of the river.

The upper parts of the fort were connected to the lower at the caveyard by a complex series of tunnels excavated out of the solid chalk, which provided the defenders with the opportunity to move under cover between the two parts and for concealed guns to be aligned along the main barrier ditch. These were an elaboration of the earlier tunnels.

The barrier ditch had been proposed for revision as early as 1796 when William Spry was the commanding engineer, and after 1803 it became a deep, straight brick-lined ditch that separated the garrison area from Chatham town (Fig 7.12). This ditch connected to the river at the Gunwharf, where it was a wet ditch and turned a right angle. Behind the walls of this stretch of the ditch, two concealed gun chambers or casemates were built so that they could fire into the river upon any attacker.[12] The upper end of the barrier ditch was controlled from Fort Amherst by six guns aligned to fire along its length (two on each of upper and lower gun floor and two in the open on the top rampart), which would have provided a devastating impact upon anyone trying to force the ditch or storm across its drawbridges.

Fig 7.10
The cavern-like underground tunnels at Fort Amherst, hewn out of solid chalk and supported in places by complicated brick vaulting.
(Tony Pullen)

Fig 7.11
An underground brick-lined tunnel at Fort Amherst.
(Tony Pullen)

A similar level of deliberate planning was exhibited on the slopes behind the former Chatham Town Hall. These were sculpted so as to make them harder for an attacker to ascend and so that they could be swept by fire from within Fort Amherst, including from the fausse braie rampart in front of the main defences. The troops could exit the safety of the main fort via a sallyport and proceed down a covered way that existed on the outer edge of the barrier ditch.

To control access to the garrison area within the lines from the direction of Chatham town, the road network was revised, with upper and lower drawbridges to cross the barrier ditch.[13] The lower one was based on the existing route

Fig 7.12
The brick-lined barrier ditch
at Fort Amherst.
(Royal Engineers Museum,
Library and Archives)

Fig 7.13
Fort Pitt (centre), Gibraltar
tower (far left) and Delce
tower (far right) in 1813.
(Detail from TNA MPHH
1/585)

to the dockyard (Dock Road) and largely served the Gunwharf. The upper drawbridge was served by a new road (Barrier Road), which became the main route for military and civilian traffic. It led through the new Amherst guardhouse with carefully planned gun and musketry positions that enabled anyone trying to force the gates to come under fire. A brick-revetted subsidiary ditch allowed these same guns to have a line of fire onto the river, and for this reason the buildings of the Gunwharf were restricted in height so that their roofs did not interfere with the operation of Fort Amherst.

Military engineering at its most calculating made Fort Amherst a tough nut for any attackers to crack. Murder pits in the ditch bases prevented the close approach of an attacker. Inside the tunnels, the defending troops could use levers to slam doors shut and isolate attackers in places where internal musketry galleries could shoot them down.

As a citadel Fort Amherst had to be able to withstand a potential siege. Its grand magazine on Belvedere battery was therefore revised, and barracks were included within the fort to hold troops. Casemated barracks at Prince William's bastion and the Spur bastion accommodated the majority of the troops. The well for the water supply and the latrines survive in the tunnel complex. The fort had many layers of defence so that if one part fell it could fight on. Belvedere battery dominated the parts to its south in case these fell. The Amherst redoubt was possibly the proposed place of last refuge, because it was defended by a new strong guardhouse and had an underground work known as a caponier. If enemy attackers had forced their way through the Spur bastion, the caponier enabled fire to be directed upon them, into an area called a tenaille.

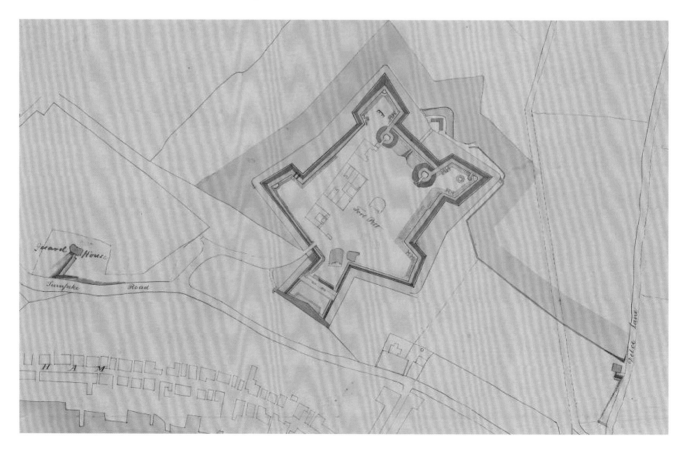

Southern defences: Fort Pitt

Land on the south hill above the town of Chatham had been acquired under the 1782 Act of Parliament, and the first building to be constructed from 1803 was a military hospital.[14] The engineer William Twiss examined the challenge of securing this ground with a fortification, and on 20 February 1804 he wrote to General Morse. Earlier criticism by the Duke of Richmond about the effectiveness of the Chatham Lines now re-emerged. Twiss considered it strange to defend the hill against an enemy force that had heavy guns, because such a force could use the same guns to bombard the dockyard. His argument was that if the attacker had heavy guns, he could 'probably take Chatham Lines and thereby entirely destroy the dockyard instead of doing it partially'.[15] He thought that the Chatham Lines were, by virtue of their location, construction and lack of casemates, 'such as to forbid us placing too much reliance on the works around Chatham dockyard if the enemy can bring heavy artillery against them'.[16]

Twiss recommended that the south hill should be occupied by fieldworks only around the new hospital and that roads should be formed to permit a safe retreat to Rochester bridge or Chatham. Others, including Robert D'Arcy, were of an entirely different opinion, and in 1805 work started on building a bastioned fort, to be known as Fort Pitt (Fig 7.13). The design of this fort is singular. It combines features that appear antiquated, such as the twin southern bastions, with casemated elements that had only been adopted at Chatham after 1803. It is just possible that, as with the Lower Lines, the earlier proposals of Hugh Debbieg were still influencing the design.

As built, the fort was a rough rectangle with bastions at each of its corners. The anticipated direction of attack was from the south and the road from Maidstone, and so the guns were concentrated there, with almost none aimed northwards to cross fire with Fort Amherst or on to the river. The south front of Fort Pitt had both a ravelin and twin raised earth mounds (referred to as cavaliers) for increased defence. The north front was given over to a major set of casemated barracks that sat within deep brick flanking walls.[17] These sat high above Chatham in the open ground that was required for a field of fire and dominated views from the town. Any guns located here could fire over the town and to the river.

Within the fort, the 1803 hospital buildings were used as supplementary barracks and were returned to medical use only after the 1815 peace. In the interior of the fort was a magazine behind the casemated barracks, and at the centre was a keep-like tower that belonged to the group of D'Arcy-inspired gun towers (Fig 7.15).[18] In the 20th century Fort Pitt saw major changes for the construction of three separate educational establishments. The south-east bastion was almost entirely removed, and its twin survives only marginally better. In addition, the counterscarps of the ditches and the surrounding glacis have been so thoroughly removed as to make it very difficult to appreciate the original form of the fort and how it would have been used. There were two detached guardhouses, built as small gun towers, that were intended to complete the control of the hill. Of these, Gibraltar tower has been demolished, with no known remains, while Delce tower survives as limited ruins. Delce tower was situated to control the route along the Delce towards Rochester and was linked to Fort Pitt by a large earthwork, of which only slight parts now remain.[19]

In his 1822 publication the French author Charles Dupin commented on Fort Pitt, based on his inspection of the military establishments of Britain:

In the centre of the spaces occupied by the fortress [Fort Pitt], there was originally built a defensive tower, armed at the summit with two long guns to batter in front, and two carronades to protect the gorge. This was at the epoch when the rage for building martello towers had seized the British government; they were not contented with placing them on the shores of the sea or large rivers, but even erected them at great expense to form parts of works in the interior of the country. The tower in Fort Pitt is very lofty, and its object is to command at a considerable distance the brow of a hill which raises itself with an insensible slope in front of Fort Pitt.[20]

The communication

The remodelling of the Chatham Lines from 1803 was as a tête de pont or defended bridge-head. The inclusion of a pontoon bridge linking the Chatham and Upnor shores of the River Medway was to be an essential part of the fortifications, as it would dispense with the bottleneck of the public bridge at Rochester. Defence of the Upnor side of the river seems not to have been a major concern despite the

Gun towers

In 1804, before Fort Pitt was constructed, Robert D'Arcy proposed a tower at St Margarets, which would become known as the Clarence Lines. This was one of several innovative forms of towers that he experimented with in his refortification of Chatham. Fort Clarence is now the only intact example, but similar keep-like towers were built at Fort Pitt (Fig 7.14) and adjacent to the obsolete fort at Gillingham. Fort Pitt also had the detached tower-like Delce and Gibraltar guardhouses, and the Clarence Lines were terminated by similar structures on the Maidstone road and another above the River Medway. A casemated guardhouse was also built at the St Mary's hornwork, and another at the sallyport near Brompton is possibly of this date.[21]

The adoption of gun towers as part of defensive schemes in England can be linked to the British experience of fighting in the Mediterranean where such towers had a long history. In particular, the resistance offered in 1794 to a British naval attack by a single tower at Mortella Point on Corsica so impressed the attackers that it influenced defensive thinking for many years. Between 1798 and 1802 the British built 11 defensive gun towers on Minorca, where the commanding Royal Engineer was Captain D'Arcy, assisted by Second Lieutenant Pasley. These two men came to have the greatest influence on the work of the Royal Engineers at Chatham in the early 19th century. Comparison of the Chatham gun towers built under D'Arcy with earlier examples that he saw on Minorca built by the Spanish, such as the Alcufar tower of 1782, shows common features. The adoption of machicolation at Chatham in a largely ornamental capacity is strikingly similar.

The Minorcan towers also influenced the design of the Martello towers (so-called after the tower at Mortella Point),[22] which were first recommended in 1803 as a chain of individual gun towers to control the possible invasion beaches of the Kent and Sussex coast. As a result of a conference called at Rochester on 21 October 1804 to discuss the defence of southern England, the potential landing beaches were made secure by the building of Martello towers from 1805. That meeting was attended by the Duke of York (Commander-in-Chief), William Pitt (Prime Minister), Pitt's brother the Earl of Chatham (Master General of the Ordnance), General Brownrigg (Quartermaster-General, responsible for the Royal Staff Corps), Major General Morse (Inspector-General of Fortifications), William Twiss (senior engineer) and General Dundas (commander southern district). Dundas had participated in the Corsican action at Mortella Point in 1794, as had Thomas Nepean. D'Arcy must have been included in the discussions of the committee, and so there was a body of senior Royal Engineers with direct experience of the Mediterranean gun towers. In this context, the decision to build Martello towers and to use gun towers in the defence of Chatham is more understandable.

vulnerability of the dockyard to bombardment from the west. Tower Hill did have guns located upon it but came to be used mainly in training.

In March 1804 William Twiss took a personal interest in the bridge design. In consultation with Thomas Nepean he rejected the option of using barges to transport troops over the river. He was the first to propose a floating bridge and

Fig 7.14 (right)
Postcard showing the gun tower at Fort Pitt.
(Keith Gulvin)

Fig 7.15 (far right)
The floating bridge with its central section moored alongside, ready to be put in place when needed, shown on an Ordnance Board survey plan of 1806.
(TNA MR 1/815)

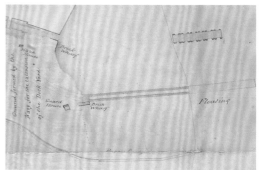

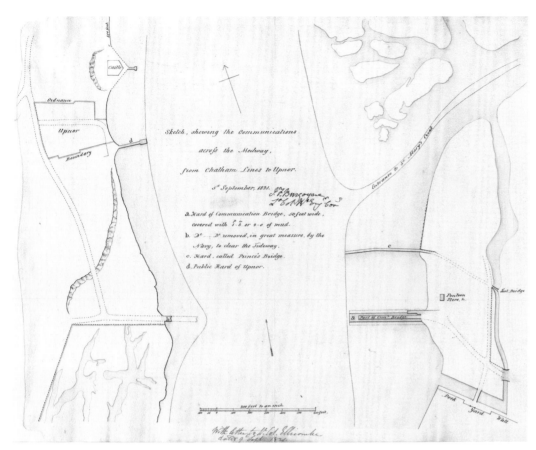

Fig 7.16
Plan of the communication
across the Medway from the
Chatham Lines to Upnor,
dated 1821. It shows the
permanent hards or
causeways built over the
tidal mudflats for the
military roads that
connected with the floating
bridge.
(TNA MFQ 1/1280)

described a structure 25ft wide over the deep part of the river and 15ft wide over the causeways. For the bridge construction, he requested and was supplied with condemned masts and new cables from the dockyard and 270 large casks from the victualling yard.[23] Work took until summer 1804 to complete, and the Royal Engineer Thomas Hyde Page took responsibility for its construction. A Board of Ordnance survey plan of 1806 appears to show the floating middle section moored and ready for use (Fig 7.15).

In July 1804 D'Arcy wrote to Morse: 'The troops (about 1,500 of the guards) passed the bridge at about 4 o'clock this evening it then being low water and very smooth, on the return of the troops the whole number halted on the bridge and everything answered perfectly well – more buoyancy will certainly be required for baggage wagons.'[24] On 21 August Twiss reported on a major inspection:

On Sunday I attended the Duke of York and Lord Chatham on horseback over the floating bridge laid across the Medway near Chatham dockyard, the party consisted of about fifty horses with Colonel Hope in his carriage and while we went over both sides of the bridge were occupied by numerous persons on foot who attended from curiosity to see his Royal Highness. Notwithstanding we passed and repassed without the smallest impediment.[25]

In 1805 the small labour force still responsible for the pontoon bridge was listed separately from that of the wider lines.[26] A map dating to 1805 gives the location of the floating bridge and shows that the permanent hards were needed across the mudflats and the salt marsh of the river edge, as well as connecting roads.[27] Guardhouses were provided, presumably to watch the barges that would have been moored up, with the bridge only put in place when its use was anticipated.[28] Another plan (Fig 7.16) shows the various hards and approach roads, but most is known about the construction of the bridge from a statement made by D'Arcy in 1816 concerning the intended disposal by sale of the floating parts and decking.

Pontooning was considered part of the duties of the Royal Engineers, and so when the bridge was dismantled at the end of the war, the hards were left *in situ* and became the basis of instruction in pontooning for the Royal Engineer establishment. This instruction sometimes included the re-creation of the communication,

Fig 7.17
A late 19th-century pontoon bridge on the Medway. (Royal Engineers Museum, Library and Archives)

Fig 7.18
The Clarence Lines. (Detail from TNA MPHH 1/585)

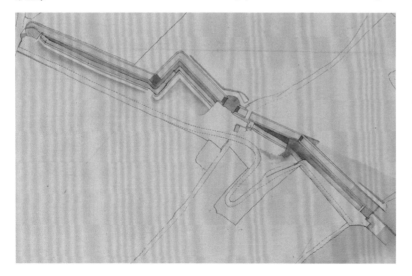

and late 19th-century photographs of these floating bridges between Upnor and Chatham dockyard (such as Fig 7.17) provide the best indication possible of what the 1804 original must have looked like.

One organisation was very pleased that the communication was removed at the end of the war. The Navy Board considered that its installation had made significantly worse the silting problems experienced by them for their river front at Chatham dockyard. John Rennie repeated this view in 1817 in a report on dockyard improvements, but recommended that more major works to the river front were needed than simply the removal of the bridge.

Southern defences: Fort Clarence (Clarence Lines)

Fort Clarence should more correctly be called the Clarence Lines, because this fortification comprised a short line of brick-revetted rampart and ditch designed to close off the approach to Rochester and its bridge from the direction of Maidstone along a high ridge (Fig 7.18). The works are also sometimes referred to as St Margarets.

Captain John Handfield of the Royal Engineers wrote to Lieutenant-General Morse on 16 August 1805 to outline what was now proposed.[29] Because the communication bridge between Chatham and Upnor was for military use only, Rochester bridge was the only publicly available bridge over the river, and it formed a target for an attacker intent on forcing a passage over the Medway. To control the bridge, a battery was proposed at Frindsbury at the head of the bend of the river, so that its guns could command the bridge. In addition, it was suggested that Rochester castle could be reoccupied for infantry 'by piercing the wall for loop holes and erecting a scaffold within'. St Margarets was considered next, as the fear was that attackers might work their way along the river bank towards Rochester and be protected by the high ground from fire from Fort Pitt. This might result in the defenders having to destroy Rochester bridge to prevent its loss to the enemy, which, in Handfield's words, would create a crisis by making 'the stores, baggage, cattle etc pass over the same bridge with the troops [the communication] which would not fail to produce very great delay if not absolute confusion in the military movements.'[30]

Handfield confirmed that D'Arcy's proposed solution to the strategic weakness at Rochester bridge was a 30ft or 35ft-high tower at St Margarets, with a ditch to connect it to the river. He thought this would cover Rochester and assist the defence of Fort Pitt. Since it would take a long time to build in brick, it was suggested that a fieldwork comparable to the shape of Fort Pitt could be hastily dug, so that the approach to Rochester from the direction of Maidstone could be secured. Handfield's letter illustrates the alarm felt in 1805 that invasion was imminent, as he excuses the sketchy nature of his proposed works on the grounds that he was busy supervising military working parties to remove all obstructions from the glacis of the Chatham Lines and Fort Pitt.

It appears that none of Handfield's proposed works was actually carried out, but in 1810 D'Arcy's original proposal was implemented at St Margarets, so creating the Clarence Lines. The central feature of the fortification was another massive gun tower sitting astride the former ditch, so that guns located on its open roof could fire southwards, and the guns on each of its two gun floors could fire east and west along the length of the ditch. This concentrated gunfire was increased by concealed gun chambers (east casemates) behind the ditch wall, to the east of the tower where the ditch was carried through a large dog-leg. The base of the gun tower formed the magazine and had tunnel connections to the above buried works and other parts of the fort.

The eastern ditch terminated with a casemated guardhouse at the Maidstone Road in the valley bottom. West of the tower there was a guarded gate with a drawbridge that carried the road through the fortification. The west ditch had further guns, located this time not behind the ditch wall but across its width (west casemates). From here the ditch ran steeply away in the direction of the river and ended in a further gun tower (Medway Tower). North of the central tower a guardhouse (since demolished) and a Governor's house with a rear boundary wall created a parade ground area.[31]

Charles Dupin recorded the appearance of the fortifications:

Fort Clarence is to be considered as one very large defensive tower, of square form, and strengthened by small towers or turrets at the four angles: these turrets contain winding staircases to communicate between the different stories of the work ... Fort Clarence is on a height very near the river, the course of which it protects; and it commands with much advantage the bridge at Rochester, which is the only communication between the opposite banks of the Medway, from that town to the sea. Lastly, the guns of this fort co-operate with those of two or three batteries, which you pass in proceeding up the opposite bank of the river. A covert-way was to have connected the two forts Pitt and Clarence, as well as an intermediate tower, to be erected at the bottom of the valley separating these works; it was also intended to prevent all passage between Fort Pitt and the citadel, by one or two other towers of defence: but, before these numerous works could be completed, England had ceased to apprehend an invasion, and the execution of them was suspended.[32]

Today the gun tower comprises the most visible remains of the complex of fortifications, but significant lengths of the east and west ditches and both sets of casemates survive. The terminal guardhouses have been demolished. The Governor's house is extant, but otherwise the features related to the crossing of the ditch at the tower have been lost.

Fig 7.19
Fort Clarence tower as it exists today.
(Author)

8

Firepower and Sieges

With the Chatham Lines being greatly increased, more firepower was needed for their defence and therefore more secure storage for gunpowder was needed. Naval powder was also stored at Chatham, for which the storage at Upnor castle was no longer sufficient. The Napoleonic Wars saw the start to the Chatham Lines being used for training in siege warfare, and this activity required access to gunpowder.

Gunpowder storage

Hugh Debbieg had recognised that if the northern end of the Chatham Lines were to be extended, an additional gunpowder magazine would be required. In 1806, as the Lower Lines approached completion, work started on a new and large magazine. The portion of the Chatham Lines from Prince Frederick's bastion westwards had been turned into a secondary defensive line by the construction of the Lower Lines, and so the land to the north could now be occupied. First of all, an earthwork ravelin (visible on Fig 7.1) to help protect the explosive contents from accidents was added between Prince Frederick's and the Duke of Cumberland's bastions, and within this a brick magazine was constructed. The Royal Engineers and their contractors were not infallible, and this element of their great project ended in tragedy, when in October 1806 part of the incomplete magazine collapsed:

OCT. 1. An unfortunate accident occurred at the new works, building for a magazine at Chatham. A large arch, eighty feet long, and sixteen feet wide, containing nearly 100,000 bricks, having been finished, in taking away the centres, which had been raised for turning it, the pressure of the brickwork proving too great for the abutments, which gave way, the arch fell in, and, melancholy to relate, killed eight men, and very materially wounded two others.[1]

The Board of Ordnance held an inquiry into what had gone wrong, and pensions were agreed for the widows and orphans of the civilian labourers killed.[2] When D'Arcy and his team built their next large magazine at Upnor, the design was changed. Remains of the ravelin magazine exist beneath the later naval barracks that make up the area known as the Collingwood triangle.

The opportunity was taken to store further dangerous material within the defended area, but away from important sites such as the barracks. A structure referred to as the fire barn was built north of the ravelin, which comprised brick-built stores within their own enclosure, but lacked the massive construction of a main magazine. Small magazines were also constructed at necessary locations along the line of the ramparts so that the guns could have a convenient supply of charges. These were known as 'ready use' or 'expense' magazines and took the form of brick structures, set wherever possible into the earth of the ramparts for protection.

The Chatham fortifications relied on the gunpowder stored in the magazines closest to the guns, while Upnor had a primary role for the storage of powder for use by the navy, including the receipt of powder off vessels being placed in ordinary – temporarily decommissioned – on the river. The castle had been turned into a magazine after the 1667 Medway raid, but it was inadequate for the demands made of it. In 1763 the Ordnance Board, faced with the need to store powder being given up from vessels returning from the Seven Years' War, had adopted the expedience of acquiring an existing storehouse at Upnor and converting it to hold 10,000 barrels of powder. This was located south of the High Street at the river's edge and was served by its own pier (Figs 8.1 and 8.2). This 'temporary' magazine remained in use for several decades despite the danger of its proximity to the growing settlement of Upnor. Floating magazines made from converted hulks were also used to cope with the demands for powder storage and were somewhat safer.

In 1806 the temporary magazine was being used as storage and stables, and we know that in 1807 the castle held 4,000 barrels of powder, while three floating magazines, *Vryheid*, *Delft* and *Wassenaer*, held a further 23,000 barrels.[3] The castle had a multiplicity of functions, many unsuitable. One tower was a laboratory, the other a store, the basement held unserviceable powder, the ground floor was a store for ammunition, the second floor contained returned rockets and blue lights, while the third floor was a lumber room. The gateway was in ruins. The other ordnance buildings included the barracks, the storekeeper's house and a combined guardhouse and ordnance office.

Downstream of the castle, a ballast wharf had created an excavated area in the riverside that could be adapted to form a natural traverse to contain a new magazine. In 1808 D'Arcy was instructed to build a magazine here to hold 10,000 barrels. Doubtless chastened by the accident at the ravelin two years earlier, D'Arcy chose catenary and not round arches for his new magazine that are very similar to the examples built by Pilkington at the contemporary ordnance depot at Weedon Bec (Northants).[4] The magazine at Upnor (*see* Fig 8.3) was completed in 1812, and by 1813 it had received 6,739 barrels of powder.[5] It has since been demolished, but the later example of 1856 that stood beside it (*see* Fig 11.4) indicates what the structure was like.

The new magazine alone was not sufficient to create a workable ordnance depot. The growth of Upnor as a settlement as a result of nearby private enterprises created problems for safety, which the storekeeper had highlighted in 1808:

In consequence of the private Yards for building ships and brickmaking in this neighbourhood, a great many disorderly and drunken people are frequently lounging about at all hours with lights, and smoking too near the magazines, and although this has in some measure been remedied by turning the path to the rear of the Storekeeper's House, yet from having been accustomed to the use of the landing place near the castle, it is impossible for the sentries to prevent these dangerous irregularities.[6]

A boundary wall to the ordnance land at Upnor High Street and an oak palisade fence around the new magazine was the solution. As

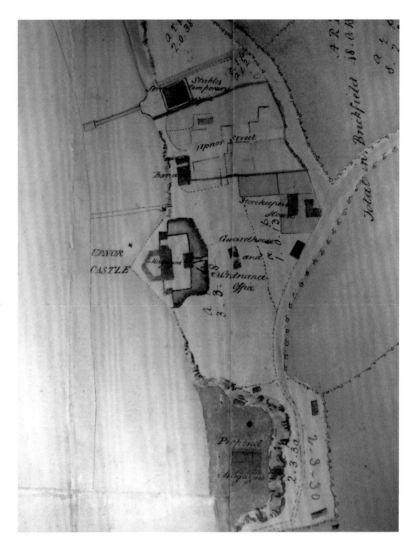

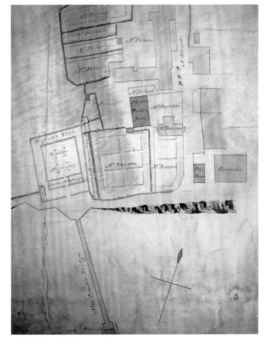

Fig 8.1
The start of Upnor as an ordnance depot larger in size than the earlier castle. Upstream of the castle is the temporary magazine with a landing stage. Downstream is the ballast quarry in which a new magazine and shifting complex were built, and further downstream is the brick wharf belonging to the Ordnance Board.
(TNA MR 1/815)

Fig 8.2
A plan of the so-called temporary gunpowder magazine at Upnor, with its own pier.
(TNA Work 41/85)

Fig 8.3
The gunpowder magazine at
Upnor designed by D'Arcy
and completed in 1812.
(TNA Work 41/89)

the temporary magazine was no longer required, its pier became a public landing place, and a new powder pier was built to serve the new magazine.

In addition to magazines, an 1807 report for the Ordnance Board recommended the construction of separate and traversed shifting houses, in which incoming barrels of powder could be more safely opened for inspection. At Upnor this task was carried out in a building built on the water bastion of the old castle, and in 1811 it was observed that 'The whole castle would most undoubtedly be destroyed by an explosion in the shifting house where there are

at times from 3 to 500 barrels of gunpowder returned from ships of war which can only be examined, weighed & coopered in this building before it is deposited in the magazine.'[7] A bad situation was made worse by the use of the shifting house at the castle to examine doubtful powder taken from the floating magazines. The solution was to construct a purpose-built examining and shifting house (Fig 8.4) between the old castle and the new magazine. The inclusion of traverses was designed to prevent any accidental explosion spreading to either magazine. The shifting house has since been reduced to its foundations.

The Gunwharf

The Ordnance Board lands at Upnor were used not just for magazines, but also as brickfields. There was also a plantation on which timber was grown for ordnance purposes, including walnut trees for musket stocks.[8] The Ordnance Board's site at the Gunwharf in 1803 was made up of the wharf with cranes, the Grand Storehouse (since demolished), the storekeeper's house (now a pub) and a long range of carriage storehouses (since demolished). As early as 1796 the then commanding engineer William Spry had prepared a proposal to expand the site southwards to incorporate the site of the former millpond (today occupied by the bus station). The enlarged site would have been surrounded by a high wall and taken in the road known as the Land Wall, which is now followed by part of Globe Lane. In 1804 the Ordnance Board ordered that Chatham Armoury should hold 17,000 stands of arms for infantry and cavalry when the summer camps were broken up. As the existing buildings could hold only 10,500 stands, additional structures were demanded, together with 'armoury workshops necessary for keeping in repair and cleaning such number of arms'.[9]

No enlargement of the Gunwharf nor any new structures are known before about 1806,[10] by which time construction of the revised Barrier Ditch as part of the post-1803 fortifications had cut the site in two. The Gunwharf was then extended with a new ordnance boundary wall separating it from the growing town of Chatham. The Land Wall road was left out of this acquisition. The additional land that became known as the New Gunwharf included a brick stage for delivering bricks to the fortifications (*see* Fig 9.9), but it was not yet fully

Fig 8.4
The combination of new
magazine and traversed
shifting house.
(TNA Work 41/84)

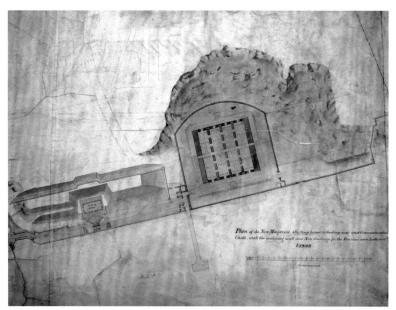

integrated with the older part of the site. These works were postponed until 1811,[11] and then a new wharf was constructed at the waterside and buildings erected on the boundaries of the site. At the Old Gunwharf 140 feet of the wharf wall was replaced, and three new cranes provided. A blacksmith's shop and a carriage workshop were also built here. The final addition to the New Gunwharf was a house for the Clerk of the Cheque, which was designed after the war in 1816 and is now referred to as the 'White House'.

Charles Dupin observed the workings of the Gunwharf and was amazed to see how rust was removed from cannonballs:

Machine for removing the Rust from Cannon-Shot.– Under sheds in front of the magazines, and on the water side, a machine is employed in taking off the rust of balls, which, from being long buried in the ground, or under water, have become oxidized, and covered with a crust more or less irregular. It is a kind of wooden drum, opening in the convex part by a little door, which serves to introduce and remove the balls. These are put into the machine in sufficient numbers for the operation, and when the drum turns on its axis, by means of two handles at the ends, the balls which are carried up by the rotatory motion, and down to the bottom of the machine again by their own weight, are in continual movement; they rub one against the other, and against circular projections formed inside the machine; and this constant friction has the effect of completely detaching from their surfaces all the heterogeneous particles which render them uneven and rugged. This apparatus has a good deal of resemblance to the barrels which we use in France to give smoothness to leaden balls.[12]

How sieges operated

Ever since they were first built, the Chatham Lines were used for training, and the field of fire is often referred to as the exercising ground, but in the early 19th century, training of a more specific kind started – for siege warfare. A siege could succeed only with the services of well-trained military engineers. The officers of the Royal Engineers had to assess the weaknesses of a fortress, plan the attack and lead their men. The men of the Royal Sappers and Miners needed specialist skills that were not found in the general infantry. They needed to be fit and strong so as to rapidly excavate earth quickly and they needed to be capable of constructing defences rapidly from sandbags, gabions and fascines. The tunnellers were even more skilled

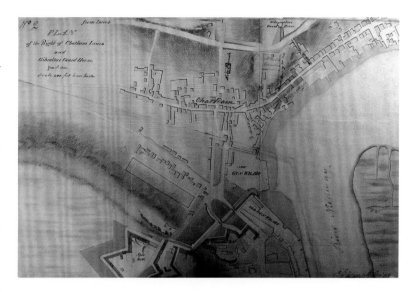

Fig 8.5
New and Old Gunwharf, Chatham.
(TNA WO 55/767)

and capable of working in the narrow confines of a mine, shoring the roof and sides in timber and preparing underground explosions. All this work took considerable practice to perfect.

Sieges and the practice of mining to bring down castle walls were an ancient method of attack,[13] but the introduction of gunpowder led to the use of explosive mines and artillery. This changed both the design of fortifications and the techniques of besieging and defending fortified sites. To attack a well-defended place, the besieging force had to surround the fortress to prevent the escape of those being besieged or their relief by friendly forces. The siege train – the equipment used by the attackers – consisted of heavy guns, ammunition, powder and entrenching tools, which all had to be moved by pack animal. The engineer and artillery officers would identify their favoured location for an attack, based on their assessment of weak points in the construction of the fortress or its cover by the defender's guns.

It was possible to bombard a defended place, but while this could cause a major loss of life and property, experience showed that only a direct assault would defeat well-constructed fortifications. This involved an attacker bringing their guns to bear by moving them close to the defences, despite the defensive fire coming from the fortress. To do so, broad trenches known as parallels (so-called because they ran parallel to the defences) were excavated, often by non-specialist infantry. The guns and other materials were placed in the parallels to give them some shelter from firing from the fortress. Several such parallels, each one closer to the fortress, might be required, and they were linked together by zig-zag communications or approaches and widened out as necessary to create siege batteries. Sapping was the name given to the task of excavating broad trenches to approach a fortress, and mining was the practice of tunnelling underground.[14] The title adopted after 1812 for the engineer soldiers, the Royal Sappers and Miners, reveals their main duties. A determined defender during this phase of a siege might seek to disrupt progress by aggressive sorties to attack the excavations and carry off the entrenching tools.

When the attackers were sufficiently close to the fortress, they could open artillery fire upon the fortress and commence the practice of mining. Their guns were used to dislodge the defenders' guns on the ramparts. Rifle pits might be dug to give cover for snipers firing at the defending troops, and the guns were also turned on the walls of the rampart and ditch. The ditch posed a considerable barrier for an attacking force to cross, particularly when under fire from the defenders. One solution was to use repeated artillery fire against the same part of the fortification to batter a breach. The aim was to destroy the ditch walls and rampart so that the dislodged material formed a makeshift ramp across the ditch and up the rampart for the attackers. The defenders might use gabions or chevaux de frise to repair the damage to their defences. The earthworks of the attackers were also protected from aggressive fire by gabions and by fascines.

Fig 8.6
Siege operations at Chatham. A mine has exploded and the engineer soldiers wait with their entrenching tools to rush forward to secure the crater before their imagined enemy has time to recover from the surprise.
(Illus London News 4 November 1871)

When mining started, this was a job for the specialist engineer soldier. If a fortress had a well-formed glacis and outworks, perhaps with countermines, it was impossible to defeat these without using mines. The miners would tunnel into the earth in the direction of the fortress, sometimes with the purpose of placing explosives under any land that had to be taken, so that on detonation a large crater was formed (Fig 8.6). The attackers could then rush such a crater before the defenders had time to recover, and by hastily improvising defences with sandbags and so on, this crater could be held against a counterattack and form the start of the next mine. In this fashion, the miners could reach the outer edge of the fortress ditch, from where further digging could undermine the rampart. A tunnel under the ditch and rampart, if packed with enough explosives, might blow a hole in the fortifications. Alternatively, the counter-scarp of the ditch might be breached by a mine and the miners then rush in under fire to commence a new mine on the scarp wall of the ramparts. To do so required hastily provided protection against the fire coming from the defenders.

The defending forces would not wait patiently for their defences to be overwhelmed. Countermine measures were designed into a fortress to provide tunnels under the glacis from which the defending engineers might detect the approach of an attacker's tunnel and destroy this by excavating their own tunnel to intercept it with explosive charges. 'Camouflets' was the term adopted for such underground defensive explosions that were designed to collapse tunnels and kill miners but not disturb the land at the surface. A cat-and-mouse game developed underground as miners on both sides sought to detect the tunnels of their enemies. Countermine galleries could themselves be destroyed by mines, and as a final desperate measure the defenders might place explosives under their own ramparts, so that if these were breached, a major explosion might then kill sufficient of the attackers to defeat an assault.

A siege might last for weeks or months before a fortress was defeated. When it was considered that a practicable breach had been made in the main defences, it was customary to offer the defenders the option to capitulate. If they did not, then the breach had to be assaulted. The attacking party that did this was known as the forlorn hope because soldiers taking part in the assault stood little chance of surviving.

Sometimes repeated assaults were necessary before a breach could be taken. The final assault on a fortress was often a bloody affair, with successful attackers venting their rage on the inhabitants of the defended place through drunken murderous looting, as was the case after the bloody assault on Badajoz during the Peninsular War.

Training for sieges

Research on Woolwich, the home of the Royal Artillery, has shown that field exercises with the guns of the Royal Artillery took place there by the late 18th century for training the gunners. The increasing professionalism of the British army during the Napoleonic Wars and after was the result of increased training regimes instituted at home, and one example was the training of light infantry from 1803 at Shorncliffe by Sir John Moore.[15]

The Corps of Royal Engineers was so few in numbers that when the British army was sent on campaign and needed the expertise to execute its own sieges, officers had to be taken from Chatham and other military establishments in Britain. During the Peninsular War (1808–14) Wellington had to storm the fortresses of Badajoz, Cuidad Rodrigo, Burgos and San Sebastian, but his army had only an improvised siege train and no heavy guns and was lacking in recent experience of a major siege. Also, too few of the engineer soldiers were siege specialists.[16] As a result the sieges were costly, bloody affairs, conducted by a small group of Royal Engineer officers, supported by the Royal Staff Corps and some artificer soldiers. Many paid with their lives. There were simply too few trained military engineers, and the manpower for siege works had to be drawn from the infantry. Wellington wrote to the Earl of Liverpool from Spain on 11 February 1812, some three weeks after the ending of the siege at Cuidad Rodrigo:

It is inconceivable with what disadvantage we undertake anything like a siege for want of assistance of this description. There is no French *corps d'armée* which has not a battalion of sappers and company of miners. But we are obliged to depend for assistance of this description upon the regiments of the line; and although the men are brave and willing, they want the knowledge and training which are necessary. Many casualities among them consequently occur, and much valuable time is lost at the most critical period of the siege.[17]

Foundation of the Royal Engineer Establishment

One Royal Engineer in particular was aware of the consequences of the lack of engineer soldiers and became determined to do something about it. He was Charles William Pasley (Fig 8.7), who in 1809 said:

The important department in which I had the honour of serving, was so imperfectly organized, that I considered the British army ... incapable of succeeding in a siege, though one of the most important operations of war, without either having recourse to the barbarous measure of incendiary bombardment, or without an enormous sacrifice of the lives of officers and men in sanguinary assaults, which might be rendered unnecessary by a more efficient organization of the Royal Engineer Department, and especially in forming a well-instructed and well-disciplined body of engineer soldiers diligently exercised in all the operations of a siege, particularly in military mining.[18]

Pasley was wounded during the 1809 Walcheren expedition, and while recovering he started to press for improved engineer training. In 1811 at Plymouth he instigated his own training regime. The views of Pasley were known from his 1810 publication *Essay on the military policy and institutions of the British Empire*. This influenced the thinking of the Ordnance Board and General Gother Mann in particular, who was now Inspector-General of Fortifications and was in a position to act. A royal warrant to establish an engineer training establishment was signed on 23 April 1812, and in May Pasley was promoted to major and ordered to Chatham. The Royal Engineer Establishment, founded at Chatham in 1812, is the direct predecessor of the existing Royal School of Military Engineering.[19]

Mann had helped Debbieg reinforce the Chatham Lines back in the 1780s and knew of their suitability as a training base, which was one reason why he had persuaded the Royal Staff Corps to suggest Chatham for their depot in 1803. Pasley and D'Arcy were also no strangers, having served together in Minorca, at Copenhagen (1807) and on the Walcheren expedition (1809). As the senior engineer at Chatham, D'Arcy was able to assist Pasley in his new command. The year after the Royal Engineer Establishment was founded, Pasley wrote an 'Account of the establishment which has

Fig 8.7
Charles William Pasley (1780–1861) by Charles Blair Leighton. (Royal Engineers Museum, Library and Archives)

been lately instituted for instructing the Corps of the Royal Sappers and Miners and the junior officers of Royal Engineers in military field-works', a lengthy, unpublished report in which he very clearly explained why such training was necessary:

> for want of men trained to the duties of sapper and miners, the greatest confusion, blunder and delay have often taken place in our sieges and … many valuable lives have been lost particularly of officers of engineers who have unavoidably been obliged to expose themselves in a manner that would otherwise have been unnecessary in teaching the working parties the most simple parts of their duty under the enemy's fire.[20]

A few years after its establishment, Pasley described the purpose of the new school:

> To qualify the NCOs and privates for the very important activity which continuously falls to their lot in services of assisting their officers to lay out field-works etc and to superintend the execution of them by giving such directions as may be necessary to working parties furnished either by regiments of the line or by peasants of the country which is the seat of war.[21]

What Pasley first taught his recruits went on to form the basis of the syllabus for siege training for the rest of the 19th century. By looking to produce educated men, capable of combat but with specialist knowledge of fortifications and how to attack them, he started the tradition of the combat engineer that is still taught today. The men learned how to cut brushwood so as to make gabions, fascines, hurdles and pickets. They built parallels and approaches, and gun and mortar platforms in batteries with field magazines, and acquired experience of various kinds of sapping when under fire. For military mining they were taught to sink shafts and drive galleries, at the head of which they would prepare a chamber in which they practised the loading, tamping and firing of explosives. Pasley also mentioned that training was given in pontooning for bridges on the river.

Pasley's intention was to train Royal Engineer officers and men from the Corps of Royal Sappers and Miners. Soldiers from the various infantry regiments stationed at Chatham might also participate in joint training with these Ordnance Board troops with the agreement of their commanding officers. Pasley wanted to educate the men more broadly, requiring them to 'give an account of the technical terms such as the interior, superior and exterior slopes of the parapet'. Those likely to be NCO foremen and overseers were trained in 'practical geometry and place drawing', for which slates and not paper were used on grounds of economy. He stressed the value of artificers who could work from plans and models when employed in garrisons on permanent works: 'Those who come entirely uneducated or imperfect are taught to read and write and others are instructed in arithmetic. A man of good abilities who arrives totally ignorant generally learns to read and write before he quits the establishment. Those who go through the course of geometry and plan drawing proceed afterwards to the study of mensuration.'[22]

The junior Royal Engineer officers who were being trained took responsibility for the supervision of the men and their field projects and for identifying the NCOs and privates who most distinguished themselves. Pasley was at pains to explain that the men should be trained first and foremost as soldiers and then as combat engineers, and that they should be able to perform the same drill as the regiments of the line:

> I consider the drill of great importance not only to the discipline and respectability of the Corps but also for another reason. Although the men are seldom likely to be called upon to use arms in the field there is no class of soldiers in whom greater courage is required in order to do justice to their duty and there can be no doubt but that a confidence in the use of fire arms adds to the courage of an individual in all cases and in all situations because although he may not be actually engaged in personal contest he feels that if it came to that point he would be equal to any adversary.[23]

The Royal Engineer officers who would be called upon to direct attacks studied the various skills needed for a siege. Pasley stated that 'it is absolutely impossible for any officer to acquire them from study and theory alone. For instance if a fortress is to be attacked an engineer who has been at the establishment on a hasty examination of the woods in the neighbourhood will be able to say whether they will furnish a sufficient quantity of gabions and fascines.'[24]

For the first 20 years of its existence, although their training establishment was based at Chatham, the training ground for the Royal Engineers was not on the Chatham Lines. In 1812 these were maintained in a state of readiness for the active defence of the

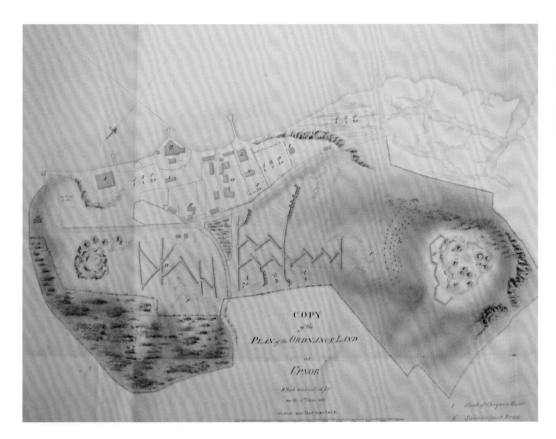

Fig 8.8
The Upnor engineer practice ground with parallels to attack Tower Hill (far right) during the course of field instruction by Lieutenant Colonel Pasley.
(TNA WO 44/143)

dockyard, and so Pasley was allocated land for training at Upnor, in the Ordnance Plantation, on the other side of the River Medway (Fig 8.8):

Colonel D'Arcy had the goodness to go over the whole of the ground at Upnor with me yesterday. Part of the Ordnance land which it will be desirable of us to have is occupied by the storekeeper and another civil officer and a portion of the brickfield is covered by unburnt bricks ... I wish eventually to have the use of the whole of the ground between the brickfield and Tower Hill, leaving untouched the small fields in the vicinity of the castle and the ground behind the hill, as also the plantation ... The whole of my detachment are at present lodged in the casemates on the left of the lines which afford excellent accommodation.[25]

Two of the St Mary's casemates were fitted out as classrooms with benches and a raised platform at one end, but Pasley's initial favourable opinion of the suitability of the St Mary's casemates for accommodation of his men was not borne out once the poor quality of these barracks became clear, and at some stage they appear to have moved to the Brompton barracks. A plan of 1822[26] shows that by this date a small proportion of the main barracks at Brompton comprising the chapel and three adjoining barrack houses was given over to the Royal Sappers and Miners, along with a small adjutant's office.

In July 1812 Pasley was requesting barrels of powder for use in practice mines and musketballs with which to prove the effectiveness of the stuffed gabions and mantlets. In September he reported that 30 officers and men had been trained in mining at Upnor by the sinking of a shaft and then principal and communication galleries. Pasley had ordered a small battery of four guns to be built over the location of the mine, so as to be able judge the impact of the detonation. Forty men had been trained on the pontoons, and their bridge had carried a light 12-pounder gun and a column of 64 men. Within a year of setting up the Royal Engineer Establishment, 250 men were undergoing training at any one time, and Pasley recommended that they should stay at Chatham for a minimum of 6 months. Officers and men who were the first graduates were available for foreign service during the final years of the Napoleonic Wars, and his cadets fought at the siege of San Sebastian in 1813.

Barracks and Brompton

Although Chatham ceased to be the main recruiting depot in 1803 and the Inspector-General moved his headquarters to Parkhurst barracks on the Isle of Wight,[1] this did not empty the existing infantry barracks that had been built in 1758 for 1,800 men and the 1777 barracks for marines. Two completely new sets of barracks – Brompton barracks and the casemates of the Lower Lines – were built during the Napoleonic Wars alongside two new hospitals, one at what became Fort Pitt and another behind the infantry barracks.

Brompton barracks

Before 1803 at Chatham, barrack accommodation was at a premium and very crowded. The Ordnance Board decided to address this problem in 1804 with an instruction to build new barracks for the artillery, which the engineers would also occupy. The existing infantry barracks could then be left for the use of recruits to the regiments of the line.

The architect James Wyatt, who had been responsible for the completion of the stupendous artillery barracks at Woolwich, was now asked to work at Chatham. Although Wyatt and his family were responsible for the designs,[2] the work was in the hands of a contractor and was supervised on site by D'Arcy and his team. The site selected was on the north side of Wood Street at Brompton, and the new barracks were on the same grid as that planned settlement. The High Street ran right through Brompton and the barracks site.

As first built, the barracks were open and remained so until the late 20th century. Civilians, including tradespeople offering services, were able to access the barrack blocks without passing through guardhouses and a high wall, as was the case with the infantry barracks from where the risk of recruits absconding was higher. The new barracks were built as three blocks ranged round three sides of a parade square. The north and south sides of the square were originally closed off by screens of ornamental railings and gates, incorporating sentry boxes, to a design by Wyatt.[3]

The style of the architecture at Brompton is Palladian in inspiration and similar to Wyatt's work at Woolwich. Two-storey accommodation is interrupted by three-storey pavilions and joined with giant Tuscan columns in antis as a colonnade at the centre of each range. Charles Dupin was full of praise: 'the engineer barracks, which by the grandeur and regularity of their construction, by the majestic beauty and simplicity of the architecture, appeared to me to be a model of their kind.'[4]

The officers have always occupied the western range, with a mess room at its northern end.[5] In 1806 4 field officers lived in the centre, with 20 captains and 12 subalterns in the rest. The remaining 28 subalterns occupied the ends of the men's ranges closest to the officers' quarters. The main accommodation for the artillery men was in the north and south ranges, 553 in the former and 659 in the latter. Though not luxurious, the individual barrack rooms offered

Fig 9.1
The Brompton barracks with the 1804–6 ranges at the top.
(© English Heritage 23187/17 04/08/2003)

Fig 9.2
The Brompton barracks of
Wyatt and D'Arcy.
(Royal Engineers Museum,
Library and Archives)

better conditions than at the older infantry barracks. Each room was 30ft long and 21ft wide, with three windows and a single fireplace. Here the men continued to live communally, even with the wives and children of married soldiers. The centre of the north block was given up to the adjutant and an armoury that was later converted to a chapel – the first such facility built for the army at Chatham.

The artillery introduced the need for a massive amount of stabling, since horses were their only form of motive power. These were exercised on the field of fire, and there were stable ranges for 400 horses behind the men's blocks.[6] At the east end of both of the men's ranges there was a gun carriage shed, each capable of holding 30 guns.

St Mary's casemated barracks

These barracks were built inside the Lower Lines as troop accommodation for the soldiers responsible for defending the adjacent fortifications. Thomas Nepean had it in mind to build casemates as part of his design for the Lower Lines in 1804, and a design was approved by the Ordnance Board. However, it fell to D'Arcy to refine the proposal and supervise the construction, and in January 1805 he wrote:

I have the honour to send you a section of the proposed casemate in the rear of the new front on the left of Chatham Lines. As the furthest removed from the works those cavaliers or casemates nearest the parapets must be sunk proportionally lower to obtain the necessary cover from them. As the casemates proposed are not merely bombproof to be retired to in the time of a siege, but to answer at all times as barracks, and to afford the necessary accommodation for troops, I have made them to consist of 2 floors to avoid the inconvenience that fixed berths would be to the men's dining with comfort, and to encourage the cleanliness that the use of boards trestles admits of, which might as well as the bedding be exposed to the open air each fine day and at all times placed sideways for the convenience of the mens dining.[7]

D'Arcy planned for the casemates to hold up to 2,000 men and made provision for a separate block for officers (Fig 9.3; *see* Figs 13.4 and 13.5). Despite his worthy aspirations to produce good barracks, these were sub-standard casemates and represented the worst accommodation at Chatham. Casemates were bombproof structures made up of brick-vaulted cellular chambers with earthen roofs (to resist the impact of gunfire) on which guns could be sited. They were used in the Lower Lines, in Fort Amherst and at Fort Pitt in situations

Fig 9.3
D'Arcy's proposal for the
casemates at the Lower
Lines.
(TNA WO 55/767)

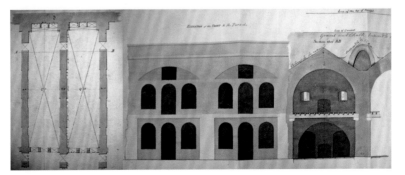

Fig 9.4
The main entrance to the
commanding officer's house
at the infantry barracks,
with a sentry and three
mortars positioned on the
lawn, photographed in
1857.
(Royal Engineers Museum,
Library and Archives)

where secure barracks were required within fortifications that might come under direct assault. These casemates at the Lower Lines were arranged side-by-side on two floors with connecting balconies. Each chamber was designed to hold 30 men but had only a single fireplace. Fenestration was inadequate at the end nearest to the fortifications and was poor at the opposite end.

Their regular use as barracks appears to have been intermittent. In 1807 when the Tunstall ammunition depot was closed, the Ordnance Board moved its contents into 'the flank casemates of the great ditch', which most probably meant the Lower Lines.[8] Although the Lower Lines casemates were used to house soldiers and their families, they were considered unsuitable for use as stores, on the grounds that they 'would contract damage from want of a due circulation of air'. In 1810 D'Arcy firmly turned down a request to use the casemates for prisoners of war, as this would prevent their use in an emergency,[9] and in fact the casemates were used in 1815 to house the families of soldiers sent on the Waterloo campaign. Though frequently condemned as a result of barracks inspections, the Lower Lines casemates remained in use until after World War II. They were then demolished.

Infantry and marines barracks

In 1799 the Chatham infantry barracks held 4 field officers, 24 captains, 68 other officers and 2,496 other ranks. Allowing for some women and children, the barrack blocks must have been crowded to bursting point.[10] The construction of the Brompton barracks between 1804 and 1806 must have provided some relief, but in 1809 there were still 4 field officers, 26 captains, 72 subalterns and 2,374 other ranks in this older set of barracks.[11] The Ordnance Board did not give up the parts that it occupied until 1811, and even then it retained its own artillery storehouse and the barrack masters house until such time as alternative buildings could be built elsewhere.[12]

The Ordnance Board storehouse at the infantry barracks was in existence by 1806. This building still survives outside the barracks wall, opposite the parish church, and was the result of the Ordnance Board needing to have a store at the barracks, despite having given up most of that site to the Barracks Department for the regular army. The Ordnance Board also gave up responsibility for the garden of the commandant's house. This house had been significantly extended after 1804 by the addition of a western wing that gave the residence a T-plan. It is seen in a mid-19th-century photograph (Fig 9.4), but has since been demolished.

Behind the infantry barracks the Ordnance Board's artificers had a garden,[13] and in 1809 this was approved as the site of a new military hospital (since demolished), capable of holding 170 patients (Fig 9.5).

Across the road from the infantry barracks the Navy Board was experiencing the same problems in housing all of its marines adequately in their barracks. In 1803 they sought royal approval for additional buildings at that site. With so many marines at Chatham, the existing barracks could not accommodate them all, and so the practice of billeting in inns had again to be relied on. It was explained that this was 'prejudicial to the good order and discipline of your Majesty's service and affording constant opportunities to the men to desert'.[14] In 1805, Samuel Bentham, assisted by Edward Holl, was able to squeeze a new range of buildings between the rear of the existing main barrack block and the Ordnance Board's property on the Gunwharf.

Chatham town from the 1790s

The phrase 'Rob'em, Starve'em and Cheat'em' was used by the soldiers to refer to the principal towns of Medway – Rochester, Strood and

Chatham. The earliest documented use is in Francis Grose's dictionary of 'the vulgar tongue' for 1785. It betrays the attitude of the men of the garrison to both the military authorities and the civilians who surrounded them. Doubtless most of the residents of these towns held an equally low opinion of the soldiers. Many of the inhabitants viewed the dockyard and the great concentration of troops, numbering as many as 7,000, as a means of earning a living by fair means or foul, lawful or not. Before the Crimean War and the rise of popular concern for the men's welfare, the common soldier was not held in high regard, and his was not a respectable profession. Garrison towns, particularly when combined with a major dockyard, suffered from many social ills. Some of these arose from overcrowding and poor housing conditions, but others were the result of behaviour involving drunkenness, licentiousness and crime.

Not only did Chatham have to contend with a sudden increase in its population to cater for the dockyard work force, it also had to absorb the impact of the fortifications and barracks. As previously described, much of the old settlement around the parish church was demolished for these new works, which caused future development to focus on the High Street area and Chatham Intra. Construction of Fort Pitt and the refusal to permit encroachment too close to Fort Amherst in the early 19th century made matters worse. It prevented Chatham from expanding onto the higher ground to the south and from occupying the valley bottom of The Brook. It is therefore not surprising that Chatham was an ill-planned and crowded town, made inevitable by the topography and government control of land.

A rather disdainful description of Chatham comes from 'Stroud, Rochester, and Chatham', an anonymous 1790 poem attributed to 'a tourist':

Old *Chatham's* a place,
That's the nation's disgrace,
Where the club and the fist prove the law, sir;
And presumption is seen to direct the marine,
Who knows not a spike from a hawser.
Here the dolts show with pride.
How the men of war ride,
Who France's proud first-rates can shiver,
And a fortified hill all the Frenchmen to kill,
That land on the banks of the river
Such a town, and such men we shall ne'er see again,
Where smuggling's a laudable function;
In some high windy day may the devil fly away
With the whole of the dirty conjunction.

Fig 9.5
An aerial view of February 1948 showing buildings that existed after the Second World War, including the substantial rectangular building of the 1809 Ordnance Board hospital (A); the upper terrace of barrack blocks for officers from the 1750s (B); the commanding officer's house from the 1750s to 1795 (C); blocks built as canteens and offices from the 1750s (D); unaltered barrack blocks for the rank and file from the 1750s (E); infantry barrack blocks of the reform period of the later 19th century (F); and the 1930s barrack blocks (G).
(© English Heritage 7568/3 04/02/1948)

Fig 9.6
Chatham from Fort Amherst
showing the development of
the town to the riverside and
how it was constrained by
the fort, the Gunwharf and
the open land around Fort
Pitt.
(Fort Amherst Collection)

Fig 9.7
The garrison area depicted
on an 1860 Ordnance Board
map with the town of
Chatham marked in red.
(TNA MR 1/1276)

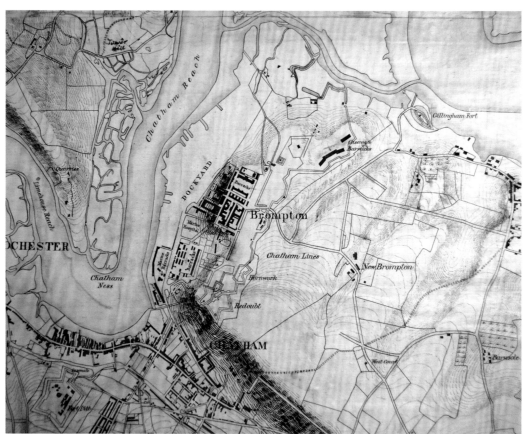

In 1798 the historian of Kent, Edward Hasted, described Chatham: 'It is like most seaports, a long, narrow, disagreeable, ill-built town, the houses in general occupied by those trades adapted to the commerce of the shipping and seafaring person, the victualling office, and the two breweries being the only tolerably built houses in it.'[15] In the 18th century the most respectable part of Chatham was the High Street closest to Rochester, where even today some surprisingly good historic interiors survive in what were once domestic houses, Hasted's 'tolerably built' houses. The Best family owned one brewery, and Chatham House (now demolished) was built as their family home in 1742. Hasted's reference to the victualling yard points to this government-owned and riverside establishment that was responsible for supplies to the navy. It was located on the Chatham–Rochester boundary and closed in 1822, with no surviving visible remains.[16] The construction of the New Road as a means of avoiding the older route close by the river allowed a more select residential quarter to develop, and Gibraltar Terrace dating to 1794 is today the best surviving part, but the construction of Fort Pitt from 1805 prevented this area from developing further.

With difficulties in expanding, Chatham became densely populated, with inevitable consequences for the health of its residents. The one place where it could grow was on the slopes of the valley. This area was known as The Brook and was described by Hasted in 1798:

It consists of a long row of houses which have of late been greatly increased with streets leading from them up the hill about the middle of which at some distance from all others is a number of houses built closely together called Slickett's Hill so as to form a little town of itself. It is exceeding populous owing to its numerous connections with the several departments of government and the shipping business carried on at it.[17]

In 1800, after a very dry period, fire broke out in the area known as Chatham Intra, killing four people and destroying 100 buildings on both sides of the High Street.[18] The military authorities were instrumental in bringing the fire under control and preventing worse harm – fire engines were despatched from the dockyard and victualling yard, the dockyard workforce and the garrison troops and marines were sent to help move possessions from the houses

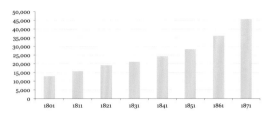

Fig 9.8
Population growth at Chatham, derived from various sources.

threatened by the fire, and the army supplied tents to the displaced residents, which were pitched on fields at New Road. A guard was also mounted over the rescued goods to prevent pilfering. Chatham was a densely developed ill-planned town built largely of timber, and it is not surprising that the fire did such great damage.[19] The town continued to expand in size, and at the first census the following year, the population (excluding the military) was 10,505, making Chatham the most populous town in Kent. The other garrison towns of the county also had large populations, Canterbury 9,500 and Maidstone 8,000, both of which were cavalry stations, while Rochester had a population of 8,000.[20]

The scale of the post-1803 constructions transformed Chatham, but one aspect in particular has continued to shape the planning of the town to the present day. This was the creation of a military road network. By 1805 a continuous road ran from the northern end of the Chatham Lines through Brompton barracks, along Brompton High Street and through the infantry barracks to Fort Amherst. It then left that fort via the guardhouse and crossed the barrier ditch on its upper drawbridge before turning west to cross the valley bottom and rise up the hill to Fort Pitt. The road passing over the valley floor was an entirely new construction, which still exists with the name Military Road.

Since the traditional route from Chatham town centre to the dockyard along the Land

Fig 9.9
A detail from an 1806 Board of Ordnance map showing the new road, known today as Military Road, running parallel to the much older Land Wall (marked here as 'Chatham').
(TNA MR 1/815)

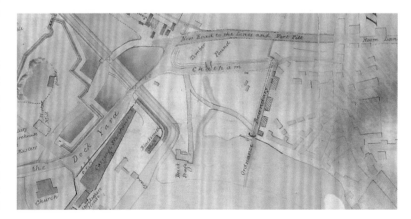

Wall continued to make use of the lower drawbridge over the barrier ditch, the valley bottom came to have two parallel roads (Fig 9.9). The space between these two roads was first used as a timber pound for the construction projects and is today the origin of the green space known as The Paddock.

As the new Military Road rose up the western side of the valley, it followed the alignment of the existing Room (Rome) Lane, which now became a proper military road. Where the New Road was carried over the top of this Military Road by a bridge, a form of guardhouse (since demolished) was constructed by Debbeig in the 1780s that was nearly identical in appearance to the Fort Amherst gatehouse (Fig 9.10). These roads were available for public use, but the military had the ability to control them so that troops could move swiftly between Fort Amherst and Fort Pitt. Guns at Fort Amherst were positioned in order to control the roads, which by their straightness could be swept by fire.

The continued expansion of Chatham prompted the civil authority to propose development along the new military road, but D'Arcy advised firmly against this in a letter of May 1808, because the town was viewed as part of the field of fire of Fort Amherst:

I have considered the proposal to erect buildings on each side of the military road leading from Chatham to the lines and find great difficulty in giving an opinion favourable to the wishes of the Mayor and Corporation of Rochester, for as the Act of 14th July 1804 gave the Ordnance possession of the space over which the new military road has been carried was passed for the better security of His Majesty's dockyard. An engineer cannot consistent with that principle agree to a street being formed (however ornamental) in the way of the defences or give encouragement to substantial buildings being erected that must be levelled when the defences are resorted to.

The valley over which the new road has been formed is 4 feet below HWM [high water mark] and at present occupied by gardens and small wooden houses and while allowed to remain in this state can be flooded to impede as much as possible the spread of fire which it is natural to suppose the enemy will attempt to destroy the posts and obstruct the communication between Fort Pitt and the lines. I am aware that the Government has no right to prevent people improving their property at the same time it cannot be forgot that the state of the ground when the Act was passed in July 1804 did not admit of any

Fig 9.10
The bridge and guardhouse at Room Lane.
(Medway Archives)

Brompton's development

Just as the development of Chatham was curtailed by the military presence, a similar situation prevailed at Brompton. Since its foundation, the gridded streets of this small town had been extended to the east, but only as far as the line of a road in use by the military that connected Townshend's redoubt with Fort Amherst (marked today by Mansion Row and Maxwell Road). Development across this line was strictly prevented, because it would have intruded into the internal fields of fire of the fortifications, in the area today known as the Inner Lines. As a result Brompton grew into a densely developed place though one much better-planned than Chatham and inhabited by better-off people. It was primarily a civilian enclave, surrounded by fortifications, the dockyard and barracks. There was a limited military presence within the town itself at this date, and a small group of buildings on the junction of Mansion Row and Garden Street was by the late 18th century in use as accommodation for the senior non-commissioned gunners and artificers and their families. These buildings remain today.

speculation in the way of buildings like those proposed by the Corporation of Rochester and therefore if the military road by becoming a causeway across the valley has implied the buildings of Chatham to advance nearer to the lines its object has been defeated and it will cease to be what the Act proposed for the better security of His Majesty's dockyard.[21]

Map evidence from 1816 shows that the Ordnance Board enforced the need to keep Chatham's civilian buildings away from the valley bottom. Some buildings were erected, but other maps show that they were all of wood, despite the danger of fire, the inference being that these would not provide cover to an enemy in the same way as substantial brick-built houses. The growth of Chatham had to be accommodated away from the new military road, on the valley sides and along the High Street in the direction of Rochester.

Fig 9.11
Engraving of 'Chatham, Kent' after J M W Turner, c 1830–1. The view is from Fort Amherst looking towards Fort Pitt (left). The military controlled the higher ground, and so the town is seen on the lower ground by the river. A hulk is moored by St Mary's church.
(Royal Engineers Museum, Library and Archives)

10

After the Napoleonic Wars

Victory in 1815 ushered in a period of stagnation for the British army as its strength at home fell. By 1830 it was down to 51,000, much of it in Ireland. Colonial wars and garrison duty created an ongoing need for new recruits, largely to replace the loss of men to disease in tropical climates. Chatham developed a role for troops at the beginning and end of their military service. In the first half of the 19th century Chatham was potentially the largest concentration of troops in Great Britain (the major training garrisons at Aldershot and elsewhere did not yet exist). It was also a place of major experimentation by the military authorities, with trials of new muskets and rifles taking place on its marshland firing ranges.

New recruits

New soldiers entered the army at Chatham barracks, which had regained its role as a recruiting depot for regiments on overseas duty. By 1830 the depots of the various regiments on overseas duty were consolidated at Chatham into a single 'Provisional Battalion' under a unified command from which newly trained recruits would then join their regiments.[1] Chatham was also a home depot for the East India Company forces and processed large numbers of their recruits,[2] although in 1843 their depot was moved to Warley in Essex because the pressure on barracks space for the regular army was so great. In 1847, 2,664 men embarked for Indian service from Chatham. The recruits spent an average of two months at Chatham before being sent abroad, but if a transport ship was ready to depart, a raw recruit might be there for a few days only.

Chatham's role in recruitment and also as a discharge centre meant that it retained its character as a major garrison town. Several accounts exist of the process by which a new recruit became a soldier in the middle of the 19th cen-

tury, and one in particular, *Camp and Barrack-Room* by John Mercier MacMullen, describes the harsh conditions endured by a private soldier. MacMullen accepted the recruitment bounty in Dublin in 1842 and sailed for Gravesend to join the depot of the 13th Regiment at Chatham. This regiment was on service in India and had just fought with distinction in the First Afghan War by breaking out of the besieged town of Jellalabad. Recruits were held in the receiving house to prevent spread of contagious diseases to the wider barracks. Once passed by the surgeon, their heads were shaved and uniforms issued. They then started to learn the drill. MacMullen described his daily routine:

I rose at five o clock in the morning, and made up my bed; which occupied at least a quarter of an hour, and was rather a troublesome job. I then made my toilet, and at six turned out for drill, from which we were dismissed at a quarter to eight, when we breakfasted. From ten till twelve we were again at drill; had dinner at one, in the shape of potatoes and meat, both usually of the most wretched quality; and at two fell in for another drill; which terminated at four; after which hour my time was at my own disposal until tattoo, provided I was not ordered on piquet. During this period of leisure, I generally amused myself by strolling in the vicinity of the garrison (no soldier being permitted to a greater distance than one mile) or by reading.[3]

Soldiers were not supplied with an evening meal. They fended for themselves and were thus drawn to the beerhouses of Chatham or the canteen within the barracks (Fig 10.1).[4] Their pay after stoppages was only just sufficient to afford food, which was a cause of frequent desertion by new recruits, as MacMullen described:

the recruit would only receive two, at the most, threepence per diem; and young lads having good appetites, this trifling sum would be expended in procuring something by way of an evening meal, their ration meals only embracing a breakfast and dinner. Having accordingly no money to spend in amusement, and imagining they must continue to be similarly situated while in the service, young soldiers become quickly disgusted with it; and, when destitute of principle, desertion on the first opportunity followed almost as a matter of course.[5]

MacMullen was damning of the way in which new and still green recruits were seen as an easy means of extracting money by the men placed in authority over them. He was charged for his uniform, though it should have been issued free of charge, and he described various other rackets of stealing from new soldiers: 'One mode of depriving the recruit of his pay, is to give him an old shattered musket, easily injured; thus there are ten chances to one, that some part of it gets broken while it is in his possession; and he has in consequence a round sum to pay on delivering it into the store, when leaving the garrison.'[6]

Once trained, the day would come for embarkation on active service overseas. Soldiers on the verge of departure were, MacMullen said, prone to riotous behaviour in the town of Chatham:

Many of the men, aware that in consequence of their being on the eve of embarkation they could not be punished for minor offences had got drunk, and quarrelling and noise were the order of the night. The authority of the non-commissioned officers was insufficient to secure order; and one sergeant left the barracks altogether, dreading some bodily harm; as he knew that he was generally disliked, owing to his own mean and tyrannous conduct.[7]

He described the departure for Gravesend and the ship to India, with one old soldier warning the new soldiers not to be too heartened by what awaited them: '"Ah!" remarked an old soldier as we passed through the gate, "You shouldn't cheer till ye were comin' back: there wont be so many of you then, I warrant, and they'll not be in a cheering humour".'[8] Men recruited and trained at Chatham were instrumental in the string of colonial wars that marked the expansion of the British Empire in the 19th century. Another description is typical of the thousands of men who left Chatham for service in the empire, principally in India:

MILITARY INTELLIGENCE. CHATHAM–Aug. 1. This morning, at 7 o'clock, eight detachments, selected from the Provisional Battalion assembled on the parade-ground, to the number of 325 men, of the following corps :–8th Foot, 17th, 22nd, 28th, 60th, 1st battalion of Rifles, 86th, 25th, King's Own Borderers, and 78th Highlanders; and, after being inspected, each man was provided with the Articles of War. They were then marched off the ground, *en route* for Gravesend, attended by the drums and fifes of the Provisional Battalion, for embarkation on board the ship *Ann*, for Bombay and Cannanore. The troops, on leaving the barracks, were cheered by their comrades assembled to witness their departure. Seven officers embarked with the above, also ten men belonging to the 10th Hussars (the Prince of Wales's Own), from the cavalry depôt at Maidstone. Capt. James Knox is in command of the ship.[9]

Fig 10.1
An army canteen (not Chatham) showing the routine drunkenness of soldiers.
(Illus London News 20 March 1847)

Barracks

No significant new barracks were built between 1815 and 1850,[10] and yet the garrison remained large. In the case of the infantry barracks, the number of men they contained increased, and overcrowding remained a major problem. The 1841 census recorded over 5,000 soldiers and marines at Chatham, 65 of them inmates at the lunatic asylum at Fort Clarence and 899 as patients in the 4 hospitals (Melville, Pitt, Ordnance and Brompton).[11] Census information counted 1,524 other members of the garrison society who were otherwise invisible from military records. Some of these were civilian employees, but the vast majority were the wives

Invalids

If subsequently their health failed in the outposts of empire, soldiers were brought back to Chatham to be assessed for discharge on medical grounds. Invalids were housed in the St Mary's casemates, and Fort Pitt became the main military hospital, having reverted to its hospital role after 1815. The oldest hospital buildings (now part of the grammar school) are most probably those from 1803. The use of Fort Pitt as part of the invalid operation at

Chatham saw the expansion of the military hospital, with 9 wards capable of holding 200 patients. The fort interior and ramparts were converted into airing grounds to speed the recovery of its occupants. In 1847 an asylum was built for cases of mental illness, though it is reported that the boundary fence was so low as to be capable of being cleared by the inmates in one bound. A museum of anatomy, pathology and other curiosities collected from across the British Empire was also established at Fort Pitt.

and children of the soldiers. Chatham barracks contained 646 such people and Brompton barracks 357. In total, the census recorded 6,558 for the military population of Chatham.[12]

The barracks were in a poor state and must have contributed to the cholera epidemic of 1849. The army surgeon of Brompton barracks wrote to Frederick Smith, then Director of the Royal Engineer Establishment, in order to report how the condition of the barracks was contributing to sickness among the soldiers and their families:

on visiting Corporal Gwynn's wife in the back lower room of this house I was disgusted with the stench that proceeded from the back yard. I enquired particularly respecting it and found that from 5 O'Clock till about 7 AM when the foul air had got partial exit through the front passage the smell was so bad and so sickening that the windows could not be opened. Notwithstanding that the windows were kept close shut the effluvium penetrated and from it and the heat the room at this period was nearly intolerable. I examined the sources from which the smell proceeded and found that it was mainly traceable to the privy and the grating nearest to it. I need scarcely remark how essential it is that attention be immediately directed to the condition of the above yard. I have had more sickness in the rooms adjoining it than in any other part of the barracks.[13]

The Royal Marines barracks were downslope of the main infantry barracks, which contributed to problems with their hygiene. A detailed report by Dr Thomas Stratton described the cholera epidemic at Chatham in 1849, and a large part was devoted to the marines barracks:

The main body of the men's barrack is a building of four floors, of which the lowest is in front, a sunk floor, a passage of four feet wide going along in front

of the windows, and separating these rooms from any dampness in the bank of earth; the wall keeping up this bank is as high as the top of the windows. In the building there is a double row of rooms, one with windows to the front, and the other with windows looking to the rear and the Medway. The front rooms in the sunk flat would not, I suppose, be occupied if the barracks were not crowded; they would probably not be thought good enough to be occupied at ordinary times.[14]

The majority of cholera cases at the marines barracks came from these 'sunk' barrack rooms. Stratton noted this but failed to properly account for it: 'we have 13 cholera cases in the lowest floor, while in the other three floors together, and all occupied to the same extent, there were only thirteen cases. This clearly shows the preference that cholera has for the lowest situations and those worst ventilated.'[15] The final comment shows that Stratton was still open to the theory that cholera was spread through the air as a result of miasmas, when it was in fact spread by contamination of water by sewage. The infantry barracks had only 2 deaths out of 2,000 men from cholera during this outbreak, whereas for the 1,000 individuals living at the marines barracks the death toll was 5.[16]

An 1851 Board of Ordnance return listed who was in each barracks.[17] The infantry barracks had quarters for four staff officers – the commandant, Brigade Major, Second Commandant of the provisional battalion and the Barrack Master. There were also 4 field officers and 85 other officers, 2,768 NCOs and privates, and 32 horses. Brompton barracks had quarters for five Staff Officers – the commandant of the Royal Engineers, director of the Royal Engineer Establishment, captain and adjutant, superintendant of surveying and the commandant of the provisional battalion. There were also 2 field officers and 58 other officers, 1,397 NCOs and privates, and 194 horses. The garrison hospital had 269 patients. Fort Amherst had a staff captain of the invalid depot, with 60 invalids living in the Spur barracks and Prince William's battery. St Mary's casemates had 2 field officers and 840 invalids, and Fort Pitt (the general hospital and the casemates) had a principal medical officer, a deputy purveyor, 10 officers and 447 patients, while 3 officers lived in the house under Fort Pitt. Fort Clarence military prison had a governor, 8 warders and 184 prisoners.

By 1851 the St Mary's casemates and Fort Clarence had each found a new purpose. The latter was in use as a military prison, and the casemates were used by the medical department for invaliding in conjunction with Fort Pitt. The regime at the military prison was harsh:

The prisoners are divided into three classes; the third or worst class are at hard labour, employed in carrying a shot of the weight of thirty-two pounds; the second class carry a twenty-four pound shot; the first or best class are not put to this kind of punishment; they are three hours a-day so employed, half of the time in the morning, and the other in the afternoon. Weakly men are not ordered this shot exercise. A few of the prisoners are employed at trades, as tailors, shoemakers, and carpenters, but only so far as any of this kind of work is required within the prison. The prisoners are not allowed to converse with each other. When they are locked up, each man is placed in a separate cell, which has an arched roof, and is quite free from damp, as over this is a slated roof; the cells are warmed by means of heated air, and gas is burnt in them till eight in the evening.[18]

Development of military engineering training

A specialist focus on siege training was to be a major part of all Royal Engineer training at Chatham for the rest of the 19th century, and after the founding of the Royal Engineer Establishment in 1812 Brompton barracks took on an increasingly significant role. Charles William Pasley held the post of director of the Royal Engineer Establishment at Chatham for 29 years, from its foundation in 1812 during the Napoleonic Wars until 1841, and for this and his other public services he was knighted in 1846.

Pasley was a true polymath and can be seen as the founding father of the Royal School of Military Engineering. He was a man of science, who was elected a Fellow of the Royal Society in 1814 and became an early member of the Institution of Civil Engineers in 1820. He was able to use his work at Chatham as the basis for experimentation in many fields of military science and construction that was transferable to civil projects.

Charles Dupin has left us with a description of the operation of the school in his 1822 work:

But it is time to speak of the studies and works of the practical school. In the distribution of hours, the utmost care is observed not to fatigue the intelligence of the men, and to avoid weakening their physical powers by excessive study. Every day, Sundays excepted, the soldiers turn out in their working dress, in summer at half past six o'clock in the morning, and in winter at half past seven. They are allowed half an hour for breakfast; after which they repair to their different classes in the school, where they remain until nine in the summer, or half past nine in the winter: the remaining portion of the day is devoted to works in the open air. When, however, the weather is such as to prevent a prosecution of this latter description of instruction, the artificers remain in the school until eleven in the morning, and return there again in the afternoon, for three hours in summer, or three and a half in winter. If either soldiers or non-commissioned officers wish to continue their studies beyond the regulated hours, books and instruments are lent to them for the purpose ...

As soon as the students are familiarized with all the elements of fortification, they are rendered equally so with the works of attack and defence. A large model of a fortified place and its environs, with all the accidental features of ground, is provided for the purpose, showing a camp at a distance, and, nearer, the parallels, approaches, and, in a word, all the operations of a siege. There are also models of boyaux-de-tranchées in relief, by means of which a line of attack is marked out, and the pupil directed to show the manner in which a sapper should advance from a given point ...

There are models showing the best means of repairing, with rough pieces of timber of moderate size, arches of bridges destroyed by an enemy.—Others represent the most advantageous point for attaching a mine to a bridge, to blow it up, with the probable breach which would appear after the explosion. Rope-bridges, and other expedients for procuring a military passage over rivers, are also placed in the same rooms. The whole of these models are made by the engineer soldiers themselves, and the very execution of them becomes a means of instruction of the most efficacious nature. Independently, also, of durable models, calculated for the permanent tuition of the school, the artificers raise small models in earth, of works of field fortification.[19]

Where no suitable textbooks existed for use in his training courses, Pasley wrote his own, and these publications became standard works of reference across the world. His three-volume work *Course of instruction; originally composed for the use of the Royal Engineer Establishment* (1814–17) would become his two-volume *A Course of Elementary Fortification* (1822). The abolition of the Barracks Department in 1822 restored responsibility for all barracks and construction on military lands back to the Board of Ordnance and thus to the Royal Engineers. There being no suitable publication with which to teach architecture at Chatham, Pasley wrote an *Outline of a course of practical architecture compiled for the Royal Engineers* (1826). In 1826 he began experiments to perfect artificial Roman cement, and some of the structures at Chatham were used as part of this work.[20] His discoveries were published in 1838 as *Observations on limes, calcareous cements, mortars, stuccos and concrete*.

The other great interest of Pasley was diving and the underwater use of explosives, including their remote detonation by electricity. The Chatham siege exercises frequently included the explosion of submarine mines and the demolition of simulated wrecks. These skills were used for real in the removal of actual wrecks that were a hazard to navigation. Between 1839 and 1843 Pasley instructed a party of engineers in demolishing the wreck of the *Royal George*, which had sunk at Spithead in 1782. His nautical interests extended to pontooning, and he designed a new form of raft for use on the River Medway. Cadets were taught surveying under the Ordnance Survey in Wales, but when this proved inappropriate, a course in surveying was started at Chatham in 1833. Pasley established the first of several observatories at the RSME in order that astronomy could also be practised.[21]

Siege training

In the early days of the Royal Engineer Establishment, the Corps headquarters remained at Woolwich. Officer cadets for the Royal Engineers first went to the Woolwich Military Academy[22] to be given theoretical instruction and some practical training alongside men des-

tined for service in the Royal Artillery. Cadets could only enter Woolwich if nominated by the Master General of the Ordnance and if they passed an entrance examination. Most cadets were 14 to 16 years old on entering the Academy, and they spent between 2 and 4 years there depending on their proficiency, which was tested by examination. Young engineer officers were then sent to Chatham for 15 months of instruction in military engineering, with a heavy emphasis on siege training. These trainees took charge of men of the Royal Sappers and Miners who were also at Chatham to learn siege craft. The Napoleonic Wars may have finished, but in the early to mid-19th century, Chatham was a centre not just for the recruitment of infantry, but also for their training, often in concert with the engineers. Such a role pre-dates the use of Aldershot and other places that were subsequently used as the main infantry schools. Although training took place at Upnor, the Chatham Lines gradually took over, perhaps from as early as 1821,[23] and so the engineers had no need to manufacture training grounds, as these fortifications provided the genuine article. In 1833 Pasley officially gave up the training grounds at Upnor and mentioned that these had not been much used for many years:

I beg to report to you that the ground allocated to us at Upnor for the practice of the Royal Sappers and Miners in military fieldworks is exceedingly inconvenient from the circumstance of the men having to cross the water and expensive in as much as it occasions a great wear and tear of boats. In fact it has proved so inconvenient and harassing to the men that for several years past we have made very little use of the ground at Upnor but have carried on the greater part of our practice on this side of the river within the lines by permission first of Major General D'Arcy and afterwards of Lieutenant Colonel Burgoyne.[24]

The siege training was on a scale and complexity not seen at any other British garrison. While stationed at Chatham, it was agreed that the infantry soldiers should make use of their time by receiving this type of training, such that

every man might, once in his life at least, form a yard of common siege trench: and the advantage of this no one can doubt; certainly no officer will doubt it, who has had to lead soldiers, in a dark night, under an enemy's walls, after having given them a pick-axe in exchange for their musket, and had to direct them, in

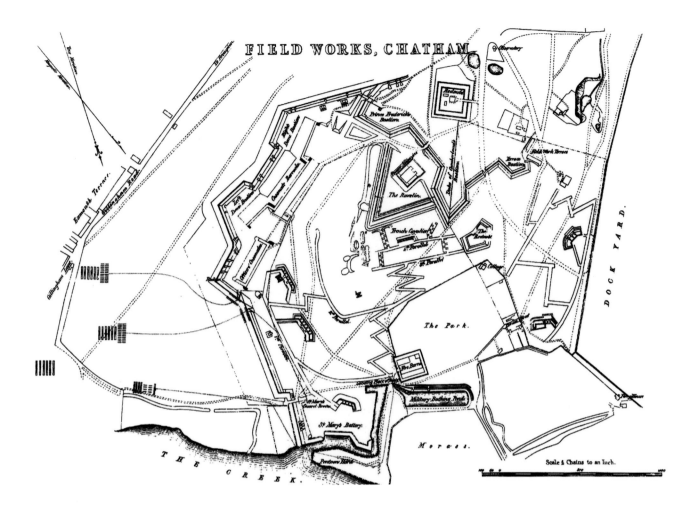

Fig 10.2
A plan of the 1848 siege
works at Chatham.
(Royal Engineers Museum,
Library and Archives)

such a situation under fire, to make what they never saw or perhaps heard of before.[25]

Engineer soldiers under instruction in field-works spent the summer months building the earthworks of a major siege and then used these as the basis of large live firing exercises to test their ability in all aspects of mounting a siege. Others of their number took the role of defenders to learn that aspect of a siege. The army garrison collaborated with the engineers, and the artillery, the navy and the marines all participated. The siege exercises followed a somewhat formulaic series of choreographed episodes, and referees were required to help ensure safety and to judge the efficiency of the various parties in the different duties they executed.

Many accounts of these siege exercises exist, particularly from the *Illustrated London News* and *The Times*. An early account appeared in Charles Dickens's novel *The Pickwick Papers* of 1836. The first well-documented major siege exercise took place in 1833[26] and consisted

of an attack by sapping and mining, driven against the Duke of Cumberland's bastion. This same location was used for at least the next 10 years. The high ground on which the Brompton barracks were located[27] acted as the focus for the assault, which was mounted from close to the north-east corner of the dockyard and from the St Mary's hornwork, as seen in engravings and printed maps, such as those of 1848 (Fig 10.2).[28]

It was feasible to allow this part of the lines to be compromised through training because it lay behind the Lower Lines. Use of land nearer to the St Mary's casemates was impossible, as they were in use as gunpowder magazines until *c* 1846 in order to cope with the quantity of naval powder that was returned to store after the 1815 peace.[29] They then reverted to barracks for use for invalids. Although training using mining and explosions appears to have been concentrated on the northern end of the lines, other parts were also used. Fort Amherst was used to practise escalading or the use of assault ladders to cross the ditches and get over

Fig 10.3
Escalade exercise against
Fort Amherst.
(Illus London News *28 July*
1849)

the ramparts. There is also evidence from as early as 1825 that the excavation of parallels was practised in the open ground outside the central section of the lines. The success of the 13th regiment in the storming of stockades in the Burmese War (1824–6) was attributed to their practice of the techniques of escalading at Chatham before their departure for India.[30]

A report in the *Illustrated London News* describes the combined use of Fort Amherst and the left of the lines for siege training in July 1849:

First part of exercise is on right of the Lines. The parapets being manned from the Gunwharf to the Spur. Attacked by three columns who are unsuccessful largely due to the depth of the ditch. Within and without the lines nothing could be more praiseworthy than the manner in which the men went through their evolutions. Without the columns exhibited the utmost daring. An impervious hedge, a high wall and short scaling ladders were the real causes of the retreat and not the slightest taint rests upon the honour of the corps engaged. In fact they seemed to court destruction and how they escaped the deadly aims taken at them by the besieged was what no one

Fig 10.4
View of the siege exercises
from St Marys Creek
(Illus London News *25 June*
1864)

Fig 10.5
The siege exercises at Chatham were open to the public and attracted huge crowds who travelled there by excursion trains and ferry.
(Illus London News *22 July 1854*)

present could perfectly understand ... The scenic effect of it was beautiful from the height at which the lines attacked stand and the evolutions of the troops in availing themselves of the shelter which the ground afforded.

Second part of the exercise was far more elaborate and was a successful assault and escalade of the left of the Lines. A portion of sailor and marines were used in 4 gun boats to capture Gillingham tower and battery. Pontoon bridge built over St Marys Creek. Assault supported by fire from the high ground at Burnt Oak Cottage and from gun boats in the Medway and St Mary's Creek.[31]

The VIPs who were invited to attend the annual field exercises included British and foreign royalty and senior army officers, and they watched the proceedings from grandstands erected on the casemates in the Lower Lines (*see* Fig 12.14). The excitement of seeing massed troops and the firing of underground mines attracted large numbers of the public, and additional transport was laid on to take people to the spectacle. The numbers in attendance created its own problems, with people pressing close to the explosions in a way that today would be unthinkable.

The report of the 1849 siege exercise in the *Annual Register* captured the danger and excitement of the event for participants, guests and spectators alike:

The 'siege operations' at Chatham, affording a military spectacle not often to be enjoyed by the people of this commercial country, drew prodigious crowds to the scene; between 40,000 and 50,000 persons were present. Prince George of Cambridge, Prince Edward of Saxe Weimar, the Marquis of Anglesey, Viscount Hardinge, and others of the nobility, took their stations in the casemates, and a vast number of ladies posted themselves in prominent positions. The 'operations' consisted of attacks by a besieging army, which had beaten a force sent to relieve the fortress besieged, and had returned to the siege operations; and of a defence by the besiegers, which was successful up to a certain point, but at last failed against the superior force and offensive *matériel* of the attacking body. The final and successful operation commenced with the repulse of a sortie made by the besieged; in following which, the besiegers entered the sally-port close on the heels of the troops from the fortress, who had not time to raise the drawbridge. The attacking party then breached a stockade by the explosion of two bags, containing 90 lbs. of gunpowder. The effect was startling – large pieces of timber were blown 100 feet into the air; and, with the great quantity of clods of earth which showered upon the spectators, it was surprising that they escaped so free of injury. The mimic warfare was, however, not unattended with danger. The Master-General, with the impetuosity of a gallant warrior, rushed with his staff through the breach in the stockade; and the Royal Sappers and Miners, and the Royal Marines, also rushed in real earnest through the breach to take possession of the lines by escalading them; forgetting, it is supposed,

Fig 10.6
A sketch of the siege works in the Royal Engineer training exercise in August 1843, drawn by J C Anderson, an engineer in the East India Company.
(Royal Engineers Museum, Library and Archives)

in the impulse of the moment, that the garrison had left slow matches at two mines under the batteries; one of which exploded when the Royal Marines were within a few feet of it, and covered them literally all over with mud and clods of earth, which caused them to retire with such haste that one poor fellow broke his leg. The Marquis of Anglesey was so near the mine when it sprung, that his hat was knocked off by a clod of earth, and several of the staff were struck with large pieces of earth, and covered with dust, which nearly blinded them, and created, in spite of the serious nature of the scene, universal laughter amongst all who were near enough to witness it ... The other mine being a few seconds later in exploding, enabled all parties to retire to a safe distance to witness the effect. Some slight mishaps occurred, chiefly from the eagerness of the spectators to join the soldiers in the attack on the trenches, and their reckless defiance of orders to beware of the explosions; altogether the affair seems to have given high satisfaction to the immense concourse of spectators.[32]

Training in explosives

Training was not just restricted to siege events. Those engineers undergoing instruction built brick walls, bridges, timber stockades and all manner of structures to study the impact of explosive charges and mining. Before the invention of photography, the only way to record the results was by watercolour and ink sketches, and so Royal Engineers were trained to observe and record in this way.[33]

The training was not just theoretical, as the British army after 1815 took part in many colonial wars across the world, with the Royal Engineers providing support. In 1847 the British were fighting the Maoris in New Zealand, and so in June of that year experiments took place at Chatham to discover the best way to breach a native *pah* (a form of double stockade) using explosives and no artillery.[34]

The use of explosives and tunnelling inevitably made training a sometimes dangerous duty. In October 1844 an experimental system of countermines designed by Lieutenant Herbert Newton Penrice was tried out under his direction, in which galleries were dug at different levels rather than in a single plane radiating out from the ditch. The form of the resulting countermine system was criticised for its lack of ease of ventilation, which probably contributed to the fatal accident:

At about 2 o'clock P.M. (that is, about 2¼ hours after the explosion,) an accident occurred which caused the deepest regret to every one engaged in these operations. At about 2 hours after the explosion of the 25 lbs. of powder, a brigade of miners commenced work in gallery C, under the orders of Lieut. Moggridge, in putting up the frames that had been knocked down. This officer, observing the lights to burn dimly, and feeling a deficiency of air, ordered his party to withdraw, and he himself retired towards the mouth of the gallery, to examine the ventilating pipes. Whilst so occupied, he heard an alarm that an

Fig 10.7
A sketch from a notebook of
a Royal Engineer officer
undergoing training at
Chatham to show the effect
on a timber stockade of a
small demolition charge.
(Royal Engineers Museum,
Library and Archives)

accident had happened at the head of the gallery, and repairing instantly to the spot, he found two of his miners senseless. A very gallant attempt was made by Lieut. Moggridge to drag out the foremost man, but, overcome by the foul air, he himself fainted, and was carried out by Colour-Serjeant G. Shepherd and Private J. Murphy, R. S. and M [Royal Sappers and Miners]. After some difficulty and delay, which may be attributed chiefly to the undulating form of the gallery, the two men were rescued, but not until a third had fainted. Medical aid was fortunately at hand, and two out of the three miners were restored, but unhappily the third (Private James Sullivan, of the East India Company's Sappers and Miners) was brought out dead, and all attempts for his recovery proved unsuccessful. From the results of a subsequent investigation before a Court of Inquiry, it appeared that the two men, instead of promptly obeying the command to retire, had loitered in the gallery, and that one of them afterwards either removed a plank, or otherwise disturbed the earth with his pick, when it is supposed that a sudden inbreak of carbonic acid gas immediately prostrated the men.[35]

The dockyard

The revolution in warship design in the first half of the 19th century focused on the adoption of steam power in combination with sail, first of all with paddle wheels (1827) and then with screw propellers (*Ajax,* 1846). These steamers were still wooden hulled, because despite the introduction of iron construction for civilian shipping, such as SS *Great Britain* (1838), such hulls were too vulnerable to gunfire due to the brittle nature of the iron. France was the only naval power to seriously challenge the Royal Navy through the adoption of steam power. A French naval renaissance started in the 1840s, which continued under Napoleon III after the hiatus of the 1848 revolution. During the period 1850–60, France built 10 combined steam- and sail-powered ships of the line and carried out 28 conversions from sail to steam and sail, while Britain built 18 new ships, converted 41 and had 9 blockships.[36]

This period of major change in warship design and construction created a similar revolution on shore in terms of the design of the British dockyards. First, the introduction of steam power in wooden hulls required new trades and structures in which to build engines and boilers, and then the massive increase in the use of iron for hulls and armour required new smitheries equipped with large machinery. As ships became larger, the dry docks and building slips of the late 18th-century wooden sail-powered navy were inadequate. Larger docks were required, either as new constructions or by lengthening the old. Steam ships required basins in which to be kept after launch for fitting out or repair.

At Chatham the pre-1815 dockyard occupied a cramped linear site with no room for expansion except to the north. Major change using new land was the only solution that could meet the new demands of a steam-age dockyard, but initially the change was accommodated within the older site. Consideration had been given during the Napoleonic Wars to a grand new naval arsenal at Northfleet in Kent, in recognition of the fact that Chatham and the Thames dockyards were becoming awkward and outdated. This scheme was not adopted.

In 1817 John Rennie reported on the suitability of the river front and docks at Chatham and recommended a major rebuild. His grandiose scheme to improve Chatham as a dockyard was by diverting the course of the Medway across the Frindsbury peninsula so as to turn the naval anchorage into a single large wet dock controlled by gates and entered via St Mary's creek. Elements of this proposal did appear in the solution eventually adopted, but attention first focused on rebuilding the river wall and on the construction of large roofs over new building slips.

The covered slips are a unique and highly visible feature of Chatham dockyard. The concept of building wooden warships under large shed-like roofs in order to protect them from premature rot was commonly used abroad, but not adopted in Britain until the early 19th century. The group of five covers illustrates the development of this building type over a very short period of time, and in this they mirror the similarly rapid development in warships.

Fig 10.8
Covered Slips 3–7 at Chatham dockyard alongside the River Medway. (Ben Found)

Fig 10.9
The interior of No. 3 Slip at
Chatham dockyard.
(Author)

The earliest surviving slip cover at Chatham (No. 3 Slip) is typical of early roofs and is constructed of timber. It dates from 1837. When three more roofs (of Slips 4, 5 and 6) were ordered in 1844, just seven years later, these were to be in iron but to a design influenced by their timber predecessors. Slip no. 7, ordered in 1851, represents the full development of the slip cover as an integrated factory space in which the iron frame does not just provide cover for the shipbuilding, but was designed to take overhead cranes and to facilitate the movement of large and heavy components.

Building under cover was no longer essential once iron took over from wood as the main component of a warship, yet No. 7 Slip continued to be used until the period of the dockyard closure (c1984), latterly for submarines. The Royal Engineers were closely involved in the design and construction of the slip covers. From 1837 the previous separation of the Navy Board with sole responsibility for dockyard projects was eroded by the creation of the Admiralty Works Department to which Royal Engineers were appointed. Slip nos 4, 5 and 6 were constructed under the direction of Henry Brandeth RE, and No. 7 Slip was designed and supervised by Colonel Godfrey Greene RE, who was also responsible for the boatstore at Sheerness dockyard.

Chatham and Brompton civilian settlements

The economy of Chatham rose and fell with the fortunes of the government establishments, especially as the dockyard was the largest local employer. Periods of war created a demand for labour and services, and the local economy benefited, but peace brought retrenchment. Enterprises grew up to support the dockyard and the barracks, but Chatham also developed other industries, many being related to the river and the private wharves. Private shipbuilding yards, some working for the navy under contract, provided some additional work. The Medway was navigable as far as Maidstone, and so before the arrival of railways the river provided a commercial artery for bringing out agricultural and other products from the Weald of Kent, such as hops, paper and timber, and delivering coal. Trade with London and down the coast to Sheerness and beyond was significant.

The social and environmental ills of Chatham as a town that had grown up primarily to serve the dockyard and the army could not be addressed until the place was able to achieve a separate identity from Rochester, along with the public institutions required of a respectable town. Chatham was not just physically one long continuous street connected to Rochester, it was seen as an adjunct to the older city. It was originally intended to have only one Member of Parliament for Rochester and Chatham, but the electorate of Rochester feared that they would be always outvoted by the larger Chatham electorate, who were nearly all linked by employment to the Government. The Great Reform Act of 1832 separated parliamentary representation by allocating a new member to Chatham. Chatham became a nomination borough where the Government could control who was returned to Westminster.

The Poor Law Amendment Act 1834 introduced a much tougher regime for the poor nationwide. The first workhouse to take the poor and homeless at Chatham was opened in 1727, but it was also possible to obtain outdoor relief by which the parish provided a subsidy to its paupers in their own homes. The 1834 Act effectively criminalised poverty and punished people for being poor. Those seeking relief had to be committed to the workhouse, where they endured a harsh regime. The Medway Union was responsible for parishes in Rochester, Chatham and Gillingham and ran two workhouse establishments. At the 1841 census, the workhouse in Chatham had 138 male paupers, 184 female paupers and 6 officers.

Chatham had no town council to regulate its business or appoint public officers. The closest it came was the Court Leet that had feudal origins and under which 24 jurors were elected from the free citizenry of the town, who were then led by a High Constable elected from their number. In 1835 the Court decided not to seek incorporation as a full borough, something that would have enabled Chatham to have a properly organised police force and its own magistracy. In 1849 a new Act of Parliament permitted the establishment of a Local Board of Health, which was effective in addressing some of the nuisances to public health, principally by constructing proper sewers and regulating polluting industries like slaughterhouses.

For a description of how Chatham had developed by the mid-19th century, a detailed and unappealing picture was provided by Dr Stratton's account of the cholera epidemic in 1849:

Chatham – This town is the lowest situated of this cluster of towns; some parts of the High Street, and some lanes and courts off it, are only a few feet above the high water level. What is called *The Brook* repre-

sents what originally was probably a beautiful and romantic riverlet or burn, but is now a ditch filled to overflowing by contributions from all the drains near it. It is an uncovered drain, about four or five feet wide, and from three to five feet deep; its contents are half solid; bubbles of gas are constantly rising to the surface, and the odour of it is, to strangers, most intolerable; and along its banks are erected a number of overhanging necessaries. This 'Brook' stagnates in a winding ditch in the bottom of the valley and for the distance of half a mile it has houses close to it. The tide rises in it; and about 150 yards from where it joins the Medway, the rise is about a foot. This so-called *Brook* ought to be arched over throughout its whole length; it is at one or two points covered in for a few yards; but this partial covering, though beneficial to those living nearest these spots, makes the exhalations more intense at other parts. Some married men of the marines live on the Brook; such ought to be recommended to live in Brompton ...

Some of the courts near Holborn Lane and the High Street are built with a marvellous attention to intricacy, small courts being, as it were, within others, and the greatest difficulties being opposed by man to any ventilation by nature. These lanes are between the High Street, and the Medway; and some of the houses the ground-floor is barely above the level of high-water. Some married men of the marines live in these courts, and, for a single small room in this low, damp, and unhealthy situation, pay the rent of two shillings and six pence a-week or six pounds four shillings a-year. In these lanes, the children have a very sickly appearance; bowel complaints are prevalent all the year round, and there are occasional outbreaks of low fever ...

Passing along the High Street of Chatham, we next see on the right hand some ground set apart for market gardens, lying between the street and the Medway; beyond this we enter the city of Rochester, and are immediately struck with the much more cleanly state of the streets than is exhibited in Chatham. The houses, also, have a better appearance; and the proportion of inhabitants in comfortable circumstances, and with habits of attention to cleanliness, is evidently much greater than it is in the former town.[37]

The diseases caused by the poor quality of the town inevitably struck mostly at the occupants of the worst areas, but disease was not discriminating and created both a fear in the better off of the town and a desire, motivated perhaps by self-interest but also by altruism, to improve the living conditions of their less well-off fellows. Dr Stratton described the death of one of the dockyard officers:

On Thursday, August 29, in the afternoon, Mr V., aged 52, one of the officers of the yard, was looking on at the cleaning of a very offensive drain near *the Brook*, and close to some houses of which he was the owner. During the evening he felt quite well, as usual, and had a party at his house. Next morning, at 4 o'clock, he was seized with cholera, and died at 2 P.M. after ten hours' illness. Perhaps if he had not exposed himself near the drain, he would not have been taken ill.[38]

Stratton's description of Chatham can be contrasted with that for Brompton:

Brompton. – The town of Brompton is pleasantly situated. It is elevated and well aired, being much more healthy than Chatham, and somewhat more so than Rochester ... The High Street and the principal other streets are kept in a tolerably clean state, although some of the arrangements for drainage are a little defective. Some of the streets are on a pretty steep incline, so that rain and other water runs off easily. Some courts and alleys were in a bad state; to improve which, a few efforts were made by the inhabitants, to which they were perhaps stimulated a little by the commandant of Brompton barracks threatening to confine the soldiers to barracks, if the town was not kept in a more cleanly state. During the epidemic, the soldiers were not allowed to enter Chatham; but Brompton was open as usual; while the arrangement was a loss to the shopkeepers in Chatham, their loss was an additional advantage to those in Brompton.[39]

By 1849 Brompton had grown into a small town in its own right. Its economy was heavily reliant on the dockyard and on the two large barracks that stood at each end of its High Street. The 19th-century commercial directories show that Brompton developed a wide range of local enterprises, both in response to the needs of the army and navy and also to support its residents. During the 1849 cholera epidemic, sentries were posted to prevent soldiers from entering Chatham, but Brompton remained open, including its public houses. Like Chatham, Brompton was curtailed in its expansion by the military land ownerships. Although there were grander terraces such as Mansion Row or Prospect Row, dense development was also inevitable on the slopes leading down to the dockyard, and these dwellings were cleared as slums from the 1960s.

Chatham and Brompton were full of military men and dockyard workers. Frequenting the same streets were men of the Royal Navy, the Royal Marines, the Royal Engineers and regi-

ments of the line for the army, each based within their own establishments. Charles Dickens spent his early life at Chatham and drew on this for his later works, giving a description of how mid-19th century Chatham would have appeared. From his 1836 novel *The Pickwick Papers* came the following description of the Medway towns:

The principal productions of these towns ... appear to be soldiers, sailors, Jews, chalk, shrimps, officers, and dockyard men. The commodities chiefly exposed for sale in the public streets are marine stores, hard-bake, apples, flat-fish, and oysters. The streets present a lively and animated appearance, occasioned chiefly by the conviviality of the military. It is truly delightful to a philanthropic mind, to see these gallant men staggering along under the influence of

Fig 10.10 (top)
Wood Street, Brompton.
(Royal Engineers Museum, Library and Archives)

Fig 10.11 (bottom)
Mansion Row, Brompton.
(Royal Engineers Museum, Library and Archives)

an overflow, both of animal and ardent spirits; more especially when we remember that the following them about, and jesting with them, affords a cheap and innocent amusement for the boy population. Nothing can exceed their good humour.

In his *Household Words* of 1851 Dickens also wrote about the military nature of Chatham:

Coming in to Chatham it appeared to me as if the feeble absurdity of an individual were made more and more manifest at every step I took. Men were only noticeable here by scores, by hundreds, by thousands, rank and file companies, regiments, detachments, vessels full for exportation. They walked about the streets in rows or bodies carrying their heads in exactly the same way, and doing exactly the same thing with their limbs. Nothing in the shape of clothing was made for an individual; everything was contracted for, by the million. The children of Israel were established in Chatham, as salesmen, outfitters, tailors, old clothesmen, army and navy accoutrement makers, bill discounters and general despoilers of the Christian world in tribes rather than in families. The cannon and pyramidal piles of cannon balls renounced the insignificance of individuality, and combined by the score. In the town barracks, if I saw one soldier pipe claying a belt, I was sure to see twenty: nineteen of whom might have been compound reflections of the first one in a combination of looking glasses. No man cooked his dinner in a saucepan, the whole regiment's dinner came out of a copper. The muskets stood in racks and even the drums were gregarious. Up in the airy Artillery Barracks Private Jones or Brown lived in a mansion labelled '120 men' or '160 men' – that was his doorplate – he had no separate existence.

Law and order

Chatham in particular had a reputation for lawlessness. Riotous behaviour was not uncommon. We can speculate how lively the town must have been at the time of the major siege exercises, the annual races on the Great Lines and the two fairs held each year. In garrison towns inter-service rivalry would result in disorder which the inadequate police force of the day was unable to control, such as in 1838 when men of the 67th and 74th regiments clashed with the marines, leaving two of the latter dead. The military were likely to fight with the local civilians as well, as in 1834 with the men of the 88th regiment:

Outrages by the military on the people are yearly becoming more frequent. At Chatham races, a dispute having taken place between some soldiers and the people, the non-commissioned officers and privates of the 88th regiment, advanced in complete battle array to the booths, where the people were enjoying themselves after the races. The soldiers were armed with bayonets, and plunged them indiscriminately into every person within their reach, thereby wounding about thirty persons. Next day a body of sailors and other persons, armed with bludgeons, having paraded the town, they were attacked by the soldiers, who sallied out of the barracks with their arms in their hands, and made a general attack.[40]

Accounts of the recruitment process at Chatham barracks describe the behaviour of soldiers on the night before embarkation for foreign service. Knowing that they would not be punished the next day, these men indulged themselves fully. It was not just on such special occasions that the pubs of Chatham were full. The canteens inside the barracks were unattractive and the prices unfavourable, because the canteen masters had to recover the fee they paid the barracks department for the right to run the establishment. As soldiers were not provided with an evening meal, it is not surprising that they frequented beer shops set up for their use. It was the need to tackle the inevitability of drunkenness that lay behind the founding of the Soldier's Institute and the army temperance societies.

11

The Crimean War and Reform

In July 1854 the siege exercises at Chatham took place against the background of a deteriorating situation in which Britain and France were allied with Turkey against the Russians. The Crimean War was the severest test yet to the value of the siege training at Chatham. In September the allies began landing troops in the Crimea and laid siege to the dockyard city of Sevastopol, which was fortified against a landward assault. The war here became a bloody conventional siege lasting almost a year, from the first bombardment in October 1854 to the allied occupation of the city in September 1855. The Russians mounted a spirited defence, including counterattacks against the siege works of the French and British. The attackers resorted to heavy artillery bombardment to soften up the Russian positions before repeated infantry assaults. The Royal Engineers made little use of underground mining in this war. Instead, in the final bombardment of Sevastopol, hundreds of allied guns were used over three days, before the final assault of the city.

The Americans sent a commission to observe the progress of the war, and their opinion of the British siege tactics was not complimentary. George Brinton McClellan of the US army observed that the French drove their parallels to within 50 yards of the Russian defences, but the British to within only 250 yards, leaving their storming columns more exposed to the defender's fire. The years after the defeat of France at Waterloo in 1815 had been essentially a period of stagnation for the British army, with little innovation and investment. When peace had been restored, criticism was voiced in Britain of the great cost of fortifications that were never put to the test. Speaking in 1816 in the House of Commons, John Calcraft, MP for Rochester, gave his opinion of the Chatham defences:

With respect to the works, the best thing we could do was to sell the materials, or suffer them to fall silently into the dust. The new kingdom of Chatham, as it had been called, was remarkable for nothing but its absurdity and expense; and we had much better get rid of Fort Amherst, Fort Chatham and Fort Pitt, and all the other nonsensical forts. As to the works across the Medway, they should be either burnt or sold, as well as the other two communications across the Thames.[1]

The Crimean War was therefore fought by a British force that was little changed in terms of equipment and organisation from the one that had fought under Wellington. The Crimean War not only exposed the inadequacy of the army and its supporting departments, but provided notice of the kind of industrialised warfare that would grow throughout the second half of the 19th century, foreshadowing the horrors of total war as fought in the 20th century. In particular, the French demonstrated in the Crimean conflict a greater openness to new technologies. This reinforced the fear held by Britain that their naval supremacy was open to challenge and that invasion from France was once again a possibility. It was therefore obvious that the army was in need of major reform and improvement.

Having exposed many failings in the British army, the Crimean War led to major reforms and reorganisation. Chief among these was the creation of a new War Department under a Secretary of State for War. The Ordnance Board was not spared, since it was abolished in June 1855 and its responsibilities for the supply of munitions, the construction of fortifications and barracks and the command of the engineers and artillery were transferred to the War Department. Another post-Crimean war reform of 1856 was the amalgamation of the officer-only Corps of Royal Engineers with the Royal Sappers and Miners to form the Royal Engineers composed of officers and all other ranks, as they are today.

The newly amalgamated officers and men of the Royal Engineers were soon called on for further active service in the suppression of the Indian Mutiny that had started in 1857. The mutineers seized Delhi, and Colonel Richard Baird Smith was sent to take command of the Royal Engineers responsible for assaulting the city. Operations here were more successful than the long drawn-out siege of Sevastopol. The storming of the Kashmir Gate was a decisive event led by the Royal Engineers, for which three VCs were awarded to the Corps. Some 250 miles from Delhi, Lucknow was also under siege, but here the Royal Engineers were in a defensive, not aggressive, role. As garrison engineer, Captain George Fulton RE organised efficient countermine defences underground against Indian attacks, but lost his life before a British relief force was able to reach Lucknow.

Inspection of barracks

Responsibility for barracks in the reforms after the Crimean War now rested with the Inspector-General of Fortifications reporting to the War Department. Before and after the 1855 army reforms this post was held by Major-General John Burgoyne, who had been commanding engineer at Chatham in the 1820s and the senior engineer for the Crimean campaign. The 1854–5 parliamentary report, *Report of the Committee on the Barrack Accommodation for the Army,* was submitted to Burgoyne and highlighted three issues. Separate eating areas were required in addition to the cooking areas, so that men did not spend all their spare time, including meal times, in their sleeping quarters. Another issue was the practice of married soldiers living with their wives and children alongside their single colleagues. Finally, the use of canteens was to be reviewed so that they were more efficiently run and more attractive to the soldiers.

In 1855 Palmerston became Prime Minister, and his new administration came under considerable pressure from public campaigners like Florence Nightingale and from his own colleagues, such as Sidney Herbert, to reform army accommodation. In 1857 Palmerston set up a Royal Commission under the direction of Herbert to examine the question, and it reported in 1861 as the *General Report of the Committee appointed for Improving the Sanitary Condition of the Barracks and Hospitals.*

Public opinion was shocked by the revelation that army barracks were severely prejudicial to the health of the troops. For those aged 20 to 40 within the general male population, the mortality rate was 9.8 per 1,000, but for soldiers in barracks it was a staggering 17.9 per 1,000, even though infirm candidates were excluded by the recruitment process. Soldiers were provided with food, shelter and regular exercise, but life in barracks was prematurely killing or incapacitating the men through illness. Alcoholism and venereal disease were factors, but the main issue was their living conditions.

The report revealed that throughout the barracks and old forts of the United Kingdom, there were 5,300 barrack rooms for sleeping in, holding a total of 75,801 men. The Royal Commission recommended that 600 cubic feet of space should be allocated for each soldier, which meant that based on this allowance there was capacity for only 53,806 men. Barracks rooms were undeniably overcrowded, and even the allocation of 600 cubic feet was less than considered appropriate for prisoners in civilian gaols.

The squalid living conditions of the British soldier were revealed to the public. Barracks were damp, draughty and poorly lit, and rooms were heated by a single, inadequate fireplace that might also be needed to warm up food. Ventilation was either non-existent or frequently blocked up. Sanitary provision was rudimentary, and there was no running water. Lighting was normally by candles, although a few sites were starting to receive gas lighting. The men spent all their waking hours in the fetid atmosphere of the barrack room, except for the time spent on parade or on drill. Most seriously of all in the eyes of the commission, the wives and children of married soldiers endured the same conditions.

The Royal Commission was to become the standing Army Sanitary Committee, and as part of its report, it inspected 162 barracks across the kingdom. Chatham's turn was in July 1858, where some of the barracks were then 100 years old and very overcrowded. For the infantry barracks, the report gave a vivid impression of how the soldiers lived:

There are 3 parallel rows of barracks separated by 30 feet. Due to falling ground the blocks are higher on their lower sides making the lower rooms unfit for use as they are dark and damp. Some are in use as latrines. Each flat of every block contains 2 ranges of barrack rooms built back to back so that there are windows on only one side. A through draft so essential where rooms are crowded can only be achieved by making openings through the partitions between ranges of rooms but this only permits the foul air of one room to intermingle with the foul air of another. Access is by wooden staircases and landings. There are 176 barrack rooms with regulation accommodation for 2,700 men. Rooms are generally 27ft 9ins long and 19ft 3ins broad with heights varying from 8ft 3ins to 10ft 4ins. They are gloomy, dark, low and encumbered with clumsy hanging shelves. Each room has generally three windows. Each room has a fireplace opposite the door but these are poorly constructed and waste a large amount of heat. The rooms are very much overcrowded. Only in three rooms did space per man exceed 500 cubic feet and some had as little as 247 cubic feet. Average per man was 351 cubic feet. The Royal Commission recommends 600 cubic feet per man and the Chatham barracks have a 50% deficiency i.e. the building would need to be doubled to hold its present complement of men with security to health.

There being no accommodation for staff sergeants or sufficient for the officers of so large an establishment. Barrack rooms are appropriated for this purpose thus reducing the accommodation for other ranks still further. Ventilation is by a slide in the windows and in the doors from the staircases. Men keep these shut so that the fireplaces become the only means of ventilating these overcrowded rooms. Lighting is by gas. There is no day room so the men occupy the barrack rooms during the day and also eat there. Walls are showing signs of want of cleanliness and some floors are asphalt which is cold and retains moisture on its surface.

Lavatories are in the ground floors of the two front ranges. They are cold, gloomy and damp and not fit for men to go washing immediately after leaving their beds. There are 11 in number each fitted with 40 basins and water laid on. There is one good ablution room but it has been appropriated as a meat store for the issuing of 3,000 rations per day. Each lavatory has a bath but no means of getting hot water. There are no lavatories or baths for the women or children in the barracks.

Chatham barracks has no separate accommodation for married NCOs or for married men whose wives are allowed. In every barrack room there is at least one married soldier amongst the 14 men and girls of 14–16 years are mixed up with the soldiers.

Apart from the demoralising tendency of such arrangements the atmosphere of barracks rooms is liable to deteriorate when activities take place when the men are on parade or other duties e.g. cooking, washing and hanging up linen to dry. Windows are kept tight shut at these times. Soldiers return to a close, heated noisome atmosphere in which they pass the night. Curtains, double beds, clothes and cooking utensils all take up space. The only remedy for an evil

of this magnitude is to provide suitable married quarters and to remove women and children from the barracks.

Until last year all cooking was done in 4 kitchens with 56 boilers. Soldiers paid to have their meat roasted for them in the town of Chatham. Last year a new kitchen with 2 large ovens came into use. There are no cleaning rooms at Chatham and no covered sheds for drill. Exposure in all weathers is a problem.

Water supply is from the dockyard whence it is pumped to a tank above the level of the barracks. The supply is inadequate for flushing out privies, drains and urinals. An additional supply is required. Drainage should be good due to the fall on the site but there are cesspools. The ash pits are open and exposed and apt to create nuisances. Collection by cart is needed. There is no proper accommodation for dirty bedding and dirty hair stores. These are placed under the sleeping rooms in two of the barrack blocks. There are no drying or airing rooms for personal linen or bedding. Beds are changed on certain days of the week regardless of the state of the weather and the Medical Officer attributes much of the catarrhal and pulmonary disease prevalent in the barracks to this.

The main evils of these infantry barracks, the report concluded, were the overcrowding and the defective ventilation. For the six-year period from 1851 to 1857, the average monthly strength was 2,810 men. In that time, admissions to hospital were 26,837, and there were 192 deaths, amounting to 10.2 per 1,000 per annum. The comparable civilian figure for this age group was 8.1 per 1,000.

For the Spur battery at Fort Amherst, the 1861 report said:

Upper rooms of the casemated barracks are appropriated for invalided gunners or married soldiers. The lower rooms are ineligible as soldier's quarters but occupied by invalided soldiers and their families or by married soldiers of Chatham garrison. There is no ventilation save windows, doors and chimneys. There is only one kitchen with no means of cooking except for boilers. Drainage is defective, it merely leads outside and discharges. Water is from a well. The latrines are defective.

Brompton barracks received a better though not glowing report:

14 school rooms are used for instruction of men at engineers school in the north wing. There is an infant and industrial school in same building with 103 scholars. Two libraries in north wing; one for sergeants and one for privates. There is an excellent museum and model room. There are 11 ablution rooms – 9 with a cast iron bath but a scarcity of water.

There is however a bathing pond. There is an excellent laundry. There is a washhouse with troughs and boilers for use of wives. Good accommodation has just been erected for married NCOs – 4 staff sergeants and 42 other families. There are 2 cook houses with 16 boilers each, but no means of roasting meat. Drainage is defective.

For additional accommodation hutted barracks had been built inside Prince Henry's bastion. These too were reported upon: 'There are 24 huts for 22 men per hut who are mostly engineer recruits. Hut barracks have the advantage in a sanitary point of view of dividing the men into small numbers, an arrangement that allows their health to be better preserved than when they are congregated together hundreds under one roof.'

Not surprisingly, St Mary's casemates were condemned:

For many years after 1815 peace it was used as a powder magazine but it has steadily been appropriated for barracks use since 1844. There are 47 casemates. Long narrow low arches placed side by side with the lower level resembling the cellar dwellings of towns. It is meant to hold 1,128 men and had 1,410 at the time of the inspection. There were about 30 men per casemate as against the regulation 24. One casemate was in use as a school room with 58 pupils and the schoolmistress living in the end of the casemate. As a place for receiving on return home from foreign-service men whose health has been injured perhaps irreparably in the service of their country the casemates of St Mary's are entirely unsuitable. We have no hesitation is stating that they should not be used for such a purpose for a single day longer than may be necessary to provide other accommodation.[2]

The statistics in the report indicated that for 1857 the St Mary's casemated barracks achieved the staggering mortality rate of 103 deaths per 1,000 men. Allowing for the fact that the casemates were then occupied by invalids, many of whom may have originated from the Crimean War, this was still a grim statistic.

Invalids

Florence Nightingale in her work at the military hospital at Scutari and afterwards back in Britain kept the plight of soldiers in the public eye. The Crimean War – particularly the way it was reported in the press – brought the inadequacy of the British army to public attention and pricked the collective conscience about the conditions under which soldiers were expected to live and fight. Even before the Crimean War was over, a select committee was appointed to examine the state of the army, and a commission reported on the supply of the forces in the Crimea. In 1855 its report stated that mortality in the army at the Crimea was 35 per cent during the winter of 1854–5, which was attributed to over-work, exposure to inclement weather, poor food and low-quality clothing.[3] British losses in the war were 19,584. Of these, only 1 out of 10 had died in action. The rest were taken by disease.

Sidney Herbert died in 1861 before the full results of the barrack reforms that he had overseen were apparent, but he lived long enough to know that he had achieved an irreversible improvement in the lives of the British soldiers. His collaborator, Florence Nightingale, with her attention to statistical detail, published mortality figures for the British army serving at home in the United Kingdom in 1862.[4] For the period 1849–54 she calculated that general male mortality in England was running at 9.8 for every 1,000 individuals. In the period 1837–46 she placed the mortality within the infantry regiments serving at home in England as nearly twice this number, at 17.9 deaths for every 1,000 soldiers. For the three-year period of 1859–61, she was able to demonstrate that the mortality rate in home barracks was down to 8.56 men out of every 1,000. This was achieved by significant decreases in the prevalence of chest and tubercular illness and in zymotic (infectious) diseases. The main reason for this fall in mortality was the introduction of barracks rooms that were less crowded and better ventilated.

Before the reforms, the mortality amongst soldiers in home barracks was worse than amongst the comparable general male population, but it was those on overseas service who suffered most. In India in 1860 the highest annual mortality rate (at Bengal) was 55.58 per 1,000, but the heaviest toll on troops was in the West Indies where yellow fever was endemic. In the Windward and Leeward Islands the rate of hospital admission was 1,903 per 1,000 per annum and the mortality rate was 93.5 men per 1,000. This rose to 143 per 1,000 in Jamaica and 200 per 1,000 in the Bahamas.[5] Men who did not die, but were unfit for continued service, became eligible to be invalided home for possible discharge or retention as an invalid on limited garrison duties. Men who had served 21 or more years were

also invalided out. Between 1830 and 1863 there were two headquarters for invaliding, Chatham and Kilmainham in Dublin.[6] The average number of men invalided out between 1839 and 1856 was around 3,000 per annum, but when the injured from the Crimean War started to arrive at Chatham in 1855, 15,707 were processed in just over two years.[7]

Soldiers from regiments at home and abroad who were judged by their own medical officers to be unfit were transferred to Chatham via Gravesend. Those requiring immediate medical attention were sent to the military hospital in Fort Pitt,[8] and those who did not were sent to the invalid depot at St Mary's casemates, where the men and their families were held, pending resolution of their cases by the principal medical officer and the board of the Chelsea hospital. The discharge process could take a long time, and the men in the depot were prone to poor behaviour. Coming from many different places, they lacked the *esprit de corps* of a single regiment, and strict discipline could not be maintained amongst men who were in poor health and who knew their army days were numbered.

During the Crimean War Queen Victoria took a personal interest in the wounded, visiting them several times at Fort Pitt hospital, and on another visit Victoria and Albert inspected 396 convalescents who were housed in one side of the parade square at Brompton barracks. Some of the men had four clasps to their Crimean war medal, indicative of participation in four separate engagements. Each held a card stating their name, length of service, their wound and where it was received, and 44 of them were amputees.

One invalid demonstrates the way in which Chatham sent men around the world. Colour

Fig 11.1
Wounded men at Chatham from the Crimean War, visited by Queen Victoria. (The Royal Collection © 2012 Her Majesty Queen Elizabeth II)

Fig 11.2
Amputees from the Crimean War at Chatham. (Royal Engineers Museum, Library and Archives)

Fig 11.3
The Chatham convict prison
of 1856.
(Royal Engineers Museum,
Library and Archives)

Sergeant Timothy Murphy of the Rifle Brigade served in the Kaffir Wars of South Africa in 1846–53 and then in the Crimea. He had four clasps to his Crimean medal and received a silver medal for distinguished conduct in the field. As an invalid at St Mary's barracks, Queen Victoria appointed him for service at the Tower of London. After 1863 the processing of invalids was discontinued at Chatham and was transferred to the Royal Victoria Hospital at Netley in Hampshire.

Prisons

One large building that opened in 1856 was to have only a short existence. This was the convict prison built to house the civilian prisoners used as labour on the dockyard extension. The prison stood on land that had been used in the earliest siege training at Chatham and was in use for only four decades. In 1861 it was the scene of a serious mutiny by its inmates protesting about prison conditions. This was brought under control only by the introduction of armed troops from Chatham garrison, and it was they who administered the floggings ordered as punishment of the ringleaders.

Convicts were a common sight around the dockyard in particular, and before the construction of the prison they were housed on prison hulks (converted former men-of-war) moored in the river. These hulks were abandoned only when the prison opened, and they were then burned due to their unhealthy state.[9] Conditions on board were very poor. During the Napoleonic Wars the number of prisoners of war taken could not be housed in the prison camps established for the purpose, and as an expedience hulks were used. Charles Dupin, in the account of his visit to inspect the British military establishments soon after the end of the war in 1815, condemned the hulks that continued to incarcerate many of his countrymen.[10] Prison hulks were a common feature of the Medway until the mid-19th century. Long after the release of prisoners of war, ordinary criminals, including those awaiting transportation to Australia, were removed from society in this way. A convict garden in which they could grow some food was permitted in Ordnance Board land south of Upnor.

Hospital reform

The Army Medical Department report of 1860 revealed that the garrison hospital built behind the infantry barracks in 1809 (since demolished) could not meet the new regulations for the standard space to be allocated to each patient, but that in other respects it was satisfactory. In the summer months marquees were used to increase the size of the hospital wards. The hospital itself was then extended in order to meet the required standard. In 1862 an additional hospital for woman (since demolished) was completed immediately behind the garrison church. This was the result of the Chatham Garrison Compassionate Institute, which was a charitable society founded for the purposes of establishing a women's hospital but also for the relief of soldiers' wives when their men were sick and for giving assistance when they travelled to Chatham before joining their husbands on foreign service.

When in 1860 it was recommended that a military medical school be established as the main training location for the medical corps, it was obvious that Fort Pitt should have this role, though the school relocated to Netley in Hampshire in 1863. Thereafter the fort remained as the main garrison hospital, and in 1865 it was possible for the hospital at the infantry barracks to be closed and the building converted into additional barracks for fit soldiers.

Advances in guns and magazines

The second half of the 19th century was also a period of major technological change, with new designs of fortifications, more accurate and long-range rifled guns and new forms of explosives. These developments contributed to a series of invasion scares, and two linked technological developments more than anything else caused the British to be fearful. The introduction of the iron steam-powered warship and the invention of rifled artillery firing improved shells, later propelled by new explosives, made wooden warships and existing fortifications armed with smooth-bore cannons obsolete.

In short, the years around 1860 were a revolutionary period for the way in which future wars would be fought and for the design of new forms of weapons, including warships and fortifications. This period of rapid change must be seen in parallel with the steps taken to transform the living conditions of soldiers in barracks and hospitals. Technological change and army reform radically altered the army in the second half of the 19th century. As a result, Chatham saw a period of major change from which no part of the existing military sites was immune.

In 1815 at the end of the Napoleonic Wars the facilities at Upnor proved inadequate for the return of gunpowder from naval vessels that were laid up in ordinary at Chatham, and use of floating magazines had to be continued.[11] The mid-19th-century military revolution saw the start of major changes to artillery, both at sea and on land, in terms of the types of gun, the shells that these fired and the propellants that provided the explosive force. Innovation in all these areas led to changes that transformed the Upnor site, with expansion into new and much larger facilities.

Rifling, by which a continuous helical groove is cut on the inside of a gun barrel so that the projectile is spun as it leaves the gun, gave artillery greater accuracy and range over the smooth-bore cannons. Experiments with rifling had taken place in the 18th century, but it was the experiences of the Crimean War that prompted George William Armstrong and Joseph Whitworth, working independently, to develop rifled artillery. A major technological advance was breech loading that allowed the gun crew to reload in relative safety and operate more efficiently in confined spaces, such as on board ships. The challenge was to adequately seal the breech when the gun was fired.

In 1859 Armstrong started to supply rifled breech loaders (RBLs), but the breech mechanisms were complicated, and breech loading would not be perfected and widely adopted until the 1880s. Rifled muzzle loaders (RMLs) were therefore adopted. The old smooth-bore weapons did not require specialist ammunition – solid shot could be stored in the open, and gunpowder could be stored in barrels in magazines before being weighed into textile bags to make up cartridges, or loaded into shells and fused. Some old smooth-bore cannons were upgraded into RMLs using a system devised by Major Sir William Palliser in 1863, by which a wrought-iron sleeve with the rifling grooves cut into it was inserted inside the existing gun barrel. In 1865 experiments showed that new designs for RMLs were superior in terms of range, accuracy, ease of working, endurance and cost, and so this type of gun was preferred. RBLs and RMLs required lead-coated iron shells that would engage with the rifling grooves. The design of these shells and their handling did not change significantly until the late 19th-century introduction of new forms of high explosives.

By the mid-19th century, the creation of a large steam-assisted navy with guns firing shells and not traditional round shot produced something of a crisis for Upnor in terms of space to take shells and cartridges off ships. The despatch of fleets to the Baltic and Black Sea during the Crimean War made matters worse, particularly as the Baltic fleet returned to home ports during the winter. Upnor had to find storage for 16,500 shells of various types, but the only available though unsafe space was in the castle itself. When the Ordnance Board was abolished in 1855 and its responsibilities transferred to the War Department, the Royal Engineers remained responsible for advising about magazines and for their construction. In 1856 a new Committee of Magazines was established, and it recommended that 300,000 barrels of powder should be kept in stores nationwide and that capacity should be increased at a number of places, including on the Medway. This led to the creation of a new, large magazine and a purpose-built shell store at Upnor.

A shell store was a new form of building, and its design was debated. Since the explosive powder was safely contained within an iron shell, it was decided that a shell store need not be bombproof as was the case with a gunpowder magazine. A brick construction under a

Fig 11.4
The A and B magazines at
Upnor.
(Royal Engineers Museum,
Library and Archives)

Review of fortifications

No new fortifications had been constructed at Chatham in the period after 1815, and in fact it appears that the existing lines were quickly placed on a care-and-maintenance basis, with the guns demounted and returned to store in the Gunwharf. No significant improvements were made to the Chatham Lines, which remained the line of defence for the dockyard and other military establishments. Although the lines were employed for siege training, this activity was not allowed to compromise the ability to bring them back into use. According to the evidence of maps, the integrity of the lines was maintained beyond 1850, but no substantial attempt was made to keep the defences up to date. Not surprisingly, by the mid-19th century the bastions were antiquated compared with the current theory of fortification, which concentrated on a polygonal form of fortress.

A renewed French invasion threat in the mid-19th century caused attention to turn to the improved defence of Kent. Between 1848 and 1850 Shornemead Fort[14] was built on a polygonal basis to guard the River Thames near Gravesend, and in 1855 Grain Tower was built as a modified form of Martello tower to strengthen the defence of the mouth of the Medway at Sheerness. It was the fear of invasion by the French after the Crimean War and their adoption of steam-propelled warships with rifled ordnance that created pressure for building new defence works. It was thought possible that steam ships not reliant on fair winds and calm seas might evade the Royal Navy and succeed in landing sufficient troops to mount either an invasion focused on London or at least a serious raid on the naval dockyards.

In view of this threat of invasion by France, the British response was to review the land defences of its strategic assets, the dockyards. This was carried out by a Royal Commission on the National Defences, with Sir William Jervois as its secretary, and it reported in 1860. Although maintenance of the Channel fleet was given utmost priority, it was accepted that the Royal Navy had commitments to protect the entire empire. There was no guarantee of preventing a steam-powered force crossing the Channel from France. The report did not set out to prevent an invasion but rather to thwart it by the defence of London and the strategic dockyards and harbours. The Royal Commission report covered all the important naval

slate roof with a lesser amount of protective traverse was agreed, and by 1857 a new shell store (since demolished) was built between the shifting house and D'Arcy's 1812 magazine. A new magazine (B magazine) capable of holding 23,000 barrels was built adjacent to the D'Arcy magazine and closely followed the design of the earlier structure.[12] It was handed over in June 1857 and, despite its date, remains the best illustration in Medway of how an early 19th-century powder magazine was constructed.

The number of steam warships and the adoption of RBLs and RMLs created a major increase in the quantity of ordnance to be stored. By the 1860s Upnor was again stretched beyond capacity, with shells once more being stored in the castle. In 1862 a second shell store was added at the northern end of the new magazine for which additional land had to be purchased. An 1864 plan (Fig 11.5) shows the ordnance facilities, dominated by the two large magazines and served by a powder pier.

On 1 October 1864 a civilian magazine at Erith, London, accidentally exploded, killing 13 people instantly and doing great damage to neighbouring buildings.[13] In response to popular concern about the safety of magazines, a Magazine Committee was set up, which reported in 1865. It advised that Upnor should be abandoned in favour of new storage at a more remote part of the river. Upnor was judged too close to the dockyard (including the caisson that gave entry to the dockyard extension then under construction) and too close to the busy river and to private property. However, nothing was done for several years.

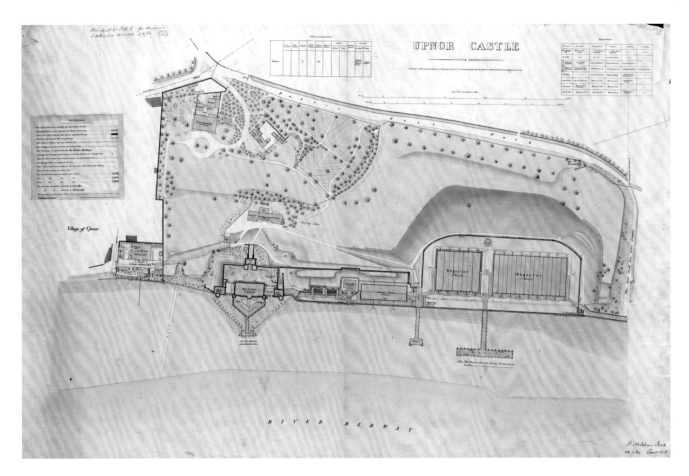

bases and anchorages – Portsmouth, Spithead, Plymouth, Pembroke, Dover, Chatham and the Medway, Woolwich and the Thames, and Cork in Ireland. The scale of the new fortifications recommended in the 1860 report was truly immense, the largest programme of fixed defences yet contemplated in the United Kingdom.

Because the new and vastly improved guns were able to fire light shells more than 8,000 yards, it was now possible to bombard Chatham dockyard over the top of its existing defences, which were no longer sufficiently strong to resist these new guns. The Royal Commission made recommendations for improved defences, which should be viewed alongside the defences for the River Medway, including Sheerness, and to some extent the Thames estuary as well. In many ways, elements of the thinking that had influenced the 17th-century defences by de Gomme after the Medway Raid of 1667 were now revived, with a new powerful fort at Sheerness and island forts in the River Medway downstream of Chatham.

While defence of the River Medway was a primary concern, the Royal Commission also

considered that a landward attack on Chatham remained credible. An invader moving on London after landing in the Deal area, for instance, would face a strong force at Chatham that could harass it. If an invasion took place in the east, such as at Harwich, the Chatham force could also move north over the Thames. This was a continuation of the concept of Chatham as a highly fortified centre of defensive forces that had been behind the rebuilding of the Chatham Lines from 1803. In the 1860 report Chatham was described as 'our greatest naval establishment in East England'.

To keep Chatham secure on its landward side, new fortifications were required, but continuous linear forms of fortification were outdated. The length of such lines at a distance from the dockyards to cope with the greater range of artillery would have been prohibitive in cost, both to build and then to man. The 1860 Royal Commission report described the inadequacy of the Chatham Lines and how they were in need of replacement:

The existing works afford some degree of protection against an attack from the eastward but their profile

Fig 11.5
An 1864 plan of Upnor Castle with the A magazine and the larger B magazine, as well as a shell store to their left.
(TNA WO 78/4488)

is for the most part so insignificant that they would be open to be carried by escalade with facility. The naval arsenal being hidden by the ground occupied by the lines a bombardment from that quarter is not much to be apprehended and the object to be kept in view in this part of the position is to strengthen it against capture. Defences are required in advance of Fort Pitt disposed to guard against bombardment and capture as there is a full view of the dockyard from several positions of the ground to southwards of the existing fortifications.

The concern was comparable to that which had prompted the post-1803 works at Chatham – that an attacker might seize the ground to the south and west of the dockyard and destroy the dockyard with relative impunity by long-range bombardment. The proposed solution at Chatham (which would not all be implemented) was to have a ring of detached but mutually supporting polygonal forts with interlocking fields of fire, estimated to cost £1.45 million. The eastern defences were planned to cover the approach from Gillingham in the north to Rochester in the south, and the western defences would link the Medway to the Thames at Shornemead by a line of forts. The eastern defences were planned to consist of 6 forts mounting 175 guns and with barracks for 1,750 men, while the western line would have 5 forts with 160 guns and accommodation for 1,800 men. The sea defences – forts either side of the Medway at Oakham Ness – were intended to have 50 guns and house 800 men.

Fig 11.6
HMS Achilles *nearing completion in No. 2 Dock – the first iron warship built in a naval dockyard. (Royal Engineers Museum, Library and Archives)*

Dockyard developments

In the Crimean War, both France and Britain built floating batteries in which the wooden hull was armoured by the addition of sheets of iron (an ironclad). After seeing how their own examples performed against Russia's Kinburn forts, the French were convinced that the wooden warship was obsolete, and they sought to challenge British naval superiority by building or converting their fleet as fast single-gundeck ironclads. The *Gloire,* launched in 1859, relied mostly on steam power, carried rifled breech-loading guns and had 4½ inches of iron armour applied to a wooden hull.

The news that France had taken the lead and that the *Gloire* was one of six proposed ironclads caused close to panic in Britain. The launch of the *Gloire* created a fear of French superiority in warship design, but it was also true that French dockyards were better equipped than the British ones. France had 76 building slips, whilst Britain had 44, of which only 9 could accommodate the largest first rates.[15] In a determination to retain superiority at sea, the British response was the *Warrior* (1860). Britain next drew on the expertise in iron ship construction that had been developed by the private sector for civilian ships and ordered the *Achilles*, the first large seagoing iron-hulled warship built in a royal dockyard. When all-iron warship construction commenced at Chatham in 1861 with the laying down of *Achilles,* the site chosen was not a covered slip but rather No. 2 Dock. To fit it for this task, the first iron shipbuilding shop in any dockyard was created (Fig 11.6). The adjacent No. 1 Dock had its timber roof removed and the dock was floored over so that iron-framed workshops could be erected close to where the *Achilles* was being constructed. A travelling crane was built to facilitate the movement of iron elements of the hull.

The *Achilles* (1863) became the first of this new type of ship to be built in the naval dockyard at Chatham and demonstrated that iron ship construction required new and purpose-built facilities. Chatham had no fitting-out basin in which to equip the ship for sea, and this work was done on the open river, at the risk of bad weather. The next major change at Chatham dockyard was therefore designed to address this gap in provision. Again, the private sector had shown the Admiralty the way, through the construction of large commercial

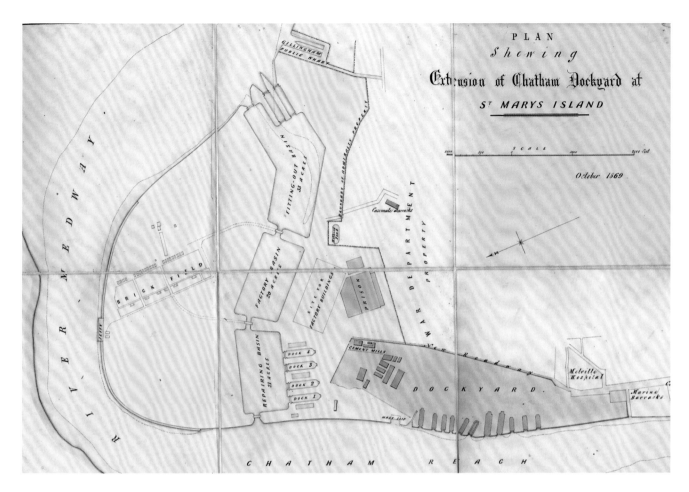

PLAN
Showing
Extension of Chatham Dockyard at
ST MARYS ISLAND

October 1869

Fig 11.7

Plan of the massive dockyard extension.

(Medway Archives)

docks, including basins, and this proven civil engineering could now be applied in a programme to equip the dockyards for steam warship manufacture.

At Chatham consideration had been given in the 1840s to construction of a boat basin at the northern end of the existing dockyard, but the proposal now put forward was on an entirely different scale, reminiscent of the ambition of Rennie's earlier scheme to use the river as a wet dock. The proposal was the work of William Scamp and Colonel Godfrey Greene RE and was based around total reclamation of St Mary's island from marshland by building a river wall around its perimeter, with convict labour, and using the line of St Mary's creek for a series of basins, with a steam factory and other dockyard structures. The scale of the dockyard extension was greater than the contemporary schemes at any of the other home dockyards. The essential components were worked out by Scamp around 1861.[16] There would be three linked basins. Ships built on new slips[17] would be taken post-launch into the repairing basin for work to be carried out on the hull when

afloat. From here they went to the factory basin for the installation of machinery and boilers and then to the fitting-out basin for the arming with guns and equipping for sea.

The Chatham Dockyard Act 1861 authorised the purchase of land at St Mary's island and its embankment for the new dockyard. It also required that a public wharf be provided at Gillingham in lieu of that lost to the basins. Land acquisition took time,[18] but by 1865 about half the embankment and 2,000 feet of river wall were complete. This major construction project led to the formation in 1866 of a massive brickfield to produce the huge number of bricks needed. Progress with the extension was slow, and key elements were moved from convict labour to private contractors. The Royal Engineers were involved throughout with the Admiralty Works Department in the supervision of the works, and a series of remarkable photographs illustrating the work is held in the Royal Engineers Museum and Library and at The National Archives.[19]

The repairing basin was the first to be finished, in May 1871. The factory basin and the fitting-out basin were not completed until 1883, with the connection to the river from the fitting-out basin at the Bull Nose as a final task. The four dry docks of the repairing basin were finished between 1871 and 1873 and the pump houses in 1874. Scamp's designs for new steam factory buildings alongside the central basin came to nothing. Instead, large slip covers that had been built at Woolwich were dismantled, and upon the disposal of that dockyard in 1872, they were re-erected at Chatham on the south side of the repairing basin.[20] The Chatham dockyard extension was not officially opened until 26 September 1885. It cost £1.75 million, covered an area of 500 acres and created combined wharfage totalling 10,000 feet.

The mid 19th-century decision to extend the dockyard at Chatham shifted the focus of dockyard activity to the north of the 17th- and 18th-century site, which undoubtedly contrib-uted to the survival of the older site as the most complete example of a dockyard from the age of sail. The extended dockyard was no longer adequately defended by the Chatham Lines, but a new and more massive approach to defence of the dockyard was being planned while the new basins were under construction. The extension did not remove any of the existing lines,[21] but it did mean the end for the 17th-century Gillingham fort. This was located on land between the fitting-out basin and the new public wharf. It is probable that buried remains of this fort and possibly of D'Arcy's gun tower still survive in what became the coaling yard for the extension and is now part of the commercial dock basin. The dockyard extension project explains why siege training on the Chatham Lines, such as a major exercise in 1877, had to relocate southwards and away from those parts of the fortifications used for the early practice sieges.

The School of Military Engineering

The year 1856 was key for the growing military school at Chatham. The Woolwich depot of the Royal Engineers was closed, and from this date the Royal Engineers headquarters was at Chatham, with the Brompton barracks increasingly given over to their needs.

Development of training

Critical review of the performance of the engineer troops in the Crimean War and the realisation that major reform was necessary in all branches of the British army probably lay behind the 1857 parliamentary commission that examined the training of officers destined for the scientific corps.[1] Its report was based on inspections of the main training establishments of the European powers, including those for engineers and artillery at Metz in France, Berlin in Prussia and Znaim in Austria. They also questioned senior serving Royal Engineer officers, including Field Marshal Sir John Burgoyne, as Inspector General of Fortifications, Colonel Sandham as the then Director at Chatham and Major Generals Sir Harry D Jones and Sir Frederick Smith as former Directors. Their report shows that the role of Chatham for Royal Engineer officer training had developed significantly since 1812. For the period 1825–35, the average number of officers completing training was only 6 per annum, but this had increased to 18 by 1845–55. On the eve of the Crimean War the school was looking to update both its facilities and what it taught in order to keep pace with scientific developments. In 1852 a cookhouse at Brompton barracks was converted as a chemical laboratory. In 1854 additional officers were appointed as instructors in fieldworks, and in 1856 training commenced in electric and magneto-electric telegraphy. That same year five NCOs were trained as instructors in photography by the London photographer, Mr Thurston Thompson.

The 1857 report recommended that the training period for Royal Engineers once they reached Chatham should be increased and that it should include more instruction in architecture and civil engineering, with visits to major civilian infrastructure projects then under way. It was realised that the focus on training for siege warfare needed to be significantly extended, with instruction in providing railways, roads, harbours and camps (including drainage).[2]

Review of training

In 1865, as part of wider consideration of army education, a further committee was appointed to report on the military school and see if any improvement was necessary. Recommendations included the introduction of sand modelling for learning fortifications, improvements to the pontoon establishment and the concentration of the workshops. Such facilities were created in what became known as the Royal Engineers Park on the site of the square Townshend's redoubt, which underwent demolition. The Royal Engineers Park functioned in close collaboration with the Field Work Practice Ground in the Lower Lines and the Field Work Depot.[3] The Royal Engineers Park was replaced in the 1960s with large workshops.[4]

It was also advised that recruits should learn about steam engines. Pasley's early interest in the use of the voltaic battery to set off underwater explosives had developed into a specific branch of training in submarine mines (torpedoes). In 1866 at Chatham there was both an electrical school teaching telegraphy and an experimental submarine mining school, based on a lighter in the river.

The year 1869 saw the Secretary of State for War order the renaming of the Royal Engineer Establishment as the School of Military

Fig 12.1
The instructors of the School of Military Engineering (c 1870) pose with the tools of their specialist subjects, including photography and telegraphy.
(Royal Engineers Museum, Library and Archives)

Engineering (SME), and its director was now known as commandant. The Royal Engineer Committee was responsible for military experiments and trials, and this was placed under the chairmanship of the commandant.[5] The SME continued the traditions established under Pasley, and by 1869 the Royal Engineers numbered 720 officers (384 for imperial service and 336 for Indian service) and 3,838 NCOs and men divided into 40 companies. There were also 474 men forming the mounted troops.

Officers, NCOs and privates (sappers) were all taught at the School of Military Engineering at the Brompton barracks. Officers passed through 6 compulsory courses lasting 21 months (exclusive of leave), after which they were examined by written paper and by a board formed by the field officers of the school. The subjects were drill and military duties (3½ months), survey course (6 months), fieldworks and military bridges (4 months), architectural course (6 months), chemistry (½ month), and telegraphy and submarine mining (1 month).

In addition to basic training, the men returned to Brompton for additional and specialist training. NCOs could volunteer for training in architecture, printing, survey, photography, telegraphy and chemistry, with each course resulting in the award of a Chatham Certificate as proof of proficiency, as Francis

Head RE described in his 1869 publication *The Royal Engineer*:

Sappers from all parts of the world voluntarily sentencing themselves to hard mental labour for from 4–9 months have converged on Brompton Barracks where by Engineer officers ranking from low to high in this corps and decorated for their services in the field, they have been cordially, patiently and efficiently instructed in the particular department of science self selected by each.[6]

By this means NCOs were trained for duties with the Ordnance Survey and for the Public Works Department in India.

Fieldwork training

The teaching of field fortifications remained a core subject at Chatham. In 1869 the senior fieldwork instructor was Colonel Wilbraham Lennox VC CB, who had won his Victoria Cross for service in the Crimea. He was assisted by two sergeant majors and six sergeant instructors. The men under instruction were formed into squads of 35–50 men and were supervised by officers who were also receiving instruction. The fieldwork course consisted of eight parts: modelling in sand, spar bridges, fieldworks of attack and defence, mining, floating bridges, railways, sundry practices and projects.

Only the works of most importance were constructed at full size in the practice ground. Many others were built at ¼ or ⅙ scale in the modelling shed using moist sand and an ample supply of model gabions, fascines, sap rollers, sandbags and gun platforms. There were also model railways and houses to form villages that could be put into a state of defence. In addition, a collection of permanent models was in use as teaching aids, and in 1869 they were kept in the model room in what is now the large lecture theatre in the barrack block on the north side of the Brompton parade square. The models included examples of every system of fortification and of civil and military projects, such as bridges. There were specimens of every type of tool used by the different trades within the Corps and of the mining and entrenching equipment. Model steam engines were displayed alongside models of types of fortification, such as the Martello tower, and there were models of specific fortresses such as one for the siege of Gibraltar, which is now on display in the Royal Engineers Museum. The centre of the model room was taken up by a low table, measuring 20ft by 15ft, which represented a bird's eye view of 'agricultural country with its houses, villages, hills, dales, high roads, by roads, hollow roads, streams etc in the centre of which appear embossed in all their details the parallels, batteries and approaches to a fortified town.'[7]

Full-scale fieldworks were constructed on the Lower Lines using material supplied from the Field Work Depot. Head commented in 1869 how encroachment by the growing town of New Brompton (Gillingham) and the increased power and range of rifled artillery had rendered the Chatham Lines inadequate and inoperable, but that these were nevertheless used for training. To avoid unnecessary labour and expense and due to lack of space, the fieldworks were constructed closer together than they would have been in a genuine situation. The practice ground included a narrow gauge railway that ran across the ditch to the Lower Lines and over Prince Arthur Road on a bridge, so that Black Lion Field could be used for training.

Fig 12.2
The constructors of this spar bridge pose with a field gun in the bridging ground near Brompton barracks. The Chatham convict prison is in the background.
(Royal Engineers Museum, Library and Archives)

Experience at the port of Balaclava in the Crimean War had demonstrated that despite the building of a railway to the front, the movement of ordnance by pack mule and manhandling for the final part of its journey was still onerous.[8] Because of the experience in that war, trench railways were also now practised at Chatham, so that guns and ammunition could be moved by trolley along the instruction trenches. Head describes how he saw 25 sappers and 25 fatigue men lay 400 yards of line at Brompton in 25 minutes. The construction and demolition of conventional railways were also practised.

Fieldwork training saw the lines of parallels, approaches, magazines and batteries traced out on the ground and then constructed using gabions, sandbags and timber. The trainees were also taught the complex tactics of attack and defence by mine and countermine, and they learned how to ventilate the mine galleries. When complete the fieldworks were used for the annual siege exercises. Other examples were subjected to demolition to observe their durability under attack.

All men were taught to swim and some to dive. The sinking of wells for fresh water was an essential skill and included the use of American Tubes as a means of raising water in the field by hand pump. Sundry practice included the construction of field kitchens, grenade throwing, escalade drill, the use of grapnels and the technique of the flying bridge to cross moats. In short, the engineers were taught not just how to assault a fortification but also how to support, transport and house the army in the field.

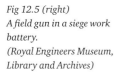

Architectural training

All Royal Engineer officers and many of the men were expected to be skilled in architecture and every aspect of building and construction. A significant part of the initial training of an officer was devoted to this task, which included railway construction, water supplies and sewerage systems. The theory of construction and materials was taught, and the use of models and drawings enabled the trainees to measure up projects, provide estimates, write specifications and prepare construction drawings of details. Each officer made a design of a selected number of works. They went on what Head described as 'short tours' to visit the extension project for the dockyard and the local cement and brick works. In addition, 14 officer recruits were sent on 40-day 'long tours' in order to visit and report on major engineering projects then under way in Great Britain, such as bridges and railways, and on the engineering required in the coal and iron industries. The NCOs received a similar but less intensive training in architecture and construction so as to fit them for service as junior clerks of work on major public projects.

Photographic training

Schooling in architecture crossed over to other areas of study. Chemistry was taught principally as materials science so that officers and NCOs would be able to analyse limes, cements, mortars, paints, metals and the principal building stones. The photographic school served several functions. Sketching had long been taught as part of field reconnaissance, and in 1868 photography was for the first time employed by the British army in the field during the Abyssinian expedition. At home photographs were used to record the state of fortifications and as an easy means of demonstrating the progress of major

Fig 12.7
Grenade practice at the Lower Lines with the narrow-gauge military railway on the skyline. (The Graphic 17 November 1877)

Fig 12.8
Instruction in techniques of diving on the River Medway. (Royal Engineers Museum, Library and Archives)

construction projects to the Heads of Department in London. Sapper photographers visited Chatham dockyard and Dover to record the major works then under way, which created a fine collection of photograph albums that are now in the Royal Engineers Museum and Library.[9] Photography was also a method of recording the destruction of fieldworks in practice sieges.

Photolithography was a means of producing multiple versions of a printed image such as a drawing, and it was taught alongside traditional printing skills, so that today the term 'lithographed at the SME' is common on many historic documents. The impact of such rapid printing and dissemination of information should not be forgotten as part of the modernisation of the army and warfare. This was arguably more significant than the development of more powerful guns and explosives.

Electrical training

The interest shown by Pasley in electricity continued in significant parts of the SME. Telegraphy was first used in the field in the Crimean War, and it now became a major part of the work of the electrical school. Officers and volunteer NCOs were taught the principles of electricity and its application to telegraphy. Trainees sat back-to-back on long tables and benches so as to send messages to each other, before graduating to sending them between separate rooms. To take telegraphy into the field required specialised horse-drawn wagons capable of distributing 4 miles of cable from drums and of carrying metal telegraph poles.

Electric lights were also experimented with as a form of signalling. Major Bolton and Captain Colomb had developed the 'Chatham Light' by which magnesium was blown by bellows into the flame of a spirit lamp in order to produce a bright flash, but it was the lime light created by burning oxygen and hydrogen as perfected by Thomas Drummond RE *c* 1820 that proved more successful, and this included flashing a message between Dover and Calais. By 1862 lights were being experimented with at the Spur battery of Fort Amherst for passing a message by relay of parties of engineers as far as Gravesend.[10] Electric lights were also experimented with as part of the attack and defence of a fortress for revealing or blinding the enemy.[11] These experiments gave rise to the Defence Electric Light, the name by which early searchlights were known. These carbon arc lights were powered by electricity generated from dynamos and were adapted for use in fixed emplacements and also as portable equipment for field use. It was experiments at Chatham that perfected the design and operation of searchlights, particularly in association with coastal defence and submarine mining.[12]

Submarine mining

Based on experience in the American Civil War and with the encouragement of Field Marshall Sir John Burgoyne in 1863, submarine mining was first adopted and became a major part of the responsibilities of the Royal Engineers as an essential way by which harbours and major rivers could be defended. The first submarine mining company was formed in 1871, and the same year saw an assistant instructor appointed at Chatham. By 1869 Francis Head was in a position to describe instruction in submarine mines or torpedoes using a lighter moored in the river. From 1873 to 1883 the submarine miners at Chatham were based on the former battleship HMS *Hood* on the River Medway. In 1883 the men transferred to the St Mary's casemates, with new submarine mining school buildings at Gillingham public wharf.

The Royal Navy had responsibility for the laying of minefields and for the ships needed for this work, but the Royal Engineers were taught to fire the mines and to control the searchlights (DELs) needed for night-time operation and to assist in the laying of coastal guns. Many of the submarine miners were volunteer companies, and by 1905 when their duties transferred to the navy, there were approaching 6,000 regulars and volunteers to defend British interests. One of the weapons used for harbour defence was the Brennan torpedo (1887). This was the world's first wire-guided torpedo that could be launched down rails from shore stations and then steered on to its target by use of shore-based winches to draw out wires carried on drums in the torpedo. The factory for the manufacture of these torpedoes (since demolished) was at Chatham, on land now occupied by the naval barracks.[13]

Steam engines and balloons

Steam engines were adopted by the Royal Engineers from at least as early as 1868. These provided power to drive electric dynamos and

Fig 12.9
A steam sapper or traction
engine as used in the 1877
siege exercise.
(Royal Engineers Museum,
Library and Archives)

other demands for motive force. Ones known as steam sappers supplied by the Rochester-based company of Aveling and Porter were used to drive machinery and for pulling heavy loads, including cannon (Fig 12.9). These were first employed in Africa during the Second Ashanti War of 1873–4. They also featured in the major 1877 siege exercise and were used in restoring the ground afterwards, so that it could be reused for training.

Without steam engines to draw the field equipment, the development of military ballooning by the Royal Engineers would have been retarded. The American Civil War saw the first extensive use of balloons for military purposes, something that was observed by Captain Frederick Beaumont RE. On his return to England he made experimental ascents in 1863 at Aldershot and Woolwich. One of the greatest challenges to be overcome was the means to safely generate and then transport the highly explosive gas hydrogen then in use. A full balloon school was established at Chatham in 1888 at the St Mary's casemates after experiences in the Sudan and Bechuanaland campaigns (1884–5) had demonstrated their value for reconnaissance, particularly using photography. The facilities included the hydrogen generating plant, a gasometer, the means to fill the portable gas cylinders and the workshops to manufacture and repair the balloon envelopes.[14] The balloons were kept safely inflated in large pits, and the ascents at Chatham were made from such a facility at Lidsing farm. By 1892 the balloon factory and school had transferred to Aldershot, but the role of Chatham in getting the Royal Engineers airborne for the first time should be remembered.[15]

Pontoon building

The final area of Royal Engineer training described by Francis Head in 1869 was the pontoon. The use for training purposes of the River Medway and St Mary's creek close to Brompton barracks was significantly curtailed by the extension of Chatham dockyard in the 1870s. Instead, convict labour helped to create a replacement pontoon facility at Upnor, on the opposite shore of the river to the dockyard, at the site known as Gundulph Pool. In addition, Wouldham (upstream of Rochester on the Medway) was established as the practice ground for pontoon bridge building in field conditions and the encampment of the pontoon train, where Head watched 60 sappers form 100 yards of pontoon bridge in just 40 minutes.

Siege training

By the late 1860s, the School of Military Engineering had significantly moved away from Pasley's initial concept of siege training. It had become a centre for military science and one of

Fig 12.10 (top)
The pontoon train of the Royal Engineers, carrying the substantial floats (known as Blanshard pontoons) for pontoon bridges and rafts.
(Royal Engineers Museum, Library and Archives)

Fig 12.11 (bottom)
The pontoon train of the Royal Engineers.
(Royal Engineers Museum, Library and Archives)

the foremost schools for the armed forces in any part of the world. It is not surprising that royalty, heads of state and senior army officers from across Europe and America were regular visitors to the establishment, and Prince Arthur, son of Queen Victoria, trained there as a Royal Engineer in 1868. The new technology in the second half of the 19th century, after the Crimean War, was reflected in the improved type of siege training undertaken at Chatham. The exercises became more complex, no doubt in response to the actual experiences of conflict, and in 1864 the *Illustrated London News* described a major exercise that began with landings from gunboats in St Mary's creek and made use of three sets of parallels to assault the redan and left demi-bastion of the Lower Lines,

all under the observation of VIPs on the officers' casemates:

The earthworks constructed during the past three months by the Royal Engineers, as part of their ordinary instruction, formed several wide-spreading angular lines of attack and defence, which were clearly visible at every point, with the troops lying close in wait behind them. Out on the Medway, beside the white hulls of the Naval Reserve ships, lay several men-of-war. Conspicuous among them was the dark hull and four lofty masts of the Achilles, round which was a fleet of little boats, armed with guns and filled with troops, waiting for the signal to make their dash at the creek and turn the works by landing in their rear. The besieged garrison were all men of the Marine Artillery and Volunteer Artillery, the besiegers Marines and Royal Engineers, so that

Laboratory

Buildings that had been provided at Brompton barracks for the artillery in 1804 were not always suitable for the increasingly technical skills taught at the SME. The Royal Engineers took over the north gun shed of the Brompton barracks as a laboratory, and here sappers under the supervision of a sergeant instructor worked on the manufacture of grenades and fuses. *The Times* for January 1861 recorded one disaster:

Everything connected with the work proceeded satisfactorily this morning until shortly before 12 o'clock, when the frightful explosion took place. Just before the accident occurred Adams noticed one of the Engineers, named Smith, performing his work in a rather careless manner, and reprimanded him for it. The same man afterwards, finding a difficulty in ramming the composition into his fuse, asked the man next him to assist him, which he did, the two giving blow and blow. Suddenly the composition of the grenade which Smith held became ignited, Smith, who appeared paralyzed with fear, continuing to retain his hold of it. The fire from the grenade then communicated with the loose composition lying about, which immediately ignited a large quantity of powder in a barrel, then the whole building blew up with a terrific explosion, resembling the discharge of artillery, and creating the utmost dismay throughout the entire establishment.[16]

Amazingly no sappers were killed in this explosion, but seven were severely burned, and the building was badly damaged. *The Times* reported how the Royal Engineers now reviewed the use of these buildings:

The north gun-shed, it ought to be stated, is a building by no means suited for the description of the work carried on within it, and, as its name implies, was never intended to be used as a laboratory for the manufacture of dangerous missiles. The only protection afforded the inmates on one

Fig 12.12
The 1861 explosion in the north gun shed.
(Illus London News *2 February 1861*)

side of the shed is a row of palings carried up to the roof, communicating with the outside, to which the public have access, and where the operations of the persons employed can be witnessed by any persons from the exterior ... Colonel Harness, C.B., after paying a visit to the factory and inspecting the damage caused by the accident, gave positive orders that no portion of the north gun-shed was ever again to be used as a laboratory, and at the same time directed that the works should be suspended until a suitable building, in which the dangerous occupations could be carried on, was provided. Two large ranges of buildings are now in course of erection at the Engineer establishment for the requirements of the officers and men, and it is probable that a portion of one of these will be ultimately used for the purpose.[17]

A court of inquiry into the explosion found the careless work of Sapper Smith to be the root cause, but was very critical of the irresponsible way in which explosive material was allowed to accumulate. It ordered that in future all work to prepare explosives should take place in the Field Work Depot, not the barracks. A catastrophe was averted, but it was clear that the military school needed new buildings if it was to be fit for purpose.

the difference between the red uniforms of the latter and the blue undress of the former marked the lines of attack and defence ... from behind earth mounds, from rifle-pits, from parapets and breastworks, from dyke and fosse, the cracking musketry kept up an incessant fire, which was answered by the assailants. After some time, a subterranean rumble was heard indicating that a mine had been sprung. A slight trembling of the ground was felt by the spectators, who crowded the roofs of the casemates ...

In the mean time, the besiegers were not idle; and the general assault was at hand. The besiegers had altogether eleven heavy guns, eight mortars, and four howitzers, and all these were going at once, when suddenly there was a lull, and on the left and centre the assaulting columns were seen hurrying across the open with scaling-ladders. In a few minutes these were planted; and the heads of the foremost men were seen above the parapet while the defenders were keeping up a heavy fire upon them.

Royal Engineers Institute

The School of Military Engineering had grown from its 1812 origins into a major military school training all Royal Engineers. To meet the tasks required of it, the infrastructure provided by the Brompton barracks as first constructed for the artillery had to be substantially adapted and improved. The parliamentary commission into military education recognised that rooms in the early 19th-century barrack blocks at Brompton were 'very unfit to be the chief place of instruction for the headquarters of a scientific corps'.[18] It recommended that the school required new and purpose-built buildings to match the Royal Artillery Institution at Woolwich. The new buildings required for the SME were concentrated east of the barracks complex on land behind Prince Henry's bastion that had previously held hutted barracks.

The most impressive new building was the 1873 Royal Engineers Institute (now the RSME headquarters), which was intended to house a museum, library, teaching facilities and offices and was also used as a test bed for experimentation in construction techniques and mortars. The formation of what was then known as the Royal Engineers Institute also lay behind its construction. This organisation had emerged from the publication of the *Professional Papers of the Corps of the Royal Engineers* dating from 1837 as the means by which the work of the Corps was communicated around the world.[19] It was a body devoted to the general advancement of military science and its promotion through publication and education. In 1923 a royal charter was granted, and the name of the organisation was changed to the Institution of Royal Engineers, the title by which it continues to be known to the present day.

The Royal Engineers Institute was built in 1873 to a design by Lieutenant Montagu Ommaney, using an Italianate style that incorporates rich decoration, including terracotta panels. The theme of terracotta decoration was continued in the new and substantial house built for the commandant of the SME, to the south of the Institute, known today as Pasley House. This building was authorised in 1873 and completed in 1876. The terracotta was supplied by the Midland Brick and Terracotta Co of Leicester.[20] Between 1876 and 1878 a pair of substantial semi-detached houses was built north of the new Institute for the senior instructional officers, and in 1891 two more houses were added alongside.

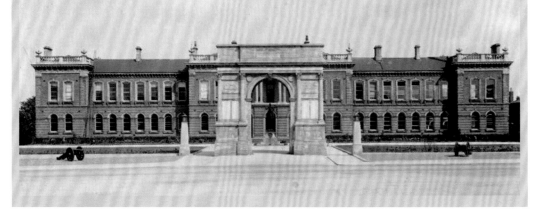

Fig 12.13
The Royal Engineers Institute built in 1873. (Royal Engineers Museum, Library and Archives)

At the same time another detachment of the attacking party was entering by the breach ... The number of those who had reached the ditch rapidly increased, and assailants and defenders kept up a rapid fire upon each other.[21]

The ditches of the lines posed a serious obstacle to an assault, but one to which the engineers had a solution by means of a flying bridge (Figs 12.15 and 12.16):

this obstacle was soon overcome by an ingeniously extemporised bridge. Covered by the fire of their comrades, a group of sappers crept round the edge of the ditch with guy-ropes, and then, once across, those left on the other side affixed the ropes to a single-legged trestle, which was hauled into the centre of the fosse and then steadied by the guy-ropes; and, with this for their centre pin, the sappers, with marvelous rapidity, proceeded to construct a bridge in almost less time than we have taken to describe it.

Fig 12.14
The officers' casemates used as the grandstand for siege exercises in 1864.
(Illus London News 18 June 1864)

The instant it was finished hundreds of men dashed across it, and even cannon was afterwards brought over it.[22]

The flying bridge was just one form of bridge practised by the Royal Engineers, and their fieldwork practice ground was also a bridging ground. The flying bridge was not without danger. In an 1868 exercise the bridge collapsed, and as the men had bayonets fixed, their fall into the ditch resulted in many injuries and the death of one man.

In 1875 a new ravelin was added to the Chatham Lines between Prince Henry's bastion and Prince Frederick's bastion. This was only ever for training purposes. The fieldwork practice ground also now contained a light railway that enabled materials for the siege works to be moved more easily.[23] It extended from within the engineers park of Brompton barracks over the ditch of the lines and across the public road to Black Lion Field. This area was also being used for siege exercises, because the decision to extend Chatham dockyard by the reclamation of St Mary's island made the use of the northern end of the lines impossible. In an 1877 exercise this was the location for the first parallel (Fig 12.17). In this exercise four parallels with associated batteries were built, but due to the limited space available, they were closer together than in a real siege.

Photographs of these late 19th-century siege exercises illustrate their large scale, with major and complex trench systems and massive

Fig 12.15
Preparing to launch a flying bridge across the ditch of the Lower Lines.
(Royal Engineers Museum, Library and Archives)

Fig 12.16
The completed flying bridge over the ditch of the Lower Lines.
(Royal Engineers Museum, Library and Archives)

Fig 12.17
Earthworks of a gun battery constructed for a major siege exercise on Black Lion Field.
(Royal Engineers Museum, Library and Archives)

damage by the use of explosives to the fabric of the Chatham Lines. The 1877 siege exercise was perhaps the largest yet undertaken, and it was reported by *The Graphic*. An account illustrated with photographs also survives.[24] A siege was practised for real, and the aim of the Royal Engineers was to create what they called a 'practicable breach'. This was achieved by destroying a section of rampart and ditch by mining and bombardment to form a ramp of debris up which the attackers could run.

Using mines to breach the fortifications required that countermine measures also be adopted by the defenders, and it is likely that an underground brick-vaulted chamber formed out of yellow bricks on the site of the new Mid Kent College was part of training in countermines at this time (*see* Figs 7.3 and 7.4). That the Lower Lines walls are today intact despite this massive disruption is due to their subse-

quent repair by Royal Engineers as part of their instruction in fortress construction. The areas of repair are today noticeable by the use of yellow brick rather than the red brick of the older lines and by the use of concrete as a backing.

The photographs of siege training at Chatham also show the use of hundreds of gabions for improvised fieldworks. Wood was cut from the Ordnance plantation at Upnor and made into gabions and fascines at the Field Work Depot at Chatham (Figs 12.20 and 12.21). The brushwood gabion was as ancient as siege warfare itself, but in the Crimean War a shortage of wood led to the iron band gabion, copying the metal straps used to bind bundles of forage for army horses. The Royal Engineers perfected this new form of gabion, and they were superior to the brushwood examples, being stronger, more regular and capable of being reused and more easily transported in their disassembled state. An experiment at Chatham showed that a sapper could assemble more of the iron band gabions in the same time taken to make a brushwood example.

War Office review 1885–6

In 1885 another War Office committee, under Lord Sandhurst, reviewed the duties, organisation and establishment of the Royal Engineers. Its 1886 report summarised the duties as:

To take the field with the army for bridging rivers; demolishing and restoring roads and bridges; rendering positions defensible; siege operations; and water supply.

- Work in fortresses to construct and maintain fortifications
- Administration of expenditure on War Department land and buildings
- Defence of ports including by submarine mines and searchlights
- Telegraphic communication
- Construction and operation of railways
- Use of balloons for observation and reconnoitring
- Survey.

To do this, the regular establishment of the Royal Engineers was set at 578 officers and 7,218 other ranks, and all the skills were to be taught at Chatham, with an increase in the numbers of NCO instructors.[25]

Fig 12.20
Making brushwood gabions
for use in siege training.
(Royal Engineers Museum,
Library and Archives)

Fig 12.21
Making fascines for use in
siege training, with gabions
stacked behind.
(Royal Engineers Museum,
Library and Archives)

Reforming Soldiers' Lives

The 1861 Royal Commission had found no garrison town with a greater deficiency of space available in its barracks for the soldiers than at Chatham, and reform of this bad situation began before the final report. Overall, the opinion of the inspection committee on barracks, including those at Chatham, was damning. It recommended a series of essential improvements: Reduce the numbers in each barrack room to give each man 600 cubic feet of space; ventilate every room; lime wash the walls; board over asphalt floors; abolish cesspools and improve drainage; provide an additional water supply; reconstruct latrines with efficient flushing and a division of seats; reconstruct urinals with a water supply; remove foul bedding and hair stores [for mattresses] from under the barrack rooms; improve the ablution rooms for men, women and children; provide baths with hot water; provide urinals in place of urine tubs for the barrack rooms; provide drying rooms; provide day rooms; provide covered drill sheds; reconstruct laundries with proper provision for washing and drying clothes and bedding; and construct married quarters.

Each of these recommendations was acted upon in the subsequent years, and the barracks at Chatham would now see the largest programme of works since their initial construction. Two measures in particular transformed conditions – a reduction in the number of men per barrack room and the provision of purpose-built married quarters.

Infantry barracks improvements

At the infantry barracks, the greatest problems identified were overcrowding, poor ventilation and the lack of married quarters. An 1864 plan of the barracks (Fig 13.1) shows the scale of the changes that were introduced to solve these and other problems, particularly when compared with that of 1795 (see Fig 4.9). Information on the 1864 plan shows that the number of soldiers was substantially reduced from that recorded in the 1851 Board of Ordnance return. The barracks in 1864 contained 2 regiments, amounting to 2 commanding officers, 4 field officers and 75 officers (32 horses), 20 staff sergeants, 1,549 NCOs and privates and 72 married soldiers.

The reduction in the total number of men in the barracks was one improvement, but another was to increase the number of barrack rooms. This was achieved not by rebuilding the original soldiers' houses dating from 1757, but by adding an entire new storey to those closest to the parade ground. These changes are visible in late 19th-century photographs and included a large thermal window and chimneys on each gable of the revised barrack blocks.[1] The officers' blocks (all now demolished) were also provided with an additional top floor, but the blocks north and south of the parade ground, whilst extended, retained the mid-18th-century form of roof. Within the barrack rooms lack of air was addressed by the construction of new ventilation shafts and the adoption of the Galton Grate, an open fireplace designed to provide both heat and ventilation, named after Douglas Galton, a Royal Engineer and barracks reformer.[2]

The challenge to remove soldiers, wives and children from the infantry barracks to purpose-built married quarters could not be met by a simple reorganisation of the existing space. Use of the available casemates and guardhouses continued, and in the cave yard of Fort Amherst, two three-storey ranges of married quarters were built (since demolished), known as the 'birdcage barracks' because of the appearance created by their continuous iron verandahs (Fig 13.3). Each family was allocated a single room, and so every block held 36 families, making a total of 72 married men.

Fig 13.1 (opposite)
Chatham infantry barracks in 1864 after the reforms. (TNA MPHH 1/356)

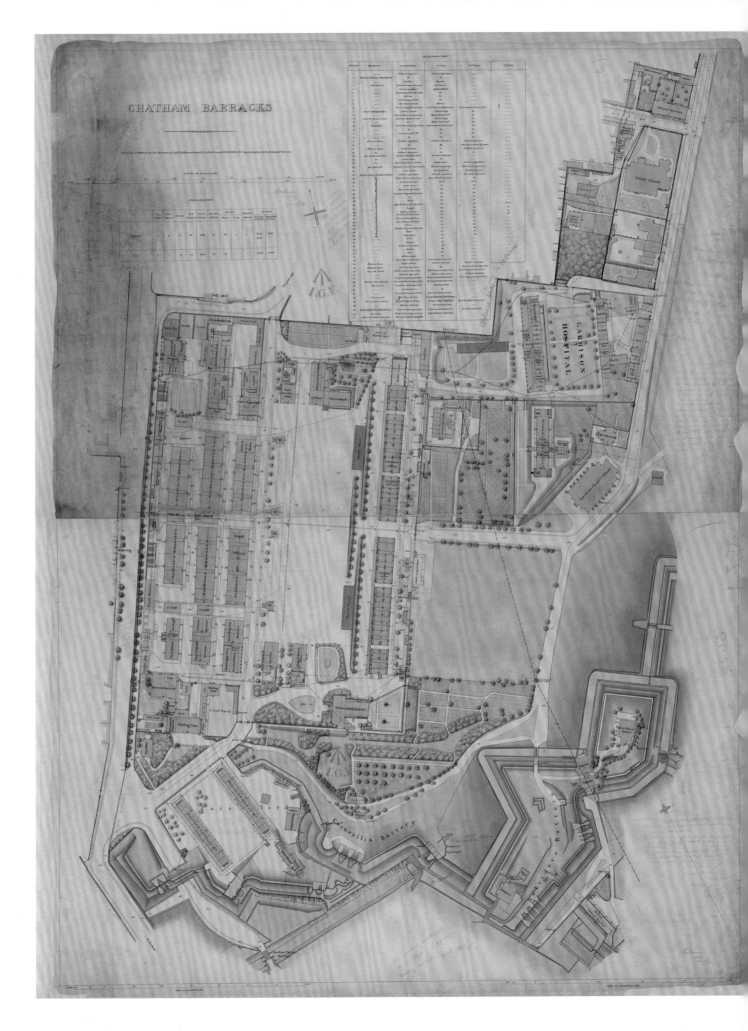

Fig 13.2
Barrack blocks at Chatham
with an added top storey.
(© English Heritage
AL0041-20-1)

The 1871 census information for the infantry barracks shows that 16 per cent of the soldiers were by that date married (compared with only 9 per cent in 1841). The staff sergeants as senior NCOs were allocated improved quarters, and the 1871 census has one such man who was living in barracks with his mother, brother, sister and a female servant. An infant school was also provided within barracks. Recognition of army families was thus much improved.

The officers continued to enjoy good-quality accommodation. The 1864 plan (Fig 13.1) shows that as there were two commanding officers, a second large residence (since demolished) was built within the Amherst redoubt in addition to the existing commanding officer's house. The latter had large landscaped gardens. The barracks master continued to live in his own residence in the south-west corner of the barracks. A new officers' mess was created by extending one of the mid-18th-century

Fig 13.3
The married quarters or
'birdcage barracks' at Fort
Amherst.
(Medway Archives)

blocks on the north side of the parade ground, and this had its own wine cellar.

A product of the 1861 recommendations was the need for improved and separate lavatories, cook houses and wash houses. These were shoehorned into the already tight site by building against the perimeter wall and in the alleys between the rows of barrack blocks. Other new buildings included a set of garrison cells and covered drill sheds for use in bad weather.

Brompton barracks improvements

The barracks at Brompton were nearly 50 years later in date than the infantry barracks, which meant that they were of better quality. The majority of the enlisted men continued to live in the north and south blocks, with the officers in the west block. Even before the inspection by the barracks committee, the Brompton site was ahead of others in the provision of purpose-built married quarters. By 1857 the first purpose-built married quarters for the Royal Engineers were built behind North Square and the former stables for the artillery. The stables had themselves been substantially rebuilt with an additional storey to provide more accommodation. South Square was also originally built as stabling, but was now converted into a canteen and quartermaster stores. North of the

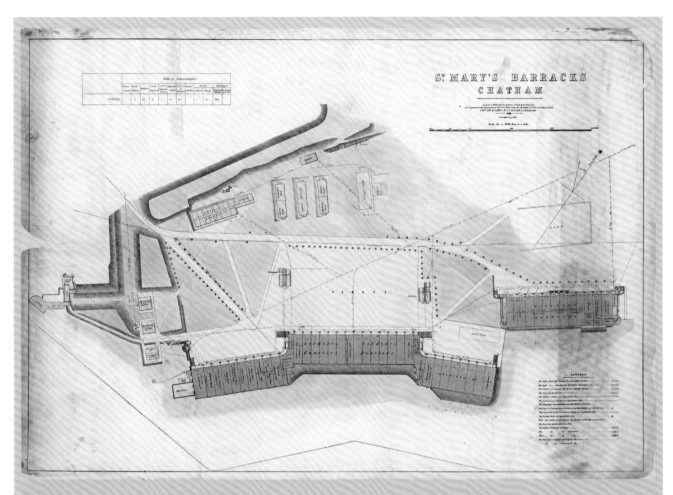

St Mary's casemated barracks improvements

By 1864 a plan of the St Mary's casemated barracks (Fig 13.4) also shows a much improved situation. One separate block of casemates housed 2 field officers and 23 other officers, while the main casemates block held 9 staff sergeants, 42 married soldiers and 816 other ranks. As at the main infantry barracks, a covered drill shed was supplied, along with a ball court, skittles alley and significantly improved latrines with a limited number reserved for women. Other additions to the barracks included new detached quarters for officers, pay

sergeants and the schoolmaster. There was an adult schoolroom for teaching the soldiers numeracy and literacy and an infants schoolroom for their children.

Fig 13.4
St Mary's casemated barracks in 1864.
(TNA WO 78/2748)

Fig 13.5
St Mary's casemated barracks (since demolished) in the late 19th century.
(Royal Engineers Museum, Library and Archives)

Royal Engineers Park, and in response to the barracks reform agenda to remove married men and their families from barrack rooms, there were from 1868 three further blocks of married mens quarters capable of holding 42 families.[3] The children of the men were catered

for by a new infant school and quarters for the schoolmistress.

In the main accommodation blocks of the barracks at Brompton, occupied by the Royal Engineers, various other improvements were carried out as part of the reform agenda. The

most significant were the adoption of ventilation shafts and inlets and the substitution of boarded floors for asphalt. Improved cooking facilities were provided, and the water supply was greatly improved by the construction of a water tower. A joint Royal Engineer and Royal Artillery mess at the infantry barracks moved to Brompton barracks in 1807 to found the mess that continues to exist today. It became a mess for Royal Engineers only in 1848. In 1861 the present dining room was carried out to a design by Captain Francis Fowke. The entrance hall was added in 1883–4, and the mess further extended by the addition of the north annexe in 1887–8.

Other major changes took place at these barracks to make them more suitable for their increasing role as the School of Military Engineering, including specific instructional buildings. The middle of the north block had been used as a chapel, but from 1854 this need was met by the new garrison church, and so this part of the barracks was used instead as the model room for instructional purposes. It was subsequently (1912–13) converted to hold the Royal Engineers Museum when this was taken out of the Institute building.[4] Nine stained glass windows were installed at this date to commemorate illustrious Royal Engineer officers.

Food supply

The 1861 recommendations for improvements to barracks included better provision for the cooking of food. The traditional method of cooking was in large boilers. For meat to be roasted it had to be sent out to the bakers' ovens in Chatham. This issue was addressed with new cookhouses and by installing the best cooking ranges then available. The quality of the rations was also attended to. It had become acceptable for contractors to supply poor-quality provisions to the army rather than the quality stipulated by contract. One report in 1862 revealed how meat supplied for the Chatham garrison was found to be unfit for consumption. An inspection regime was instituted to prevent this abuse:

the Assistant Commissary General of the garrison, accompanied by an officer specially selected for that duty, and one of the Sergeants connected with the barrack department, will attend the slaughter-houses of the contractor each morning, and after inspecting the animals selected to be killed, in order to ascertain from personal inspection that they are in all respects fit for food, will witness their being killed, and as soon as they are dressed will place his seal on the carcass of each. On the arrival of the meat at the several barracks for distribution to the troops, the seals will be examined in order to ascertain that they have not been tampered with, after which it will be cut up for the troops. By these precautions, none but really good meat will in future be allowed to be sent to the barracks for the use of the soldiers.[5]

A more satisfactory solution was for the army commissariat to slaughter and butcher its own meat, and a commissariat depot (since demolished) was constructed at Southhill Road near Chatham railway station for this purpose.[6] It also contained a bakehouse so that the twin staples of the military diet, bread and meat, could be supplied.

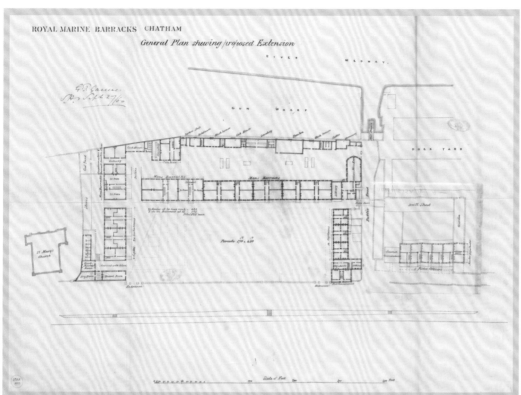

Fig 13.7
Plan of the extension of the
Royal Marines barracks.
Compare this plan with that
of the barracks when first
constructed in 1779
(see Fig 4.9).
(TNA MFQ 1/58)

Royal Marines barracks

In 1857 by Act of Parliament additional land was compulsorily acquired with which to extend the Royal Marines barracks, and in 1862 work began on improving and enlarging the barracks. The southern end of the site closest to the parish church at Chatham was rebuilt (Fig 13.7), which meant demolishing the last surviving parts of the settlement that predated the construction of the fortifications and barracks. This included Cat Lane, where civilian cholera deaths had occurred in 1849 in what were clearly substandard dwellings. To expand the barracks the main accommodation block at the rear of the site was extended southwards, and the officers' block was demolished and a new version built against the boundary of the churchyard.

A terrace of grand houses (since demolished) for the use of Royal Marine officers was also built facing Dock Road and opposite the Soldiers' Institute (Fig 13.9). In 1879 a school and schoolmaster's house for the children of marines were built on Dock Road, immediately outside the barrier ditch (Fig 13.10).

Fig 13.8
The remodelled Royal
Marines barracks at
Chatham.
(© English Heritage
AL00-21-1)

Fig 13.9
Royal Marine officers'
terrace.
(Royal Engineers Museum,
Library and Archives)

Fig 13.10
The Royal Marines' school of
1879.
(Royal Engineers Museum,
Library and Archives)

Recreation and leisure

The 1861 recommendations also called for increased attention to what the men did with their off-duty hours and for deliberate attempts to make them pass less time in the low beer-houses common in garrison towns. The 1864 plan of the infantry barracks (Fig 13.1) shows that both skittle alleys and rackets courts were built for the soldiers' recreation, but the most significant new building in this regard was the Soldiers' Institute in the north-west corner of the infantry barracks, with its grand front facing Dock Road. The purpose of a Soldiers' Institute can be summed up from an 1869–70 Royal Commission on army education, which said that it was to create for soldiers 'the beneficial effects by innocent recreation counteracting the low and vicious amusements to which they are so much exposed'. The key difference between Soldiers' Institutes and barracks canteens was how they were set up and managed. Soldiers' Institutes were 'to be distinguished from regimental recreation rooms ... as ... establishments beyond the precincts of the barracks and are founded in certain large garrisons and owe their origin almost entirely to private liberality. Even where Government aid has been afforded in the erection of buildings they are under private management and not subject to official control.'[7]

The Chatham Soldiers' Institute was the first of its kind as a purpose-built structure in any British garrison town. It was also known as the Buckley Institute after its first honorary secretary, John Buckley, who as the former barracks master at Chatham was instrumental in persuading the War Department to permit its construction and contribute to its cost.[8] This was not, however, a Government-owned or -run building. It was managed by a committee of NCOs overseen by some officers, and it was available to all men of the garrison upon payment of a small subscription. The best description comes from the 1862 publication *Red, White and Blue*:

In the north west corner of the Chatham barracks, fronting to the road leading from the Engineer barracks, and overlooking the dock-yard, there is rapidly approaching completion a handsome building, which, under the name of the Soldiers' Institute, is intended to afford the soldier the means of harmless recreation, which at present are almost entirely wanting in the station. It is, in fact, to be the Soldiers' Clubhouse, where he will meet his comrades, smoke his pipe, drink his cup of coffee, and take his ease generally, without restraint or interference ... It consists of two stories, and will afford accommodation for pretty nearly 1,000 men. The ground floor is divided into two spacious coffee-rooms, separated by a bar, at which tea, coffee, cold meats, bread and butter, and eggs, may be obtained at cost price. They will be well furnished with comfortable chairs and settees, and a plentiful supply of little marble-topped tables, such as we see in French *cafés* or *estaminets*. In one room there will be a supply of newspapers and popular periodicals, and in the other there will be chess, back-gammon and solitaire boards, bagatelle and German billiard tables, with other games; and the men will be allowed to smoke their pipes in both rooms, and both will be well warmed, ventilated and lighted. A portion of the upper floor will be occupied by the barrack library, consisting of 4,000 volumes, which is to be moved into it from its present quarters; and on the other side is the lecture theatre – a very handsome room, some twenty-six feet high, and brilliantly lighted with star pendants, after the fashion of St. James's Hall. Some 600 men may be accommodated in it. This is to be used principally for evening classes, for instruction in singing, drawing, Hindustani, &c., but occasionally lectures will be delivered by the officers and men, or by lecturers specially engaged, if the funds are forthcoming; and, by an ingenious arrangement, the tables are so contrived that they back together, and form a convenient platform for the lecturer, or a stage for private theatricals when there may be sufficient supply of dramatic talent in the garrison. The room is not yet finished, but it is to be very handsomely decorated. On panels round the walls will be inscribed the names of the principal victories in the Peninsular, Indian, and Crimean wars, and under each, in their proper order, will be ranged the busts of the victorious generals. Quarters for the librarian are provided on the ground floor. Some objection has been taken to the building, as being too highly ornamented; but here we think the Building Committee have shown their knowledge of the soldiers' way of thinking. It is always the most splendid and best-fitted gin-palace which attracts him the readiest, and he will take all the more pride in his club-house for its not being a mere long, low, corrugated iron excrescence, little differing in outward appearance from the shed in which the Armstrongs are housed in the neighbouring barracks. Next to the Convicts' Prison, it is about the handsomest building of which Chatham can boast. Close by, a large American bowling-alley is pretty nearly finished; two fives-courts are already in use, and there is room in the corner for a spacious skittle-alley, which appears to be the game most affected by the men.[9]

In 1872 permission was sought to extend the Institute through the addition of a larger lecture hall, which became known as the Buckley Theatre. Major-General Brownrigg as commandant of the garrison supported the proposal:

The success of this institution has been very great and the means of innocent recreation and amusement it affords have kept many a soldier out of the public house and canteen during the day and I feel sure that the establishment of the proposed lecture hall would have the same beneficial effect at a later period of the evening when the soldier is exposed to greater temptation and from having no means of amusing himself in barracks, resorts to the low tap room or public house in the town.[10]

Today precious little survives of the pioneering Soldiers' Institute. It has been largely demolished so that only the lower portions of the ground-floor front elevations remain, forming part of the barracks perimeter wall. These are sufficient to show what a grand building the Institute once was, but old photographs (Fig 13.11) provide a full understanding of its appearance.

Head's 1869 description of the Brompton barracks includes other buildings that reflect the greater attention now paid to the morals and well-being of the men. These include an NCOs' subscription library and an NCOs' mess room. There was a recreation and reading room for all ranks and a coffee and refreshment room that did not serve alcohol. The canteen had an enhanced role providing groceries to army families, though it still sold 160 barrels of porter per month, as well as 23 of ale and 6 of stout, with a turnover of £14,000 per annum. There was also a skittle alley.

One further new building, a military gymnasium, was added in Wood Street, opposite the Brompton barracks, and was also used by troops at the infantry barracks. It was built in 1863 to a design by Archibald Maclaren, author of *A Military System of Gymnastic Exercise for the use of Instructors* (1862). Six such gymnasia were built at the major garrisons, and Chatham's is unique because it continues in use, with some of the original folding wall-mounted equipment.

Increasing attention was paid to the physical fitness of the soldiers in the second half of the 19th century. The exercise ground of the Great Lines started to be used as sports fields, and open land at the Inner Lines was used for military sports days, which included improbable events like the egg-and-ladle and the three-legged race.[11] The first cricket ground

Fig 13.11
The Soldiers' Institute at Chatham infantry barracks. (Royal Engineers Museum, Library and Archives)

was fenced off on the Great Lines in 1863, and a tennis club was founded near Fort Amherst in 1864. The Royal Engineers football team won the FA cup 1875, and the first Corps rugby team was founded in 1886.

Like the gymnasium, another significant building was provided in a location where it could be shared by both of the main barrack sites. This was the garrison church that was authorised in 1851 and completed in 1854 (Fig 13.14). It is dedicated to St Barbara, the patron saint of artillerymen, military engineers and miners. When first constructed, the chapel was also used as a schoolroom, with a schoolmaster's house built alongside.

On the opposite side of the road to the garrison church, land that was once part of the internal field of fire of Amherst redoubt was laid out as a park in 1869, using sapper labour, with specimen tree planting. It became known as the Garrison Recreation Ground.[12] The recreation ground extended into the adjacent Prince of Wales bastion, and there is evidence here of how the firestep of the fortifications was converted with steps into a promenade. Before the end of the 19th century there would also be a bandstand. Once it was clear that the Chatham Lines would not be required as a first line of defence, the policy of keeping the land totally

Fig 13.12
The military gymnasium near Brompton barracks. (Royal Engineers Museum, Library and Archives)

Fig 13.13
Military sports at the Inner Lines, Chatham, including the three-legged race and the egg and ladle race.
(The Graphic 20 October 1877)

clear inside and outside of the bastions was relaxed. The 1879 1:2500 Ordnance Survey map shows systematic tree planting in avenues along the ramparts, the outer edge of the ditch and the Inner Lines.

Drink and prostitution

Other leisure activities did not meet with universal approval. In the aftermath of the Crimean War, steps were taken to try to persuade the military personnel of garrison and dockyard towns to lead a more upright and healthy lifestyle. Similar actions were taken by non-military bodies. The temperance movement targeted the military establishments, and in parallel the nonconformist churches struggled to establish themselves with the mili-

Fig 13.14
The garrison church of St Barbara on the Inner Lines.
(Royal Engineers Museum, Library and Archives)

tary authorities. It was the Wesleyan chaplain Charles Henry Kelly who, despite active opposition from the garrison commander, established a soldiers' home at Chatham in 1861. Several campaigning publications also pressed the case for moral and social reform of the army. One of these, aimed at the Indian army, described the Medway towns in relation to recruits destined for service there:

Close and smoky, and rickety and narrow, huddled together at the bottom of a hill, which seems to be cut and carved and pierced into the semblance of a woman's crochet pattern, lies a maze of streets and alleys. If you unwisely penetrate into these streets you will find all the evils and all the vices of the metropolis you have for one day left, and you will find them compressed and intensified. The gin-shop is here more frequent in its recurrence and more gross and shameless in its allurements, and it will be strange if your modesty be not shocked by other sights which obtrude themselves in forms still more revolting. This place is Chatham.[13]

The anonymous author pressed for new recruits to be removed from the temptations of Chatham and for them to be trained at Aldershot, or better still to become accustomed to the heat of the tropics by spending time at the Cape in South Africa.

Despite the efforts at social reform, drink remained freely available to soldiers, sailors and dockyard men in their off-duty hours. When 4,500 sq m of additional land[14] for extending the barracks of the Royal Marines was acquired in 1857, the plan (Fig 13.7) shows that it had contained 4 drinking establishments (Army and Navy Hotel, the Queens Head and Red Lion public houses, as well as a house used as a beer shop called The Royal Marine).[15] Proximity to the two major barracks for the infantry and marines helps explain the number of drinking establishments, but these were amongst tightly packed houses with inadequate sanitation that was a contributory factor to the ill-health of the inhabitants.

Public houses were just some of the places where soldiers and marines could spend their evenings. Prostitution was an inevitable part of life in a dockyard and garrison town. It was almost certainly present from the beginning of the government establishments, but the clearest evidence comes from the later 19th century when the awakening of the public conscience led to a determined attempt to eradicate the evil of venereal disease that was spread by this means. In 1864 the Contagious Diseases Act was passed as harsh legislation to give the police in named dockyard and garrison towns the right to stop and forcibly examine women thought to be prostitutes and if necessary to enforce upon them compulsory medical treatment in a lock hospital. At Chatham the lock hospital was built adjacent to the commissariat depot on the Maidstone road near the railway station.[16]

The *British Medical Journal* for 1867 published a review of the 1864 Act, with information about the extent and nature of prostitution at Chatham and the morals of the place. The police were keeping under surveillance 200 women who they considered to be 'notorious prostitutes', but there were in addition many factory workers, servant girls and married women who practised clandestine prostitution. The author of the 1867 review was Dr Berkeley Hill, and he had no doubt that it was the loose morals of the Chatham population that made prostitution and its attendant diseases such a problem: 'There is no fixed class of gentry to give a tone, and set an example, to society. The morals of the lower classes are extremely low; but though still a crying disgrace in this respect, public decency has been greatly improved since the Act has been enforced. The frightful abandonment to all kinds of foul debauchery is now lessened.'[17]

The Act was not as effective as it was hoped in reducing disease, which was attributed to the fact that the law applied only to Chatham, and yet women travelled between Chatham and Gravesend, and they would also come to Chatham from Maidstone and Canterbury, such as when ships were paid off. Soldiers from the Chatham garrison also moved around, and up to 500 were sent each month for target practice at Gravesend.[18] The Royal Engineers did spend longer in their depot at Chatham, but they were better paid than the average soldier and could easily go up to London, only 30 miles away, to pass their free time. Medical returns showed an upsurge in disease after the granting of leave to the sappers for public holidays and after their annual major exercise.

Hill blamed not the women but the 'low and loathsome' beer shop owners who profited from their misery. These beer shops were common in Chatham High Street, with slum-like lodging houses to their rear in which the women rented a room and to which the soldiers were drawn by drinking, eating and music. The lowest types of prostitutes operated outside the barracks, near Fort Pitt or in an area known as the orchards close to Melville hospital. These women would sell themselves for a few pence, a drink of gin or even a share of a soldier's bread. One beer shop owner built one-room huts behind his premises, which he rented out at 2s a week to the girls, on condition that they pass their evenings in his tap room and encouraged soldiers to drink and spend money there. The clandestine prostitutes included the wives of soldiers and sailors, who out of financial necessity were forced to survive as best they could, particularly when their men were on overseas service.

The police in Chatham were convinced that the 1864 Act was effective in controlling prostitution and therefore the prevalence of venereal disease, a view that was shared by an 1868 meeting of the clergy of Chatham. Not surprisingly, the Act was hated by women who were its victims, whether or not they were prostitutes. It embodied in legislation the sexual double standards of the day. It assumed soldiers and sailors needed prostitutes to service their natural sexual impulses and that the Government had a responsibility to ensure that there were healthy women to do so. Yet it criminalised women who worked as prostitutes, whilst leaving the men blameless. Women in the towns to which the Act applied were denied basic civil rights. They were subject to a form of arrest, despite prostitution itself not being a crime. They might have to undergo an enforced examination by male doctors, and if found to be suffering from disease, they were incarcerated in the lock hospital until they were judged to have been cured. Perhaps the worst injustice of all was that there is little evidence that the Acts helped to control sexually transmitted diseases.

In 1869 Mrs Josephine Butler, with the support of Florence Nightingale, founded the Ladies National Association for the Repeal of the Contagious Diseases Acts[19] on the grounds that they were unfair and one-sided, ignoring the role of men in the spread of the diseases. Nightingale considered the acts ineffective and advocated more support for the wives and children of soldiers and sailors and the provision at barracks of rest-rooms and leisure activities. The Acts were suspended in 1883 and repealed in 1886 (except in the colonies). At Chatham the lock hospital became a barracks associated with the commissary. It has since been demolished.

Punishments

Although in the mid-19th century the conditions of the British soldier and his family, including at Chatham, were significantly improved, it would be wrong to equate this with a soft military regime. The life of a soldier and in particular the imposition of discipline could remain brutal. Punishment by flogging continued and was normally carried out at the Spur battery of Fort Amherst in front of the assembled garrison, such as one incident in May 1857:

Yesterday morning the troops belonging to the provisional battalion at Chatham were marched to the fortifications at the Spur Battery for the purpose of witnessing the infliction of corporal punishment on a soldier of the 1st Battalion of the 60th Rifles, named John Quantrill, who had been sentenced by a district court-martial to receive 50 lashes for having robbed a comrade, named Evans, belonging to the 53rd Regiment, of a silver medal. The battalion having been formed into three sides of a square the sentence was read to the troops in the presence of the prisoner, who was then fastened to the triangles, and the punishment inflicted. The prisoner was afterwards removed to the garrison hospital.[20]

Army reform also began to address punishment. The number of lashes administered during a flogging was initially restricted, then in 1868 flogging was completely abolished during peacetime. It could still be administered on campaign until 1881 and in military prisons until 1907.[21] A further brutal but unusual means of punishment was the process of drumming out for bad conduct, which could involve branding the prisoner. The *Penny Illustrated Magazine* for 1864 records just such a scene at Chatham:

The unusual ceremony of 'drumming out' one of the corps of Royal Engineers took place at Brompton Barracks, Chatham, last Saturday morning. In accordance with an order from the Horse Guards, a full-dress parade of the whole of the officers and men now at head-quarters was held on the barrack parade-ground for the purpose of witnessing the proceedings. The prisoner, William Watkins, of the thirty-seventh company, although he has only been in the corps about three years, has been tried eleven times by court-martial for various offences, and has hardly done a single day's duty since he has been in the service, almost his whole time having been spent in prison and under punishment. On the last occasion of his being tried by court-martial – which was for desertion and making away with his uniform and regimental necessaries – he was sentenced to be branded with the letters 'B.C.' (bad conduct), to be marked with the letter 'D.' to be imprisoned for three months in Canterbury Gaol, and to be dismissed the service with ignominy.[22]

It would take until the end of the 19th century for the reform of the army to be completed such that it could attract and retain capable men rather than relying on recruiting from the lower levels of society and using brutality to keep the soldiers under control.

Later 19th-century Chatham

The simplistic view is that Chatham's economic fortunes were based on the activity within the dockyard and the barracks and that they rose and fell in periods of war and peace, investment or retrenchment. For residents engaged in trade, this was undoubtedly true, and they looked to the health of the public establishments to sustain their activities. Not everybody, however, was as welcoming of a local economy so based on government expenditure. The people who did not earn their living directly from that source faced an increased poor rate as a consequence of the impact of so many establishments. This imposed a burden upon local people, who were not adequately reimbursed by the Government because its land had an exemption from rates. One in four paupers at Chatham were the widows and children of soldiers or dockyard workers. Each year £1,200 was excused in rates on the grounds that the tenements were so small and the people too poor to pay the charge. Two-thirds of these were the families of soldiers, sailors or dockyard men.

The lack of a significant middle class at Chatham undoubtedly affected the character of the place and retarded its improvement. The dockyard and garrison influenced not only the kind of person who lived in Chatham, but continued to physically shape the character of the town. Major fires in 1800 and 1820 had destroyed many properties and in part allowed some of the haphazard areas of the High Street to be rebuilt as lodgings, while some of the structures expected of a mid- to late 19th-century town were built.

A further problem was that the presence of so many government establishments depressed rents and created a disincentive for landlords to invest. In 1858, 100 acres of the town of Chatham were exempt from paying parish rates as they were occupied by the Government. That same year a Parliamentary Select Committee examined whether government-run public establishments should continue to be exempt from local rates and taxes, by which poor relief and other services were funded.[23] The rents in Chatham in 1858 were the lowest of any town in Kent.

The Government's occupation of the best land prevented it from being used for alternative commercial purposes, which was regarded as the biggest single disincentive for 'persons of property' settling there, and one view was that 'there was no inducement for gentlemen to reside in Chatham and that 6,000 or 7,000 troops in garrison walking about the streets during the day and much more still at night, deters respectable people from taking residence in the town.'[24] A description of Chatham as a town written in 1882 by a special correspondent for use in colonial newspapers shows that whilst social reforms may have had some impact, it nevertheless remained an unruly place dominated by the military.

Chatham is a half-military, half-maritime town, with a superabundance of slop-sellers and of public-houses ... There are cheap concert-rooms for the recreation of 'Jack ashore' and tawdry sirens leering at him from the first-floor windows of low lodging houses in obscure lanes and alleys. The footpaths are bright with scarlet uniforms, and the windows of the barbers' shops are radiant with many-coloured bills setting forth the marvellous attractions of this or that place of public resort, and of the wonderful performances of this or that 'great' comic singer, character actor, mimic, or female dancer — all of which are intended to be auxiliary to the sale of rum by the publican who provides the entertainment.[25]

14

New Fortifications and World War I

The 1860 Royal Commission report had recommended a huge number of fortifications, but the proposals were too ambitious, and financial restrictions meant that the number of new works actually built was reduced. The first rings of forts were implemented at Portsmouth, Plymouth and Dover, and 76 new forts were completed nationwide by 1867. On the Medway the greatest emphasis was placed on keeping the enemy out of the river. At Garrison Point at Sheerness a massive double-tiered and casemated fort was constructed in 1872, and this crossed its fire with another new fort and separate battery at Grain, built in 1867–8. The landward approach to Sheerness was defended by the Queenborough Lines, composed of a wide, wet ditch, an earthen rampart and a military road running for 2 miles from one side of

the Isle of Sheppey to the other, with batteries securing its ends. Experience in the American Civil War (1861–5) and experiments by the Royal Engineers on the impact of improved guns against the obsolete Martello towers of the south coast had shown the vulnerability of brickwork to modern artillery, and so these new forts were built with granite faces and gun shields made of sheets of iron in each casemate.

Two circular forts were proposed further up the Medway, on either side of the navigable channel, with a boom defence stretched between them. A new fort was built at Cliffe on the Kentish side of the Thames in 1870 and another on the Essex shore at Coalhouse Point, East Tilbury, in 1874. The innovative polygonal fort at Shornemead was replaced by a new one in 1870, and the existing works at New Tavern Fort (Gravesend) and Tilbury were strengthened. A small fort (Slough Fort) was also built in 1868 at Allhallows on the western side of the Hoo peninsula to guard against a possible landing on the flats in this part of the Thames estuary and a subsequent march on Chatham.

Once the River Medway was considered secure, the planned eastern and western defences were not given priority. Two forts had been proposed either side of the Medway at Oakham Ness, but the original estuarine location was found to be too soft to take the immense weight, and so the sites were moved closer to Chatham dockyard. Instead, the twin forts of Hoo and Darnet were built in 1871, located on islands in the Medway that had first been fortified in the aftermath of the 1667 Dutch raid. Even so, great difficulty was encountered when the foundations of both forts cracked. The design of the forts had to be altered, and in place of the proposed three-tier circular forts that would have mounted 25 guns in the upper two tiers, with magazines in the tier below, only 11 guns were provided in each fort on a single tier, with the magazines below.

Chatham Ring Forts

Funds were not available for the land fortresses to defend Chatham until 1875, when construction started using a modifed design. The western defences that would have linked to the River Thames were not built, and the eastern group was revised to form an arc of polygonal forts – the Chatham Ring Forts – running from near Borstal to Twydall. Situated 1½ miles in

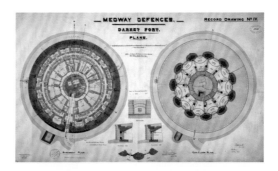

Fig 14.3
The plan of Darnet Fort, one of a pair of circular forts built on islands in the Medway to control the navigable approach to the dockyard.
(TNA ADM 140/1351)

front of the Chatham Lines, the new forts were based on the thinking of 1860, but by the 1870s the range and accuracy of artillery had so improved that they were now wrongly sited. Nevertheless, Forts Borstal, Bridgewoods, Horsted and Luton were all started, but work was suspended at the end of the 1870s due to lack of funds. Had the forts been finished at that stage, they would almost certainly have taken the form of those built at Portsmouth and Plymouth, with fixed gun positions on their ramparts and caponiers for ditch defence.

The delay in resuming construction enabled the final form of the forts to reflect the latest thinking in fixed fortifications. These Chatham

land forts span a period in which the approach to defence moved away from fixed artillery fortresses in favour of more mobile forces that could operate in open country from improvised fieldworks, infantry redoubts, trench systems and field batteries. As such, these forts were some of the last substantial, permanent land fortifications built in Great Britain. The Chatham Ring Forts were therefore no longer a fixed means of defence and had no fixed gun positions. Instead, they were secure bases from which to mobilise defenders. Magazines deep within the fort could serve shells to the rampart by means of hoists, and the guns here were fully mobile and could be taken outside the fort. The

Fig 14.4
Aerial view of Darnet Fort, nearly identical to its twin, Hoo Fort.
(© English Heritage, 26600/28 18/10/2010)

Fig 14.5
Aerial view of Fort Horsted,
one of the late 19th-century
Chatham Ring Forts.
(Avondale)

forts were also unusual in being built of mass concrete, not brickwork. Casemates for the housing of troops were integrated into the designs and were protected by turf-covered chalk mounding that had been excavated from the ditch. The ditch was defended by counter-scarp galleries rather than caponiers, which were judged too vulnerable to high-angle fire. Fort Horsted is the largest of the Chatham Ring Forts, and its design is best understood from the air (Fig 14.5).

The emergence of this new approach to land defences was the precursor to the approaches adopted in the 20th century, with a reliance on excavating fieldworks at the times of heightened threat and otherwise using land forts as mobilisation bases and strong points for the fieldworks. This can best be seen in the completion of the Twydall end of the Chatham Ring. Here, the two northernmost works built from 1886 were not true forts but were infantry redoubts of an exceptionally low profile that became known as the Twydall profile. The redoubts were designed for the use of magazine rifles and machine guns by infantry on long fronts, with the supporting artillery removed to concealed sunken field batteries. An earthen rampart provided a firestep behind which there were open-backed concrete casemates in which troops could shelter from bombardment.

The last ring fort to be built was Fort Darland. It was completed in 1899, and it also reflected the increased emphasis on forts for infantry. There were 11 emplacements for machine guns and also separate casemates in which to store moveable guns that could be deployed to a wing battery on its right flank.

Almost before they were complete, the Chatham Ring Forts were obsolete, and by as early as 1907 Forts Luton and Bridgewoods were used for siege training that involved their partial destruction by mines.

Shells and magazines

It had been recommended in 1865 that bulk storage of gunpowder should be moved away from Upnor, and in 1872 land was purchased in a natural valley at Chattenden, on the Hoo peninsula. Advantage was taken of the sloping land here to create the basis of a traverse that could be enhanced by earthworks to take five new magazines. This became the Chattenden Magazine Enclosure, completed in 1875 and connected to Upnor by railway. The hillside was geologically unstable, which from early on caused problems that persist to the present day.

To provide accommodation for troops to guard the new facility at Chattenden, barracks (since demolished) were built that reflected the new standards.[1] Terraced housing was also constructed for some of the workforce and the police. The Chattenden site was intended as a storage adjunct to Upnor, and so it never had structures for handling powder for use in cartridges or for filling shells. Such activity continued to take place at Upnor.

At Upnor a further shell store was added in 1882–3 alongside the one built in 1862, and another was subsequently squeezed in between the shifting house and the castle.[2] In 1885 the War Office resumed the use of Upnor as a magazine depot, but not for loose powder, restricting its use to gun ammunition in metal cases. At the same time it was thought best to stop laboratory use of the site and to seek a new and safer location for the filling of shells and cartridges. Such a site was identified in 1890 between Upnor and Chattenden, but was not taken forward.

Separate ammunition in which the cartridges and the shells were introduced to the gun as discrete elements was replaced in the late 19th century by fixed ammunition that combined the projectile and the propellant as one piece, giving rise to the metal cartridge case. The motivation for this was the quick fire gun (QF), which belongs to a similar development in artillery as machine gun technology does to small arms. High rates of fire were needed to counter such threats as fast-moving

Fig 14.6
Aerial view of the
Chattenden magazine
enclosure.
(© English Heritage
23189/22 04/8/2003)

torpedo boats. The metal cartridge case was essential for speed of handling and avoided the need for guns to be sponged out between firings in order to prevent premature ignition of cartridge bags. To be effective QF guns needed smokeless powders, because the copious smoke from black powder would not disperse with the rapid firing, nor was concealed fire possible because smoke betrayed the presence of guns. The development of cordite at Woolwich Arsenal saw its manufacture as a propellant start in *c* 1888, and in the 1890s it replaced powder as the main propellant. It was a mixture of guncotton, nitroglycerine and stabilisers. Not only was it smokeless, but it was more powerful and much safer to handle and store than other existing explosives.

The developments in guns and ammunition meant that by the end of the 19th century, the places in which ordnance was manufactured and stored were very different from earlier magazines built for gunpowder. At this time there was a massive increase in the size of the Royal Navy and with it demands for naval ordnance storage. Scares that naval superiority was once again in danger of being lost to France led to a £21.5 million investment programme under the Naval Defence Act of 1889. In 1890 a complex dispute between the War Department and the Admiralty about naval ordnance facilities was resolved by a committee. This divided the existing ordnance sites between the army and the navy. Chattenden went to the army and Upnor to the navy. This created a crisis for the navy, because Upnor was not suitable for bulk storage and did not have space for all the cartridges required for QF guns or for the largest cartridges for big guns. The magazines at Upnor had been built for black powder storage and were now deemed unsuitable as they consisted of ranges of joined magazines, not separate magazines divided by traverses. Only the use of floating magazines made it possible to meet the demands placed on the Upnor site, but these were seen as a stopgap, and their unsuitability was demonstrated in 1894 when the *Leonidas* caught fire, though an explosion was prevented by the fire fighters who bravely went on board.

Gun-cotton is nitro-cellulose and was used from the 1860s as an explosive that was more powerful and less bulky than gunpowder. Its use as a propellant was never perfected, but it was used to fill shells, mines and torpedo heads. It could be stored either wet or dry, the latter being a more dangerous form. At Upnor the gun-cotton was initially stored in the castle, but in 1895–6 a wet gun-cotton store, a dry gun-cotton store (since demolished) and a detonator store were added to the northern group of shell stores.

Obtaining the Chattenden magazines from the army would have significantly eased the navy's problems, but this could not be negotiated, and so additional land was purchased at Upnor in 1899 to extend the site for a final time. This included the site of the 17th-century 10-gun battery built after the Dutch raid and also parts of the Ordnance Board's former brickyard, which had developed as an area of

privately owned housing and included the Boatswain and Call public house. There was also a small privately run boatyard. The houses were retained as offices and were not demolished until the 1960s, but a filled mine store and a very large filled shell store were built in 1903–4 on the site of the boatyard.

Some of the last purpose-built ordnance structures at Upnor were built in 1906–7, when work was transferred from Woolwich Arsenal. These were a suite of six shell-filling stores protected by concrete traverses that were squeezed in along the rear of the large magazines (Fig 14.7). They were modelled on structures built in 1888 at Priddy's Hard, Portsmouth. The delay in their construction at Upnor was because shells were initially filled at Woolwich, and the navy had plans for a new filling site downstream of Upnor at Tea Pot Hard, an intention that was abandoned only in 1905.

Any description of the Medway ordnance sites in the 19th century requires consideration of Lodge Hill as the largest such site (Fig 14.8). It was thought that cordite could be stored in much lighter structures than conventional magazines, and a shared army and navy magazine was built at Crossness on Erith marshes in 1896–7, but proved less than perfect. The navy therefore resolved to build its own facility at

Fig 14.7
Upnor ordnance depot at its most developed form just before World War I.
(Royal Engineers Museum, Library and Archives)

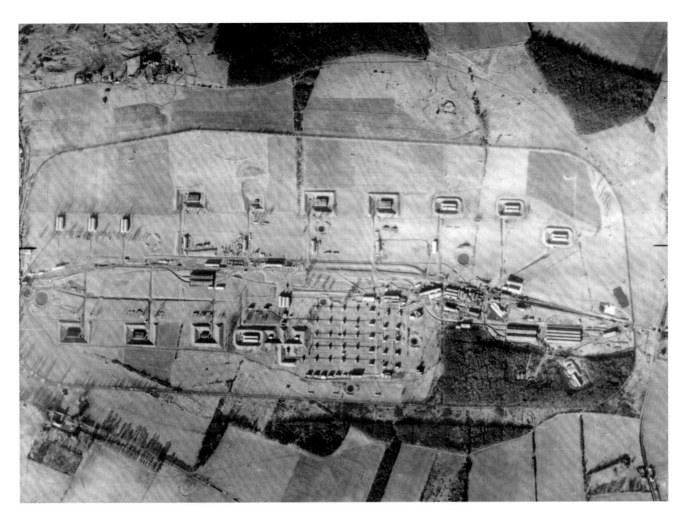

Fig 14.8
Aerial view of the Lodge Hill ordnance depot in Kent. (English Heritage (RAF Photography) RAF/CPE/ UK/1923 4082 16/01/1947)

Lodge Hill. The first land acquisition took place in 1898 adjacent to the Chattenden magazine enclosure. Here shelter was provided by the naturally secluded site, and it was possible to connect the facility to Upnor by light railway and to the national rail network.

Lodge Hill became the first naval ordnance depot that could be accessed independently of seaborne transport and was designed around a different concept to the very crowded Upnor site and the other old depots. The amount of space available enabled safety to be achieved by spreading out the magazines, so that these did not have to rely on massive traverses or heavy construction. A central railway and road formed the spine of the site, with buildings laid out either side of it. Earth traverses were built around the magazines, and deliberate tree planting as a screen against blast was used to enhance safety. By 1904 much of the Lodge Hill site was complete. In 1903 a cartridge-filling laboratory was ordered, which finally removed this hazardous activity from Upnor.[3]

The old Chatham Lines

The building of the Chatham land forts was not completed until the end of the 19th century, and until then the old Chatham Lines remained the theoretical defence line for the dockyard. Reliance on the Chatham Lines was, however, significantly reduced from the mid-19th century. Large-scale practice siege works destroyed the integrity of the lines, particularly those at the Lower Lines, although they were repaired and reinstated after each event. In 1882 the Defence Committee considered whether a portion of the lines should be demolished. They were described by the committee as being a material obstacle to any advance by an attacker, but incapable of providing protection from bombardment.[4] The senior officers responsible for Chatham were divided in their opinions. The Royal Artillery considered that the lines were 'perfectly useless', because the power of modern artillery meant that the dockyard could be shelled and burnt by an enemy who had seized the high ground where the Chatham Ring Forts were then being constructed. Rather than place any reliance on the Chatham Lines, they recommended that in an emergency, earthwork forts should be hastily built to plug any gaps in the unfinished outer defence line.

Colonel Charles J Fowler, the Commanding Royal Engineer, argued that as the new defence line was incomplete, there was a large gap between Darnet Fort in the river and the first completed fort in the outer line (by which he probably meant Fort Luton). He stated that although the Chatham Lines were weak and could not withstand the heavy fire of modern artillery, they would be of some use, particularly as the Spur battery at Fort Amherst offered a good command of the country and in an emergency could be reinforced with heavy guns. He also said that the Spur battery offered bombproof accommodation in its early 19th-century casemates, as did the St Mary's casemates in the Lower Lines, and that the Belvedere magazine at Fort Amherst was also still valuable.

The commandant of the School of Military Engineering was adamant that the old lines from Prince Edward's bastion to the river were still required as the practice ground for the Royal Engineers. Finally, the Major-General commanding the Chatham district was firmly of the view that Fort Amherst could be retained as a citadel and be reinforced and re-armed as necessary. It was therefore decided to keep the Chatham Lines, as they could be of some service for defence, even after completion of the outer line of detached forts. This decision prevented demolition of the old fortifications, and so many of them survive to this day. A comment by one of the officers perhaps betrays the true reason for their retention. He stated that a great deal of convict labour would be needed to demolish the solidly built fortifications, but the available labour from the convict prison at Chatham and the establishment at Borstal[5] was already required to build the new outer line of defences.

In 1886 there remained a small number of guns mounted at the Chatham Lines, but these were outdated pieces and were most likely for training and for military ceremonies. On Prince Henry's bastion (behind the Commandant of the School of Military Engineering's quarters), there were four 12-pounder smooth-barrel guns, and at Fort Amherst there were eleven 12-pounder and two 32-pounder muzzle-loading smooth-bore cannons.[6] In 1919 a gun list was provided for Fort Amherst, which recorded that there were then seven 32-pounder smooth-bore breech-loading guns mounted.[7] These must also have been for training purposes, as in the early 20th century they represented completely outdated technology.

End of siege training

It is not entirely clear when siege training ceased at the Chatham Lines. Concern about the effectiveness of siege guns in breaching defences led the Siege Operations Committee in 1881 to conduct practical experiments.[8] There was insufficient space at Chatham to exercise the powerful guns then in use, and so the site chosen was at Dungeness. In 1885 the War Department committee that reviewed the training required of Royal Engineer officers highlighted the continued need to teach the rules of a siege,[9] even though military tactics were changing towards more mobile forces and away from fixed fortifications. Late 19th-century press accounts describe how volunteer soldiers trained in fieldworks on both sides of the River Medway, including in land around the ordnance sites and barracks at Chattenden. Evidence for trenching that may be the product of such training is visible on air photographs. Land at Darland Banks, Gillingham, was first used as an alternative training ground in about 1900, and this use continued throughout World War I. In 1907 there was a major siege exercise involving the Chatham garrison, but although this used the familiar techniques of sapping and mining, it took place against the Chatham Ring Forts and not the Chatham Lines.

In 1911 a report stated how the ground at Chatham was incessantly worked, no doubt the reason why the Chatham Lines were no longer suitable for siege training: 'all ground which is constantly used for digging must be periodically rested. In former days much of the field work ground about Chatham had become almost useless from being so incessantly worked and also was on such a level site that it only allowed for instruction in types of works and not in their adaptation to the ground.'[10] The encroachment around the Chatham Lines by residential development, especially at Gillingham, must also have made it unsafe to continue to train with live ammunition and explosives. By the start of the 20th century major siege exercises were finished at the

Chatham Lines, but its use as a training ground for other purposes by the Royal Engineers continued.

During archaeological investigations at the Lower Lines for the building of a new college, the remains of many backfilled trenches, some gabions and several collapsed tunnels were recorded, alongside the evidence for the earlier system of countermine galleries (*see* Figs 7.3 and 7.4). Similar evidence was found on Black Lion Field when new sports facilities were constructed. The excavated results do not form recognisable patterns that can be related to the known extent of siege works from major exercises like that of 1877. Nevertheless, the excavated evidence from the site includes broad

Borough status

By 1871 the population of Chatham had increased to 45,792, but until *c*1880 the growth of the town continued to be held in check by the lines at Fort Amherst. Development occurred either side of the Military Road and hard against the boundary wall of New Gunwharf, but no closer. This changed with the shift of the defence to the Chatham Ring Forts. In 1875 the Court Leet once more declined to seek incorporation as a borough, and it was not until 1888 that a meeting of Chatham ratepayers unanimously voted to seek borough status. This would allow local control through a single body of education, health, sanitation and the police. The charter creating Chatham a new borough with a town council was granted in 1890, making possible buildings indicative of municipal status. At last Chatham the town and Chatham the garrison were joined by continuous development.

Former military land, now surplus to army requirements, was acquired by the new local authority and laid out as public spaces, including Town Hall Gardens and Victoria Gardens on the hill, on which also stands Fort Pitt and the Paddock, adjacent to the Gunwharf. The 19th century ended with the construction of Chatham Town Hall (now the Brook theatre), occupying land that had until then been kept clear of development on the orders of the military.

Chatham entered the 20th century with the enthusiasm of a newly incorporated place determined to throw off some of the worst aspects of its unruly past. Militarily the new century saw the combined presence of the army and navy reach its peak in the years around 1900. This great military concentration was about to be subject to a new form of warfare from the air, which would yet again change the approach to its defence and its character.

Fig 14.9
Early 20th-century growth of Chatham with the new Town Hall.
(Medway Archives)

trenches consistent with these being the remains of parallels or batteries, as well as much smaller tunnels that were the result of work to lay mines. Some of the smaller tunnels were for countermines, and they included tunnels with partial timber lining *in situ* that connected with the more permanent system of brick-built galleries. This physical evidence of the Royal Engineer training is so far unique in Britain and sheds important light on the nature of siege warfare above and below ground.

The navy barracks and hospital

The garrison area of Chatham reached its largest permanent extent in the first decade of the 20th century through the addition of new sites. The main projects were for the navy – a major set of barracks and a hospital. In the 18th century and for much of the 19th the navy, with the exception of the Royal Marines, had no need of permanent barracks. Chatham was a building and repair yard, not a base for a permanent fleet, and any sailors needing to be housed traditionally made use of the hulks, even after their abandonment as floating prisons *c* 1860. Circumstances changed in the late 19th century with the adoption of increasingly large and technically complex steam-powered iron warships. Chatham became a manning port with

ships based there, and the sailors needed to learn their skills in shore establishments and not just at sea. To attract and retain the kind of intelligent and skilled men that some departments of the navy now demanded meant providing decent accommodation in purpose-built naval barracks. The navy needed substantial barracks long after the army had first addressed the same issue. Keyham at Devonport led the way from 1879 as the first new naval barracks, with those at Portsmouth and Chatham being completed in the first years of the 20th century.

The Chatham barracks were named HMS *Pembroke* (Fig 14.10), after one of the three hulks they replaced that had until then served as the naval depot and been moored in No. 2 basin of the Victorian dockyard extension. Construction of the permanent barracks took place from 1897 to 1903, to an architectural design by Sir Henry Pilkington RE. Their magnificence and scale were not matched by any other barracks at Chatham. Built to contain 3,500 sailors, the site chosen was between the new dockyard extension and the rising ground on which the Chatham Lines and Brompton barracks stood. This land was that used for the first siege warfare training in the 1830s and then for the convict prison associated with the dockyard extension (*see* Fig 11.3). That prison was now

Fig 14.10
The wardroom of the naval barracks of HMS Pembroke.
(Author)

completely demolished, making it one of the shortest-lived major government buildings at Chatham. These barracks also necessitated the demolition and rebuilding of the factory that manufactured Brennan torpedoes,[11] the rebuilding in a new location of the soldier's bathing pond and the alteration of the railway connection to the dockyard.

HMS *Pembroke* was divided into upper and lower parts. The upper part contained six accommodation blocks for the ratings and the officers' wardroom. The lower part, reached down a monumental flight of stairs, had a major parade ground and service buildings such as the dining rooms, gymnasium, swimming pool and a massive covered drill hall. The chapel, dedicated to St George, and the commodore's house completed the barrack buildings.[12] These buildings are nearly all extant and today form the campus of the universities at Medway. The significance of their construction for the Chatham fortifications lies in the way in which they expanded to take in the northern end of the Lower Lines and the St Mary's hornwork in particular. The dockyard extension had left these fortifications intact, but in the late 19th century the completion of the Chatham Ring Forts meant that the older defensive line could be permanently compromised.

Proof that the Lower Lines would not be required in future as a defence was provided by the navy's decision *c*1900 to construct a substantial house (since demolished) for the admiral on a plateau created in front of the 1803 ditch and rampart. The entire southern half of the couvre porte hornwork was also excavated after 1898 to form a reservoir for storing brown water for sluicing and firefighting purposes for the new naval barracks.[13] This further compromised the integrity of the early 19th-century fortifications.

Investment in major shore facilities for its Chatham division by the navy included the new Royal Navy Hospital that opened in 1905, replacing Melville Hospital. It stood on land adjoining the south-east corner of the Great Lines and could hold 588 patients in separate general and infectious groups of wards, while 228 staff were housed in a curving avenue of quarters for sick berth attendants and substantial houses for senior officers. The naval hospital is today the Medway Maritime Hospital, but very few of the original buildings survive.[14]

Royal Engineers training

In contrast to the navy, the army spent comparatively little on new facilities at Chatham in the period 1890–1914. The most impressive new building was the electrical school, completed in 1906 at a cost of £43,405, which now houses the Royal Engineers Museum. Also known as the Ravelin building, this structure highlighted the enhanced importance to the engineers of electrical skills for lighting, telegraphy and detonation of explosives. This included

Fig 14.12
The Ravelin building, now
the Royal Engineers
Museum.
(Medway Council)

experimental searchlights from the 1890s, evidence for which was found when the Lower Lines park was being created. Constructed to the design of Major E C S Moore RE, the Ravelin building was the first building of the Royal Engineers with a reinforced concrete structure. The domed corner turrets were intended to accommodate searchlights used in training.

Between 1899 and 1902 the South African or Boer War provided a foretaste of the demands that the great conflicts of the 20th century would place on the Royal Engineers. Armed with modern weapons mainly purchased from Germany, the Boers fought an irregular war, and only by mass mobilisation of the might of the British army was it eventually possible to overcome them. The syllabus of the School of Military Engineering was adjusted to speed up the provision of trained men. Eight thousand Royal Engineers served in the conflict, and in addition to fighting, they provided the services of bridging, telegraphy, ballooning, searchlights, railways, photography and steam traction. A Royal Commission in 1903 examined the performance of the British forces in South Africa and criticised every aspect of the army. It started a process of further reform and change, influencing how 20th-century wars would be fought.

The Russo-Japanese War of 1904–5 fought in Manchuria and Korea was observed by many western nations and provided a precursor to what World War I would mean. It involved mass infantry attacks against well-defended fortified positions containing machine guns. It also saw the extensive use of mining techniques by the Japanese against the Russian-held concrete forts of Port Arthur (Manchuria). The realisation by the British army that the next major conflict was likely to require traditional siege tactics, but under the conditions of modern warfare, lay behind the major siege exercises held at Chatham using the ring forts in 1907.

Royal Engineers in World War I

Despite the experience of wars in the previous decades, the army was unready for the challenges of World War I. The Corps of Royal Engineers had to be increased massively in numbers and became ever more technically diverse, with the formation of many different specialist units. In 1914 the Corps numbered 25,000 officers and men in 24 types of 205 different units. Royal Engineers went to France with the British Expeditionary Force in 1914, and the call went out for volunteers to swell the ranks. The response was almost overwhelming for the depot at Chatham. In the first 6 weeks of the war, 15,000 men answered Kitchener's call for a new army by volunteering for the Royal Engineers, and at its peak 800 men were arriving at Chatham every day. By 1918 the strength of the Royal Engineers had expanded to 230,000 officers and men, made up of 59 types of 1,832 units. Chatham as the home of the Royal Engineers played a major role in the expansion of the Corps. Along with the depot at Aldershot, it was also responsible for the training of new soldiers, but could not meet all of the demands, and so wartime training depots were also established at Newark in Nottinghamshire and Deganwy in Wales.

In October 1914 a royal review of over 12,000 men took place on the Great Lines. Only by the use of billeting in Brompton and Chatham and by resorting to huge tented camps could the volunteers be housed. At any one time Chatham had 100–150 officers and 2,500–3,500 sappers receiving initial training. The officers received 5 months training in drill, musketry and field engineering and the non-commissioned men 12 weeks of basic training (5 weeks of drill, 1 week of musketry and 6 weeks of field engineering).

The war on the western front was in stalemate by November 1914, with the opposing armies taking up increasingly complex trenched positions. Trench warfare was not the form of war for which the British had most prepared, but in the siege-like conditions, underground warfare based on the traditional techniques of mining was under consideration as a way of breaking the stalemate. The Germans were the first to exploit mines on a large scale, and from late 1914 British preparations were under way to form specialist mining troops within the Royal Engineers.

Fig 14.13
Royal Engineer recruits in the Great Lines in 1914. (Medway Archives)

The formation of RE Tunnelling Companies in February 1915 was largely the responsibility of John Norton Griffiths MP, a civil engineer who specialised in major sewer projects constructed by tunnelling. Lord Kitchener as a Royal Engineer appreciated the value of Griffiths's proposal to recruit specialist tunnellers. Given the rank of major in the Royal Engineers, Griffiths selected his first recruits from the civilian contractors engaged on sewer work at Manchester. On 18 February 1915 the first tunnellers arrived at Chatham to receive their uniforms, and the next week they were at work in France. By 1918 the number of Royal Engineers employed in tunnelling companies had increased to many thousands.[15] It is not possible to provide here a detailed description of their activities, but the 19 gigantic mines laid by them in June 1917 as part of the offensive to shatter the German front line at the Messines Ridge symbolise the immense contribution they made.[16]

Fig 14.14
An outdoor lecture to World War I sappers on the Chatham Lines. (Royal Engineers Museum, Library and Archives)

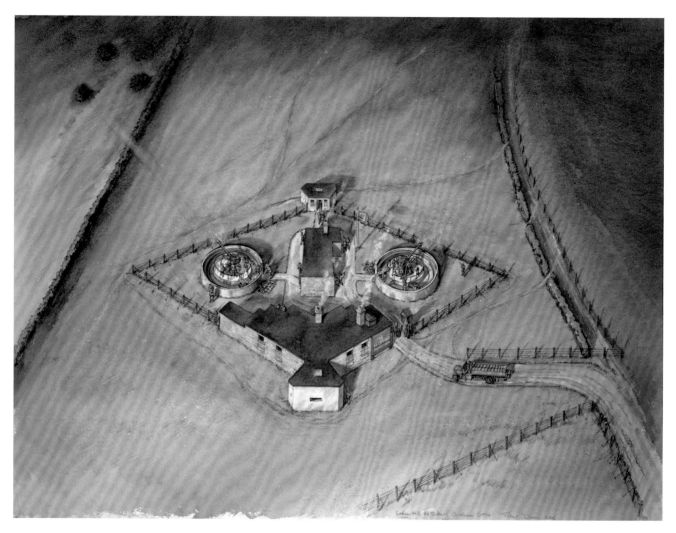

Fig 14.15
*An artist's reconstruction of
the First World War AA site
at Lodge Hill.*
*(© English Heritage
N060479)*

The techniques employed on the western front differed little from the methods that had been taught at Chatham as part of the 19th-century siege exercises.[17] The physical surviving evidence of wooden-lined narrow galleries is common to both. It is almost impossible to describe the nerve-racking and extremely dangerous nature of this aspect of trench warfare. The actual training of tunnellers took place behind the front on the Continent, and there are as yet no known remains of mine tunnels at Chatham for the 1914–18 period.

Tunnelling was not the only form of underground works for which the Royal Engineers were responsible in World War I. They built many of the trench systems, and as it became necessary to seek shelter from artillery barrage by going ever deeper underground, they built the major dugouts and subways that enabled the army to stay safely at the front and to move around. One example of this kind of large dugout, based on a grid of tunnels and chambers,

existed in the fieldwork practice ground at Chatham. It was removed by the recent construction of Mid Kent College and could not be safely explored in detail. It may have been of First World War date, but was more probably the product of interwar-period training based on experience of the western front.

The demands placed on the Royal Engineers by the First World War were very varied and included searchlights, gas attack, survey and camouflage. Most of all they were required to carry out major construction projects to keep the army capable of fighting. This meant road and rail communication to supply the troops, and the construction of major army camps behind the front to house them. The Nissen hut designed by Major Peter Nissen RE was one response to the need for accommodation.

Army camps were also required across Britain for troops undergoing training and as hospitals, and huge numbers of huts were built for this purpose, based on designs by Major

B H O Armstrong RE. The available barracks at Chatham and the use of the older forts could not keep pace with the increased need for housing men, and so huts and tents were used on open land around the Chatham Lines. A major fire in 1916 at the Brompton barracks (North Square) made the shortage of space more severe, and so hutments were also erected on the Great Lines.[18]

World War I defences

World War I initiated a new phase in warfare, because the late 19th-century experiments with ballooning gave rise to both airships and airplanes for use in aerial bombardment. From this war onwards, the conflict overseas was brought to the home front, and civilians would find themselves victims of the fighting. This required action to cope with air attacks, taking the form of passive defence in the shape of shelters and active defence through anti-aircraft measures. The Chatham garrison has very early examples of both. In September 1917 four Gotha bombers flew from Belgium to bomb the dockyards of Kent. At Chatham the lights were not extinguished, and the German airmen found several targets within the town and at Brompton. The worst impact was from a single bomb that fell on the Drill Hall of the naval barracks at HMS *Pembroke*, which was in use as overflow sleeping accommodation. There were 136 sailors killed and 90 seriously injured, most as a result of the glass used in the drill hall roof.

As early as 1912 in Britain, air attack against obvious targets such as the major static facilities of dockyards and ordnance depots had been feared. Searchlights and anti-aircraft (AA) guns were part of the response, and Chatham had some of the earliest-known examples. An AA gun emplacement was added to the roof of the casemates at St Mary's barracks (since demolished),[19] and by 1914 the ridge above the ordnance depot at Lodge Hill received two similar gun emplacements and blockhouses in an arrangement that can claim to be the world's oldest surviving purpose-built anti-aircraft site (Figs 14.15 and 14.16). At the same time, another AA gun emplacement site was created at Beacon Hill near Upnor, where the blockhouse is still visible, but not the gun emplacements.

Fig 14.16
An artist's reconstruction of the AA site Lodge Hill as it fires at a German zeppelin. (© English Heritage N060478)

Evidence for large-scale air-raid shelters is not known at Chatham for World War I, but there are single-man concrete shelters of a design that appears to be peculiar to this part of Kent. Examples are known at the Bull Nose of the Victorian dockyard, the Royal Navy Hospital, the Chattenden magazine enclosure and the Lodge Hill and Upnor ordnance depots. At ordnance sites where the late 19th-century magazines were of lightweight construction and not traversed, it is easy to understand why a sentry would require such shelter should the site come under air attack.

The fighting in Europe during World War I is indelibly associated with the horrors of trench warfare, but military planning did not assume that invasion of Britain was impossible should the enemy break through. Preparations were made to repulse any invasion, much of which consisted of coastal artillery and minefields. The introduction of the submarine demonstrated that surface naval strength was no guarantee of invincibility, and there remained a role for fixed land defences around vulnerable military installations, including Chatham. Known as 'land fronts', they can be seen as a precursor of the stop lines of World War II and were based not on major forts but on the late 19th-century thinking of improvised field defences using trenches and barbed wire entanglements. There is evidence from Chatham of several layers of trench-and-wire-based defences.

It is not clear whether the Chatham Lines were pressed back into service during World War I, but map and survey evidence shows that secure perimeters were created around places such as the ordnance depots and between the fixed forts of the Chatham ring. Even these were not the outermost layer of defence for the dockyard. The Chatham Land Front was constructed as a stop line between the Swale and the land to the north of Maidstone at Detling Hill. In the event of an invasion this is where the attack was designed to be halted. Coastal guns of forts in places such as the Isle of Grain could turn their fire inland to support troops in the stop line, and additional gun fasts for large guns were provided at several locations behind the line, to be occupied in the event of danger.

Some concrete pillboxes from the stop line survive, though much of the stop line consisted of less solid features such as earth and timber systems of trenches, dugouts and machine gun emplacements protected by barbed wire. Physical evidence of the stop line is known, but it has not been systematically surveyed. The best evidence comes from an album of photographs in the Royal Engineers library. These images include a very large dugout built in front of Prince Edward's bastion (Fig 14.18) and entered from the ditch of the Chatham Lines. Described as capable of holding 3,000 men, it was presumably constructed to accommodate the forces who would have moved forward to man the Chatham Land Front.[20]

15

World War II to the present day

The Royal Engineer depot at Chatham had a major role in the demobilisation of troops as they returned home from the First World War. The subsequent inter-war years were not a period of major investment at Chatham. In 1928 the infantry barracks were renamed the Kitchener barracks to commemorate Lord Kitchener, who was a former Royal Engineer and until his death in 1916 the commander of British forces.[1] At these barracks a substantial part of the accommodation blocks, first built in 1757 and adapted during the reform of barracks over a century later, were now demolished and replaced by the major blocks that exist today.[2] Near Brompton barracks, the 1930s saw the site of the magazine in the 1806 ravelin rebuilt as naval barracks and a technical school, HMS *Collingwood*, also known as the Collingwood triangle because it followed the shape of the ravelin.[3]

World War II defences

In the late 1930s, when it became clear that renewed European warfare was unavoidable, there was increased activity to prepare Chatham for its expected role. Air attack had been demonstrated as a major new threat to military and civilian targets, including the possible use of gas. This created a new and massive response by driving people underground. Much of the new construction at Chatham relating to World War II cannot be easily seen as it consisted of substantial buried works. The naval barracks of HMS *Pembroke* were provided with large shelter tunnels excavated in the high ground to the rear.[4] At Amherst Hill, the Kitchener barracks were served by a group of air-raid shelters, and single examples were also constructed on the Inner Lines. A tunnel complex was built below the parade ground of the barracks that connected in one direction with the Melville hospital and in the other with the Royal Marines

barracks. An underground operating theatre was designed in 1939 for the naval hospital.[5] As the ordnance depots were particularly vulnerable to bombing, Chattenden, Lodge Hill and Upnor were equipped with a large number of surface air-raid shelters for their workforce.

In the dockyard, air-raid shelters and an underground telephone exchange were provided. Protected accommodation in the form of command bunkers was ordered at each of the four main naval ports. At Chatham, protected accommodation was constructed for the Nore command in what had been the former Royal Engineers field practice ground in front of the ditch of the Lower Lines. A complex was built by private contractors at a depth of 80–100ft using steel mine hoops. It was designed to hold 60 officers and 90 other ranks so that the work of the command could be continued, even if bombing was taking place. Two wooden radio masts were for communication, though the main communication centre for the Nore was the wireless station at Beacon Hill near Upnor. At the core of the command bunker was the plotting room, in which activity throughout the area of the Nore command could be monitored by staff composed mainly of WRENs.[6] This naval command was established in 1752 and was based around Chatham and Sheerness, taking its name from the naval anchorage at the mouth of the Medway. Until 1961 it was responsible for activity in most of the southern North Sea, taking in Chatham, Sheerness, London, Harwich and the Humber.

One feature of Chatham during the Second World War was the proliferation of temporary hutted camps to increase the capacity of the military establishments. Huts were squeezed in wherever it was possible to do so. Wartime air photographs show huts at St Mary's barracks and Nissen huts on the parade ground of the Kitchener barracks. The Medway Road camp was a large collection of huts used primarily by

Fig 15.1
The plotting table of the
Nore command bunker,
which was constructed on
the site of the Lower Lines.
(Imperial War Museum
A28255)

staff who worked in the underground Nore command centre. Physical remains still survive of foundation walls and an unusual double-level air-raid shelter.

During the war, the School of Military Engineering did not remain at Chatham, but relocated to Ripon, North Yorkshire, turning over the regimental home for use by the Royal Navy. The establishment of the Corps rose from 89,301 in 1939 to 280,632 in 1945, and the Royal Engineers had to provide even more specialised skills, making a substantial contribution to the achievements of the western allies. The First World War had demonstrated that the tank was a means of breaking the stalemate of trench warfare, and their use by the German army for blitzkrieg tactics highlighted how Britain would need to be defended against invasion. After the retreat from Dunkirk in 1940, the Royal Engineers played a major role in forming emergency anti-invasion defences as stop lines. Some of this work was for the defence of Chatham as a strategically vital combination of dockyard, garrison and ordnance sites.

As in previous wars, the strategic route inland from the coast to London was of concern. If invasion took place, the bridge over the Medway at Rochester would need to be secured for a counterattack or destroyed to prevent an enemy advance. Enemy bombing of the bridge

was thought likely to render it unusable, and so in a move reminiscent of the communication bridge of 1803, a secondary relief bridge was built at Wouldham, first as a pontoon-based structure and then as a fixed bridge.

Faced with the fear of imminent invasion, the existing defences at Chatham that had been built over 200 years were pressed back into service. Fort Luton acted as a coordination centre for anti-aircraft measures, and Fort Bridgewood had a covert function as a special signal station by MI5 for gathering radio intelligence to pass to Bletchley Park. The Chatham Lines formed a ready-made deep anti-tank ditch and were used as an inner defence line. At Fort Pitt the old fort was integrated with anti-tank ditches dug across the hillside. A military 'Chatham Garrison Plan to Defeat Invasion' of 1940, with updates for 1941 and 1942, exists in the Medway Archives, providing detail of how the defences were intended to be used.[7] The war diary of the 179 RE Tunnelling Company also demonstrates their role in putting the Chatham Lines back into a 'state of defence' in September 1940.[8]

General Sir Charles Tolver Paget was the officer responsible for south-eastern defences, including Chatham, and in March 1941 he reported on his lack of resources, saying that he had 2,500 Royal Navy or Royal Marines personnel, 1,170 army men who were mostly undergoing training and 1,600 members of the Home Guard. These defenders had few weapons at their disposal – 162 automatic guns, 6 6-pounder guns, 21 anti-tank rifles and 3 flame throwers.[9] After visiting Chatham, Paget reported in July that it was still inadequately defended and that he was fearful of a paratroop invasion of the Isle of Grain. He was informed that No. 5 Commando would move to Chatham from Falmouth to bolster its defence in the event of an invasion.

The anti-invasion defences at the Chatham Lines demonstrate very clearly the improvised nature of such works using scarce resources at the time when invasion was first thought probable, followed by more considered works as Britain recovered in its ability to resist. Being positioned in front of the ditch of the Lower Lines, the Nore command bunker with its associated sites presented a defensive challenge, as it had to be defended by its own secure perimeter. During recent works to construct Mid Kent College, remains of this secure perimeter were identified, comprising a V-section ditch revetted with corrugated iron sheets held in place by verticals made of cut-up rail track. The line of this anti-tank obstacle was continued by pyramidal concrete blocks known as dragon's teeth,

Fig 15.2
One of the spigot mortar positions on the Chatham Lines.
(© English Heritage)

some of which survive near Medway Road.[10]

On the Lower Lines itself, the rampart was armed by the addition of two 12-pounder naval deck guns, which were possibly the only guns then available. These formed two separate emplacements, and the southern example still has lockers salvaged from ships set into the brick of the older firestep in order to store ammunition for immediate use. Both gun positions had a dugout, formed out of railway sleepers and corrugated sheeting, set in the earth of the rampart for the shelter of the gun crews. Improvised defences are still visible in other parts of the Chatham Lines. At Sallyport Gardens there is a pillbox that was added to the rampart to cover the road through the defences.

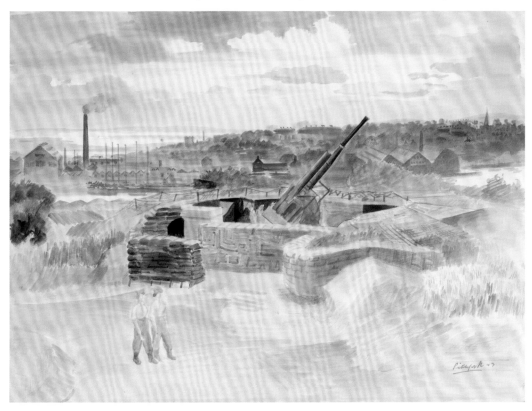

Fig 15.3
One of the 1939–45 AA sites on Tower Hill, with the dockyard in the background, depicted in 'An AA battery' by the war artist Roland Vivian Pitchforth RA.
(Imperial War Museum Art LD 3411)

This had an unconventional gun mounting, which, according to the defence plan in the Medway archives, was possibly for a 3-pounder gun. Another such gun was sited at the Gymnasium to cover that road.

The most common type of World War II defensive gun positions on the Chatham Lines was the spigot mortar position (Fig 15.2), also known as the Blacker Bombard. Named after its inventor, Lieutenant Colonel Stewart Blacker, this weapon was peculiar because it did not have a barrel like a conventional mortar, but instead relied on a spigot or pin attached to a base plate, often mounted on a concrete pedestal. The mortar bomb had an explosive propellant charge that was detonated by engaging with the spigot. This weapon was much used by the Home Guard and fired a finned bomb a distance of 75–200 yards. Several examples survive at Chatham, and detailed earthwork survey of parts of the rampart has also suggested the presence of smaller weapons pits. The 18th-century defended gateway to the couvre porte was blocked by a wedge-shaped concrete block to prevent its use by tanks. A gun emplacement was added to Prince William's battery at Fort Amherst, and the tunnel complex there provided a ready-made location for the civil defence headquarters.[11]

Anti-aircraft guns were also placed on the higher ground around the Medway (Fig 15.3), and there were some anti-aircraft towers in the dockyard itself. The defences went beyond protecting the dockyard. At Lodge Hill, for example, part of the national stop line known as the GHQ Line abutted the ordnance depot and consisted of an anti-tank ditch with associated concrete pillboxes. Additional pillboxes were built to provide a perimeter defence to the magazines and ordnance factory. During the war, Chatham was not subject to the heavy bombing that did so much damage to the dockyards of Devonport (Plymouth) and Portsmouth. The reason for this is unclear, given Chatham's proximity to London. Some damage and indeed loss of life were inevitable, but the dockyard and its associated sites emerged from the war substantially unscathed.[12]

Beyond World War II

As Britain reduced the size of her army and navy and retreated from her colonies, Chatham could not remain unscathed in the post-war, post-imperial situation. The Gunwharf at Chatham, the Royal Marines barracks, Melville hospital and St Mary's barracks were all early casualties and have been almost entirely demolished, with little or no surviving visible evidence of their once great size or even their very existence.

The site of the Kitchener barracks has remained in military use, but almost all the historic buildings have been replaced, driven by a further adjustment in how the army sought to accommodate its married soldiers. By 1939 some married quarters for officers had been built as pairs of semi-detached houses at the sallyport of Chatham Lines and near St Mary's barracks. In the post-war period this movement gained momentum and was applied to all ranks. It was considered inappropriate to house army families in the single rooms of the married quarters that had first been built as part of the 19th-century barracks reform. As a result, none of those purpose-built married quarter blocks survive today. Army housing expanded over parts of the Great Lines that had until then been considered sacrosanct as open ground, and in addition much land within the Chatham Lines was similarly occupied.

The major blow to the military presence at Chatham came in 1984 with the decision to close the dockyard. The historic core of the site has been preserved and regenerated by a trust established for this purpose. The naval barracks have found a new use as university buildings, and the Victorian dockyard has been taken forward as a regeneration area, which has kept the dockyard infrastructure of the three basins, but only a few of the historic buildings. At the time of writing the Chatham Lines are in the course of conservation as a major public open space as part of Medway Council's regeneration agenda. Fort Amherst has been saved by a trust devoted to its future.

Fort Pitt suffered significant demolition in the later 20th century, when it contained three educational establishments. Fort Clarence retains its main gun tower, which has been converted to flats. The ordnance sites at Chattenden, Lodge Hill and Upnor are all surplus to military requirements, and it is anticipated that they will form the basis of major new development on the west bank of the Medway. Upnor Castle has found a secure future in state guardianship. The only site of any great size that currently remains in military use is the Royal School of Military Engineering (*see* Chapter 16), based around the Brompton barracks. This

continues as the home of the Corps of Royal Engineers and is therefore the last remaining link to Chatham's proud service to the nation as a major dockyard and garrison town.

In memory

The Royal School of Military Engineering maintains Chatham's vital military role to the present day, while the heritage sites and memorials are a reminder of the valuable work and sacrifice of thousands of men and women. Men were often sent to conflicts overseas with exuberant fanfare, as reflected in one description, by the Royal Engineer Major-General Robert Murdoch Smith. He watched trained sappers leaving Chatham for the Crimea in March 1856:

Three hundred men and eight officers left for the Crimea on Tuesday morning ... The parade was

before 5 in the morning, when of course it was quite dark. The scene was quite striking. All the men in heavy marching order and with their haversacks and calerbashes as well. After the roll was called and inspections made, when the word Quick March was given, the band struck up the Grenadiers and the men gave quite a deafening huzza. All the way down the men's wives who were left were continually rushing into the ranks to bid their husbands good bye, comrades were shaking hands and whenever we passed a group of people another shout was raised all along the column. The band went with them to Southampton to play them through London.[13]

As in all wars, many of them would of course never make it home. In earlier conflicts, soldiers who died were regarded as anonymous, not requiring individual commemoration, but from the mid-19th century those who lost their lives began to be remembered by various memorials at Chatham. On the east side of the parade

Fig 15.4
Chatham in 1948 showing the now demolished major structures of Melville hospital, the 18th-century blocks at Kitchener barracks, the Ordnance hospital, the married quarters at Fort Amherst, the Royal Marines barracks and the Grand Storehouse and Carriage sheds at Gunwharf.
(© English Heritage TQ7568/3 04/02/1948)

Fig 15.5
Postcard of the Crimean
War memorial arch.
(Ben Levick)

Fig 15.6
The Crimean-period
monument at Fort Pitt
cemetery.
(Author)

and were buried in the cemetery. The monument is topped with a mortar, gun barrel and entrenching tools, appropriate to the work of ordnance troops.[14]

Another memorial is a bronze statue of General Charles Gordon, mounted on a camel, which was designed by Onslow Ford ARA and erected in front of the Institute in 1890.[15] The South African War memorial arch commemorating those Royal Engineers killed in the Boer War was unveiled on 26 July 1905, and some of the activities of the Royal Engineers in that conflict are recorded on it. During this war, 420 officers and men of the Corps lost their lives.

Memorials were next erected for those who died in the First World War. On 19 July 1922 the Royal Engineer war memorial in the shape of an obelisk was dedicated between the two existing memorial arches to commemorate the 19,800 Royal Engineers who had lost their lives. There is a second monument to the dead from the First World War in the Fort Pitt cemetery, when the hospital was again used to treat the injured from the front, not all of whom survived. The most prominent memorial at Chatham is the naval war memorial erected on the Great Lines, and similar monuments were also erected at the other two manning ports, Portsmouth and Devonport, as a means of recognising the naval war dead, many of whom had no known grave. The memorial at Chatham, designed by Sir Robert Lorimer, was unveiled in 1922. It takes the form of a 100-foot high Portland stone column topped by a large copper ball supported by four figures representing the four winds. It displays the names of the 8,515 naval dead of Chatham-based ships from the First World War.

A simple inscription added to the obelisk at the Brompton barracks after the Second World War records the 10,800 Royal Engineers who were killed in that conflict, as it was not thought appropriate to erect a further monument. The naval war dead from Chatham-based ships numbered 10,098, and their names were inscribed on screen walls and end pavilions, to a design by Sir Edward Maufe, that were added to the existing naval memorial.

Those lucky enough to survive warfare were often feted on their return, with much celebration, as in December 1846, when victorious troops arrived home from India:

RETURN OF THE 31ST. — The head-quarters of this gallant regiment arrived at Gravesend on the 4th, in the *Madagascar*, having sailed from Calcutta in

square at the Brompton barracks, the Crimea memorial arch was erected to a design by Matthew Digby Wyatt. The foundation stone was laid on 1 March 1860, and it recorded the names of the 23 Royal Engineers and 161 Royal Sappers and Miners who died in that conflict. This memorial arch started a tradition of monuments that form an alignment centred on the Royal Engineers Institute.

To the north of Fort Pitt is a military cemetery that was associated with the hospital there, and it contains a monument to the soldiers who were invalided back to Chatham in the period 1854–8, victims of the Crimean War, the Indian mutiny and the Persian, Mughal and Opium wars. These invalids did not recover but died

Fig 15.7 (far left)
The unveiling of the South
African war memorial in
1905.
(Royal Engineers Museum,
Library and Archives)

Fig 15.8 (left)
The Chatham naval war
memorial to the dead of
1914–18.
(Ben Levick)

August last. On the passage they lost four men and one officer. Its strength consists of 19 sergeants, 7 drummers, 15 corporals, and 174 rank and file, with 21 women, and 30 children ... On the evening of the 6th they marched to Chatham. On their arrival at the Rochester terminus, the band struck up 'God save the Queen.' They were loudly greeted as they went through the streets by thousands of spectators, who vociferously cheered the return of these gallant soldiers. This regiment ... was present throughout the Punjub campaign, and bears testimony of its gallant conduct in trophies taken from the enemy. It brings home four flags; one taken at Ferozeshah, one at Aliwal, and two at Sobraon; these were landed amid tremendous cheers. The colours of the regiment are torn to shreds by the shower of grape-shot. Ten officers fell in the different engagements; fifteen were wounded, and six were present in all the battles unhurt.[16]

Major-General Robert Murdoch Smith described a similarly joyful reception over a decade later, when Royal Engineer survivors came home from the Crimean War:

We had a grand day today in the barracks on the occasion of the return of the companies of Sappers from the Crimea. We all paraded in full dress and were drawn up in line at open order to receive them. Our band met them at the station and marched them up to Auld Lang Syne, See the Conquering Hero Comes and Home Sweet Home. The streets were decorated with flags, mottoes etc and the populace cheered the men most lustily. When they came in to the square they formed in line the same as we and facing us. One can't imagine a nobler sight than they presented. They were all great, broad, burly fellows; for alas their companions less sturdy than themselves had fallen victims to the hardships they had to undergo. When they had formed we gave General salute Present arms and the band played God Save the Queen. They then returned the compliment in a similar way. When they had done so we gave them three times three and loud as our cheer of 1,000 men

was, when their commander Major Nicholson, gave the word Crimean Sappers three cheers we were thrown quite into the shade by the thundering cheers they gave in reply. It was splendid to see them with their weather beaten faces and great shaggy beards and breasts covered with medals.[17]

The Royal Engineers lost 23 officers and had 161 sappers and miners killed in the Crimean

Fig 15.9
Additions to the naval war
memorial for the 1939–45
conflict.
(Ben Levick)

War. The Victoria Cross was first awarded in that war, and eight of these medals were won by Royal Engineers.

A few years later, one commentator described the event when Lord Robert Napier was entertained at the Royal Engineers mess at the Brompton barracks, upon his return from the Abyssinian campaign in Africa (1867–8):

Here were gathered together, red-coated records of almost every English battle of the present century. Veterans of the Peninsula and of Waterloo; the less mature soldiers of Sobraon, Chillianwalla, and Meeane; a fresher group still representing those who laid out the batteries at Sebastopol; and here too were the sharers of the siege of Delhi and other operations of the Indian Mutiny campaign; along with engineers who had fought in China, New Zealand, and at the Cape.[18]

The officers present at this gathering had a combined military service that summed up the worldwide reach of the Corps of Royal Engineers in the first half of the 19th century. This was a poignant scene that contained so much history, tradition and bravery relating to Chatham. Military traditions remain strong today, and they continue to resonate down the years through the generations of men and women who have provided service to the nation. Few if any places can match the traditions and history of the Royal Engineers at Chatham as discussed in this book.

Fig 15.10
The Royal Engineers
memorials by night.
(Holdfast Training Services
Ltd)

16

21st-Century Royal Engineers and the Royal School of Military Engineering

In 1962, in recognition of the 150th anniversary of its foundation, the School of Military Engineering was renamed the Royal School of Military Engineering (RSME). As a result, it received substantial new teaching facilities, including the large workshop classrooms still in use today. After the closure of the ordnance sites at Lodge Hill, the School made use of this ground for outdoor training, such as construction or bridging, much like the Lower Lines had been used in the 19th century. Training facilities were built here so that new skills could be learned that were appropriate to the counter-insurgency activities dominating post-war conflicts.

The Royal School of Military Engineering is today a centre of excellence for military engineering, and in this it continues a 200-year-old tradition. Remaining at the cutting edge of technology and ensuring that the British army is equipped and supported by its Engineers for the varied tasks that it is today called on to perform are the central functions of the Royal Engineers.

Two hundred years after its foundation, the Royal School of Military Engineering at Chatham remains the regimental home of the Corps of Royal Engineers and one of the principal locations for military engineer training. The RSME is also responsible for the training of combat or battlefield engineering at Minley in Surrey, the Defence EOD, Munitions and Search School based at Chatham (Bicester from mid-2012) and Kineton and the Defence Animal Centre at Melton Mowbray in Leicestershire. The traditions for military training established in 1812 are ongoing. Today the RSME Chatham is the largest residential construction college in Europe and, between the RSME's Chatham and Minley sites, currently runs 427 courses per year, of 142 varying types, delivering over 256,882 training days to 8,758 trainees.

Fig 16.1
Present-day Royal Engineers at Brompton barracks demonstrate the wide range of tasks they are called on to perform. This can be compared with Fig 12.1, which shows the technology in existence some 140 years earlier.
(Holdfast Training Services Ltd)

In partnership with Holdfast Training Services Ltd, the RSME looks to lead military engineering science and its real-world application with an undisputed worldwide reputation. Holdfast Training Services Ltd is the private sector partner to the RSME. A 30-year agreement known as a Public Private Partnership (PPP) was entered into in 2008, by which Holdfast will provide the RSME with training and training support services, including a major investment in new buildings and infrastructure. Today the RSME sites at Chatham are undergoing major change and a degree of modernisation not seen since the post-Crimean period, that marked the very first construction of purpose-built educational facilities.

One of the early Holdfast projects is the construction of new accommodation for junior ranks at Minley and Brompton barracks,

Fig 16.2
The civilian staff of Holdfast now work alongside the Royal Engineers in a Public Private Partnership. Here some Holdfast staff pose with their vehicles at Brompton barracks.
(Holdfast Training Services Ltd)

Fig 16.3
A Holdfast chef supervises
meal times in a present-day
Junior Ranks' Mess.
(Holdfast Training Services
Ltd)

Chatham. The living conditions of serving soldiers are a theme running through this book, and the story of improvement continues so that the modern-day soldier is well cared for. The private en-suite bedrooms being created would be unrecognisable to the early occupants of the overcrowded and basic barracks. Soldiers are today provided with food and facilities that are in stark contrast to the starvation wages of the 18th and early 19th centuries and the cooking of food by soldiers' wives for a whole barrack room on a single fire.

Despite the complexity of the technological world in which the modern-day sapper operates, there is a great deal that is in common with the traditional role of the Corps. First and foremost the sapper is a trained soldier and receives the same basic infantry training as other branches of the army. This initial training no longer takes place at Chatham, but is instead mainly conducted by the Army Training Regiment (Bassingbourn) in Cambridgeshire. Training in battlefield engineering next takes place at Minley before a sapper is sent to Chatham to learn a trade. Once qualified in their trades, sappers are posted to their first unit.

Charles William Pasley, the founder of the RSME, stressed the importance of the engineers going through the same drill as other soldiers, but his 1812 school focused on the specialist role of combat engineering. This remains the generic term given to all military engineering techniques and procedures used primarily but not exclusively on the modern-day battlefield by the Royal Engineers. Combat engineering is the mainstay of what the Royal Engineers do in support of the rest of the army, be it the use of explosives to remove obstacles, clearance of minefields or the bridging of rivers and other barriers. Behind the front line the Royal Engineers retain their historic role for providing all forces with secure camps from which to operate and for improving communications by build-

ing or repairing roads and runways. They also carry out the essential task of bomb disposal. Dealing with the consequences of conflict and natural disasters is also part of the traditional skills of a sapper. The ability to provide clean water supplies and to repair electrical supplies and other infrastructure is of equal relevance to humanitarian tasks as to supporting the army in the field.

The motto of the Royal Engineers is 'ubique', meaning everywhere, and this reflects their ability to take their unique skills into every theatre of operation for the British Armed Services. As recent conflicts have demonstrated, wherever the British army is engaged there will be a sapper element, often in the front line and at the scene of action. To provide this support, the Royal Engineers include parachute- and commando-trained elements and also diving experts. In the 21st century the Corps motto continues to apply not just to anywhere in the world but to any set of circumstances.

For combat engineering, the training addresses a number of basic areas of expertise:

- Field engineering
- Water supply – production and distribution of safe drinking water
- Demolitions – use of explosives
- Force protection – construction of protective structures and defensive obstacles
- Watermanship – use of small military boats
- Mine warfare – location and clearance of explosive devices
- Bridging – overcoming wet and dry gap obstacles.

Whilst Royal Engineers from the past might not recognise some of the modern terminology, they would certainly identify with these tasks and the support of the army so that it can move, fight and survive.

Fig 16.4
An Armoured Vehicle Royal
Engineer or AVRE, known as
Trojan.
(© Crown Copyright. EH)

Helping the army to move (mobility) is today carried out using specialised armoured, amphibious and plant machines. The modern soldier moves about by armoured vehicle and not by route march or horse power. To keep pace with them and to open the way forward, the Royal Engineers use their own specialist tracked and armoured vehicles (known as Titan and Trojan and Terrier in future). These are sometimes still referred to as sappers, continuing the terminology of when traction engines were first introduced at Chatham and known as steam sappers. The current vehicles are fitted with an excavator arm and bulldozer blades, replacing the need for sappers to excavate trenches by hand. They do, however, still rely on traditional techniques to overcome obstacles, such as the laying of fascines to cross ditches.

Bridging, including when under fire, has always been a major skill of the Engineers. It can today be carried out using Titan as an armoured bridge-laying tank, without exposing the sappers to the high risks inherent in such techniques as the 'flying bridge', formerly practised at Chatham in the Lower Lines. Other types of bridging exist for the modern sapper so as to meet the varied circumstances that they face. Some of these are carried by and deployed from armoured transport, but others that are expected to remain in use for longer periods are moved to where they are required by more conventional vehicles. Modular systems are essential for flexibility. Trackway to create roads for immediate use is made up of aluminium or fabric materials and deployed with launching and recovery equipment so as to rapidly provide reinforced surfaces capable of taking armoured vehicles.

Training with the specialist armoured vehicles used by the modern sapper requires much more land than is now available at Chatham, and this training takes place largely at Bovington in Dorset. Likewise, bridging skills are today practised elsewhere. A Mabey and Johnson bridge of the type in use by the present-day army has been erected over the ditch of the Lower Lines as part of a new park (Fig 16.7), celebrating the many types of bridge once practised here.

The pontoon depot on the west bank of the Medway, known as Gundulph Pool, continues in use. Today the Royal Engineers retain the ability to cross major rivers by the modern-day version of a pontoon bridge. Such crossings

Fig 16.5
Sappers train with the modular elements of a modern bridging system. (Holdfast Training Services Ltd)

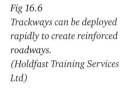

Fig 16.6
Trackways can be deployed rapidly to create reinforced roadways. (Holdfast Training Services Ltd)

Fig 16.7
A Mabey and Johnson bridge erected over the ditch at the Lower Lines. (Author)

make use of the M3 Rig as amphibious vehicles that drive into the water and then connect together to form a bridge or ferry raft. The largest rivers can be crossed using the modern equivalent of pontoons, which are delivered to the water from transport vehicles and then powered into position by their own inboard engines. Pontooning is no longer practised on the Medway, but waterman skills are taught. The Mark VI Assault Boat is taught to all Royal Engineers during their basic Combat Engineer Training at Minley. At Chatham more advanced watermanship skills are taught to selected individuals on the Mark II Combat Support Boat and the Mark III large Rigid Raider craft, both of which can frequently be seen powering about the River Medway.

The opposite of mobility training is counter mobility, to deny an enemy freedom of movement. This encompasses the use of engineering

Fig 16.8
Waterman skills are
acquired by the use of fast
craft on the River Medway.
(Holdfast Training Services
Ltd)

skills and equipment to lay minefields, dig anti-tank ditches and create obstacles. Such training is no longer carried out at Chatham, but an important part of the mobility and counter-mobility aspects of modern warfare is to overcome the limitations imposed by either deliberately laid explosive devices (land mines) or the presence of unexploded ordnance left by combat. The term Improvised Explosive Device or IED has entered the lexicon of modern English, particularly for their use in guerrilla or insurgency-style conflicts, such as in Afghanistan. The Royal Engineers train to deal with all types of explosive device in the specialist role known as Explosive Ordnance Disposal or EOD. They share the responsibility for tackling such threats with the staff of the Royal Logistics Corps. A bomb disposal engineer is also trained in the skills needed to clear places of threats, in order to keep their comrades safe, for example, or to enable civilian populations to get on with their lives safely. Counter terrorism is a significant part of this work, not only for dealing with *in situ* devices but for detecting illegal caches of arms and explosives. The EOD school is currently sited at Chattenden/Lodge Hill, where there is an important collection of ordnance of all types and periods, since the weapons of past conflicts remain lethal to the present day and continue to be found on land and at sea. There is also a training facility based around civilian housing, known as Cupar Street, where counter terrorism skills first gained in the context of the Northern Ireland troubles can be learned and adapted to meet present-day needs.

When not fighting or moving, the Armed Forces must be able to live in their theatre of operations, and this is often referred to as survivability. The Royal Logistic Corps has close affiliations with the Royal Engineers and is responsible for most of the supplies needed to keep the army working, moving and communicating. Many of these responsibilities were formerly carried out by the Royal Engineers and before them the Ordnance Board. Today the division of responsibilities means that the Royal Engineers are required to provide the infrastructure needed to support the army wherever it is and whatever it is doing. In recent conflicts, the army has operated from secure bases built by the Royal Engineers, which incorporate living accommodation, messing facilities, sanitary arrangements, hospitals, safe ordnance and fuel storage and logistical stores of everything a field force needs. These camps (Forward Operating Bases or FOBs) have much in common with those built by the Royal Engineers in earlier overseas deployments. Their secure perimeters are frequently formed from the present-day equivalent of a 19th-century gabion, using modular gabions of various materials. Because camps require more than security and accommodation, water supply including the drilling of wells continues to be taught as a specialist skill. To this must be added the mobile electrical supply and electrically powered equipment on which a modern force is reliant.

On completion of infantry and combat engineering training, the sapper recruit is today sent to the RSME at Chatham where they receive tradesman training in one of 18 trades. Most of these trade training regimes result in a civilian-recognised qualification that is essential for when a sapper's army career is over. The Royal Military artificers and then the Royal Sappers and Miners were the direct predecessors of the modern-day tradesman sappers. With increasing diversity of the tasks demanded of the engineer soldier and technological advances, it has become impossible for a single individual to be expert in everything, and specialism in a particular trade has been part of Royal Engineer training for well over a century.

Today many of the trades taught at the RSME Chatham would be familiar to 19th-century

Fig 16.9
A Holdfast instructor shares
his knowledge and skills
with two Sappers
undergoing trade training at
the Royal School of Military
Engineering.
(Holdfast Training Services
Ltd)

Fig 16.10
Traditional construction skills continue to be taught in the classrooms of the Royal School of Military Engineering. (Holdfast Training Services Ltd)

Fig 16.11 (far left)
Techniques such as arc welding are taught at the Royal School of Military Engineering. (Holdfast Training Services Ltd)

Fig 16.12 (left)
Undergoing instruction in the use of a mechanical excavator arm at the Royal School of Military Engineering. (Holdfast Training Services Ltd)

Royal Engineers. Carpentry, bricklaying, concreting and metalwork fabrication are all such examples, and by the end of the 19th century the role of electrician had been added to this list. Perhaps much less familiar would be the modern-day roles of heating, air conditioning and refrigeration fitters, required not just to ensure comfort in harsh climates for the troops, but also to ensure that sensitive highly technological equipment can function.

The 19th-century training establishment was proud of its role in training men capable of supporting the Royal Engineer officers as Clerks of Work for major construction programmes. This tradition continues with materials technicians, design draughtsmen and surveyors. A trade not taught in the past is that of geographic technician, which covers the use of IT and Geographical Information Systems for 3D terrain data on the modern battlefield, a natural extension of much older skills: satellite imagery is a progression from aerial reconnaissance and photography as pioneered by the use of tethered balloons, and map making is a skill that has always been central to Royal Engineer activities, as evidenced by the very name 'Ordnance Survey'.

The role of plant operator/mechanic has replaced digging by hand. Today earthmoving and construction vehicles are used, and the skills of Large Goods Vehicle (LGV) drivers are directly transferable to the civilian context. The Royal Engineers are also committed to ensuring that all ranks are able to maintain their continuous professional development throughout their army careers. Once they are trained in a trade, sappers receive army certificates as confirmation, but they are also encouraged to deepen their knowledge and experience by obtaining civilian qualifications. This includes completing apprenticeships through the Learning and Skills Council and obtaining National Vocational Qualifications (NVQs).

Officers and men have trained together at Chatham since the very earliest days of Pasley's school, and they continue to do so. Today 80 per cent of officer cadets are university graduates, and after an initial 48 weeks of officer training at the Royal Military Academy, Sandhurst, they spend a further 6 months at Chatham and Minley on a Troop Commanders Course. After this they are posted to their first units, but training is a process of continuous professional development. Studying for an MSc is encouraged, which is a step towards application for the status of Chartered Engineer, applicable to the civilian spheres of engineering. The Institution of Royal Engineers (InstRE) was founded in 1875 and continues with a Royal Charter to promote the science of military engineering and the military efficiency of the Corps. Membership is open to officers, warrant officers, senior and junior NCOs and exceptionally to sappers.

The Public Private Partnership entered into with Holdfast Training Service Ltd is applicable to all aspects of Royal Engineer training and support. Approximately 50 per cent of all training is delivered by about 200 Holdfast instructors. They concentrate on Royal Engineer training, but also deliver programmes to the wider army. In 2009 the Corps of Royal Engineers had a regular army establishment of some 9,700 individuals worldwide, and of these 4,000 were in receipt of some form of training via the RSME. This makes the Holdfast and Royal Engineer collaboration one of the largest training initiatives in existence, and Holdfast has responsibility for providing and maintaining the infrastructure needed for training. Much of the property at the RSME locations, and no more so than at Chatham, is old and in need of investment. A 7-year design-and-build programme of construction is under way to modernise the teaching and living facilities of the RSME in order that it can remain a centre for engineering excellence. This programme will respect the historically significant buildings at Chatham as described in this book, but is set to produce major changes across the military estate on a scale not seen since the 19th century.

When the next major anniversary of the RSME is celebrated, there will be at Chatham buildings from the early 21st century that our successors will undoubtedly value and see as part of the long story of the development of the School that started in 1812. It is a matter of pride for the present-day Royal Engineers and their partner organisations that the traditions of the Corps are sustained often by the use of the historic buildings built for and by their predecessors. Meticulous repair and clever modernisation have ensured that the oldest accommodation at Brompton barracks, built in 1804–6, remains the focus of the site, including the Officer's Mess, the Institution of Royal Engineers and the impressive range of commemorative monuments. The historic army gymnasium (*see* Fig 13.12) remains in use for its original purpose, as does the garrison chapel (*see* Fig 13.14).

The Ravelin building, constructed as an electrical school, is an early example of the need to create specialist buildings in which to teach the new skills required of the sappers in the late 19th and early 20th centuries. Today it houses

Fig 16.13
Preparations for a Corps Guest Night dinner in the Officers' Mess at Brompton barracks.
(Holdfast Training Services Ltd)

the Royal Engineers Museum, to which a visit will explain the history of the Corps and its contribution to events that have shaped the modern world. The museum makes a good starting point for visiting the world-class military heritage of the Medway area. The dockyard is a major site in its own right, but to be fully understood it must be seen alongside the fortifications that defended it and the barracks of the Chatham Garrison.

The Chatham Lines are undergoing conservation, with Fort Amherst as a major focus, for those wishing to see a restored fortress and experience its hidden underground parts. The Great Lines, the open land outside the fortifications, is being improved and managed as public open space. Its use for recreation and sports continues the purpose that it served for most of the 19th century. The Lower Lines as the 1803 extension to the fortifications and later the Royal Engineers fieldwork practice ground is now a public park.

At Chatham today it is the Royal Engineers who provide a living link to the tradition of military service to the nation that the Medway area can so proudly demonstrate over a period in excess of 400 years. There are other major military garrison and dockyard towns in Eng-

land, but for its completeness and significance Chatham is outstanding. As the Royal School of Military Engineering and its partner, Holdfast, strive to maintain world-class standards for the Royal Engineers, they can look back on their illustrious heritage and the fact that the school has always been at the leading edge of technology. There have been major changes in the 200 years of history of the Royal School of Military Engineering, and this tradition looks set to continue.

Fig 16.14
Brompton barracks have been conserved to keep them fit for purpose. Compare this photograph with Fig 9.3. (Holdfast Training Services Ltd)

Fig 16.15
Armoured vehicles used by the Royal Engineers on display outside the Ravelin building, which houses the Royal Engineers Museum. (Holdfast Training Services Ltd)

ENDNOTES

1 Unpublished archive reports by P Kendall 'Defending the Dockyard: the story of the Chatham Lines' (2005) and 'Historic Barracks in Medway' (2006).

Chapter 1

1 TNA MPH 1/247.
2 Morris 1983, section 5 no. 89.
3 Douglas 1793.
4 1633 map in the collection of the Duke of Northumberland, Alnwick Castle.
5 In 1738 the Navy Board had repaired the Land Wall as the principal route to the dockyard. They proposed to recover their costs by making the road a toll road, which brought forth protests from the local residents and business people (TNA ADM 106/897). The Land Wall is today represented by Globe Lane.
6 MacDougall 1999, 7.
7 In the 17th century high-ranking dockyard officials were likely to live in Rochester and travel by boat to their place of work.
8 Page (ed) 1926, 240.
9 Oppenheim 1914, 5.
10 Saunders 1985.
11 Adams 1990.
12 Scott and Hildesley 1920.
13 The 1633 Alnwick Castle map shows these sconces and also the chain, which it refers to as *the barricado* – a blocking of all but the central channel of the river by linked hulks. The cost in 1635 of this *barricado* was stated as £2,305 to supply a 28-ton chain with 11 anchors for the lighters and £624 per annum to maintain it.
14 *Calendar of State Papers, Domestic – (Edward, Mary and Elizabeth)*, vol. **260**, November 1596.
15 Saunders 1985.
16 BL Kings MS 43.
17 TNA ADM 214/48.
18 TNA ADM 214/48, records of land held by the Admiralty at Chatham.
19 Figures taken from Cruden (1843, 356). During construction of the late 19th-century dockyard basins in 1876, the substantial remains of an unnamed wooden warship were uncovered. This was identified as a casualty of the Dutch raid. It had been destroyed by fire and an explosion, which had scattered the guns that were still on board. It is thought that the ship was the *Mathias* a Dutch prize used by the English at the chain. For drawings and photographs of the discovery, *see* TNA ADM 195/7.
20 BL Kings MS 43.
21 Bray (ed) 1863, 180 – a letter of 26 March 1666 from Evelyn to Pepys.

Chapter 2

1 Barker 2002.
2 *Building New and Architectural Review* 1862 records the demolition of this fort by the Royal and Indian Engineers using gunpowder.
3 Saunders 1985.
4 TNA MPHH 1/25. This 1688 survey shows a 27-gun battery at Howness (Upper Pinam or Folly Point), a battery at Lower Pinam, a 40-gun battery on Bishops Ness, a battery at Oakham Ness and 50 guns in 3 batteries on the Isle of Grain.
5 Longmate 1991, 103.
6 TNA PC 1/2/85.
7 TNA ADM 140/3, MR 1/357 and MFC 1/85/5 and 8.
8 TNA MFC 1/85.
9 In The National Archives.
10 Now the Command House public house.
11 BL Maps KingsTop 16.42.
12 Defoe 1824, 20–1, 24.
13 Shrubsole and Denne 1772, 268 fn gives a date of 1695, but research by Ben Levick confirms 1699 for the deed of sale of the land on which it stood.
14 Ben Levick pers comm.
15 TNA MPHH 1/50.
16 Parliament was generally against barrack building, thinking that a standing army might be used to try to restore absolute monarchy. It preferred to billet troops in inns amongst the general population.

Chapter 3

1 *Gentleman's Monthly Intelligencer* **22**, 1753, 104.
2 TNA WO 55/356.
3 Both documents exist. The estimate is BL Lansdowne 660, and the plans are TNA MR 1/358.
4 TNA T 1/419/45 indicates that 86 houses were pulled down in January 1756, leaving about another 40 standing. These were also later demolished.

Archaeological remains of these 126 houses may exist within the car park area of Fort Amherst (Keith Gulvin pers comm).
5 *See also* BL Add MS 15532 as a bound volume of maps for various locations showing troop encampments.
6 Cormack and Jones (eds) 2001.
7 TNA WO 55.
8 TNA WO 55/276. Writing in 1780, Debbieg later increased this figure to £17,000.
9 The image may also show burial mounds under antiquarian investigation.

Chapter 4

1 TNA WO 30/49 is a 1756 return of available space in inns for billeting, and for Rochester it records 357 beds and stabling for 635 horses. TNA PC 1/8/57 is a 1767 petition to the king by the innkeepers of Chatham and Brompton to be excused the quartering upon each of them of between 6 and 12 marines.
2 TNA WO 55/357.
3 From the Orders in Council by the Privy Council 10 February 1758.
4 TNA WO 55/276.
5 TNA MPF 1/349 drawings nos 2–5 (no. 1 appears to be missing)
6 A further proposal drawing in the National Army Museum collection confirms the cut and fill operation needed to build on this sloping site.
7 Not allowing for any wives or children.
8 This is also the design seen in drawings under reference TNA ADM 140/120.
9 Soldiers were supplied with coal for heat and with candles for light.
10 Reitzel (ed) 1947.
11 Cobbett 1829, letter 44.
12 Medway Archives DE0022.
13 From the 1816 warrant appointing a civilian comptroller to the barracks department, TNA T 1/3436.
14 Haythornthwaite 1994, 126.
15 Militia were part of the solution to a shortage of recruits for the army. Each county was responsible for raising a regiment, if necessary by ballot of adult males, and this could be called to arms and used on home service so as to release regular troops for overseas duty.

16 *Weekly Chronicle Chatham* August 1759 reported that 'the Surrey militia are now very expert in performing all parts of their exercise and evolutions; the regiment being 10 companies. Those fit for grenadiers are picked out and accoutred with caps.'

17 Medway Archives DE0022.

18 BL India Select Office Papers, papers collected by Fry.

19 BL India Select Office Papers, papers collected by Fry. This was advice previously issued by General James Wolfe to his troops, and was of particular relevance to the Chatham Lines as a fortification that could have come under attack.

20 Hill House had become a pay office, but by 1762 was surplus to the Navy Board's needs and was leased out.

21 TNA ADM 106/897. The Land Wall served the dockyard but was also the public highway to the church and Brompton. In 1738 the Navy Board outraged local opinion by an unsuccessful attempt to recover their investment in the repair of the carriageway by making it a toll road.

22 The *London Gazette* contains the adverts for contractors to deal with the navy to construct the barracks – in 1777 for construction works, in 1778 for paving and in 1780 for carpentry.

23 It was thought that construction of the marines barracks possibly led to the demolition of Hill House, but there is evidence that it was still standing after the barracks were built. In 1783, a bloody affray took place in the Hill House public house between Hessian troops and the Royal Marines with swords and bayonets drawn (*Universal Magazine* 1784).

24 TNA ADM 140/120.

25 TNA WO 12/12295.

26 Serial enlistment and then desertion in order to obtain the enlistment bounty were not unknown.

27 Reitzel (ed) 1947.

28 TNA WO 12/12300.

Chapter 5

1 TNA ADM 7/660.

2 Defoe 1762, 142.

3 TNA WO 55/276.

4 TNA T 1/408/300–302.

5 TNA WO 55/365.

6 From 1777 to 1784 Debbieg was the senior engineer responsible for many works in southern England, including defence of public buildings in London during the Gordon Riots of 1780. In 1779 he built the pontoon bridge at Gravesend to connect with Tilbury Fort and designed the Royal Engineers pontoon that remained in service until another great military engineer, Pasley, came forward with an alternative after 1812.

7 TNA WO 55/374.

8 The 1779 proposal was for a fort near Chatham Hill and not the later site of Fort Pitt.

9 TNA WO 396/7 is an 1859 report by the Chief Draughtsman of the War Office to establish how and when the Ordnance Board acquired land for its fortifications. That for Chatham shows this 1782 acquisition of land north of the then lines at Gillingham, an extension of the field of fire and the south hill above Chatham.

10 RE Museum and Library, letter books.

11 RE Museum and Library, letter books.

12 RE Museum and Library, letter books. Debbieg stated that a further magazine would be required at the north end of the lines, but this was not built at this date.

13 The 1786 plan (Fig 5.3) shows a square redoubt at the northern termination of the lines where these meet the dockyard. In the 1806 plan (TNA MR 1/815) this is shown as an 'old' redoubt and with water-filled ditches.

14 RE Museum and Library, letter books.

15 RE Museum and Library, letter books.

16 *The Parliamentary History of England from the earliest period to the year 1803*, **22**, Period 26th March 1781 to 7th May 1782, p 652 (London: T C Hansard).

17 The Chatham Lines proposed in 1708 by Talbot Edwards had been conceived as earthworks to defend the dockyard, not to withstand a major siege.

18 *Twelfth report of the Commissioners appointed to examine, take and state the public accounts of the Kingdom*, 1784.

19 RE Museum and Library, letter books.

20 RE Museum and Library, letter books.

21 TNA WO 30/60.

22 TNA WO 30/60.

23 TNA MPHH 1/703 are 1780 maps signed by Debbeig to show the Greater Thames estuary with troop positions marked where an invasion might be broken up.

24 TNA WO 30/60.

25 *The European Magazine and London Review* **16**, 1789, 140.

26 *Parliamentary Register of The History of the Proceedings and Debates of the House of Commons*, **19**, 1786.

27 These were some of the 8 million bricks delivered under contract to the Ordnance Board at Chatham between 1781 and 1783 by William Adam, for which he was paid 1 guinea per 1,000 bricks and 3s for transport.

Chapter 6

1 These costs are derived from figures quoted in TNA WO 55/767, but even then do not reflect the full cost of the works carried out. Bills payable to private contractors were presented at the Tower of London direct to the Ordnance Board. These costs are not included, but were substantial.

2 The British made preparations to drive all cattle and horses inland from the invasion site to hinder French progress.

3 O'Meara 1822, 349.

4 On the announcement of invasion, it was intended to defend London by hastily executed fieldworks and also to abandon the capital and continue resistance from the Midlands should things not go well.

5 Burnham and McGuigan 2010, 2.

6 Corr 8597 in *Correspondance de Napoleon 1er publié par ordre de l'empereur Napoleon III* vol **X**, 1857 (Paris).

7 George 1899, 13.

8 Land was identified for this project and proposal drawings made. TNA WO 55/767 contains references to the Royal Engineers being asked to propose fortifications for its defence. MacDougall (2000) is an article on this proposal.

9 TNA WO 30/57.

10 TNA WO 30/57.

11 TNA WO 55/1563/2.

12 TNA WO 55/767 and WO 30/57; letters passed by coach from Chatham to London and received a reply the next day.

13 TNA WO 55/767.

14 TNA WO 103/1.

15 TNA WO 103/1.

16 TNA WO 55/767.

17 TNA WO 55/767.

18 TNA WO 55/767. In 1802 the entire Corps of Royal Engineers consisted of fewer than 100 officers with responsibility for all Ordnance Board work at fortifications home and abroad.

19 TNA WO 55/767.

20 TNA WO 55/767.

21 TNA WO 55/767.

22 TNA WO 55/767.

23 TNA WO 55/767.

24 TNA WO 55/767.

25 The list is in Whitworth's papers in the Kent County Council Archives at Maidstone.

26 By 1815, and with the completion of a massive programme of new fortifications at Chatham, there were at least 220 guns mounted for its defence. Their locations are recorded in TNA WO 55/1750.

Chapter 7

1 TNA MR 815, Board of Ordnance Survey 1806.

2 Archaeological evaluation at Lower Upnor Ordnance Depot has identified a brick kiln that is most probably part of the massive brickmaking operation at Chatham.

3 Shortages were experienced at harvest time when the horses were needed elsewhere.

4 TNA WO 55/767.

5 TNA WO 30/78.

6 A boat basin proposed in the hornwork on an 1804 map, BL Add MS 11643, was not implemented, but the ditches here were wet.

7 *Aide Memoire to the Military Sciences*, 1847–9 (London: John Weale).

8 Board of Ordnance surveys show that this was called the exercising ground for use by men and horses and that there were gated routes leading to it.

9 *The Times* on 30 December 1874 recorded how the drawbridge had become a nuisance due to increased traffic and that convict labour was used to create a wider replacement bridge, taking land from the SME to do so.

10 An English Heritage archaeological survey of this part of the Chatham Lines is forthcoming.

11 Archaeological evaluation at Amherst Hill has confirmed the survival of part of the glacis for the defences.

12 TNA WO 55/2920, Board of Ordnance Survey 1851.

13 *The Times* records that the draw or drop bridges were replaced by fixed bridges in 1867. That at the Gunwharf was widened in the late 19th century with the introduction of trams.

14 TNA WO 55/767 contains a letter from Twiss that refers to the newly erected hospital. An 1803 description of it explains that it was on the high ground for the state of the air and that it was an H-plan building with windows high in the walls that let in only a little light.

15 TNA WO 55/767.

16 TNA WO 55/767.

17 Medway Archives has a sequence of photographs that show these barracks with their massive construction being demolished after World War II. Parts survive today beneath modern buildings.

18 This tower was raised over the main well of the fort from which water could be drawn by an engine worked by horses.

19 English Heritage Research Department Report 5-2008 'Fort Pitt, Chatham – An earthwork analysis of Jackson recreation ground' (unpublished report, 2008).

20 Dupin 1822a, 334.

21 The 1806 plan (TNA MR 1/815) records a guardhouse but no bridge or road over the ditch at the present sallyport. At this date the public road crossed through the lines between Prince Henry's and Prince Edward's bastions. The sallyport guardhouse may thus have been the product of a decision to create an additional road through the lines at a later date.

22 This is sometimes claimed as a corruption of the name Mortella.

23 TNA WO 55/973.

24 TNA WO 55/767.

25 TNA WO 55/767.

26 TNA WO 55/767.

27 BL Add MS 11643.

28 The Medway was a busy commercial river and a naval anchorage, so the bridge cannot have been permanently *in situ*.

29 TNA WO 55/767.

30 TNA WO 55/767.

31 Pattison (2002) describes the Fort Clarence site.

32 Dupin 1822a, 335–6. Dupin's reference to the opposite bank of the river is a rare mention of batteries on the Strood bank of the Medway. He realised that a determined enemy who could force their way to this side of the river would have been free to bombard the dockyard with relative impunity.

Chapter 8

1 *The European Magazine and London Review* **50**, 1806, 410.

2 TNA WO 55/767 contains an anonymous letter signed by 'A mechanic' calling on the Ordnance Board to hold an inquiry and suggesting that the foremen of the carpenters held the answer to what went wrong.

3 TNA ADM 160/11.

4 These arches are based on a parabola and not a circle, and TNA 55/767 records the results of experiments made by D'Arcy to establish the benefits of the catenary system.

5 TNA ADM 160/12.

6 TNA WO 55/767.

7 TNA WO 55/767.

8 TNA WO 55/767 lists 100 walnut trees, 300 alder seedlings and 5,000 red willows for D'Arcy to plant.

9 TNA WO 55/973.

10 TNA MR 815 Board of Ordnance Survey 1806.

11 TNA WO 55/767.

12 Dupin 1822a, 277–9.

13 The 1215 siege that brought down part of the keep at Rochester castle is a Medway example of this.

14 Sapping is derived from the Italian for a hoe or zappa.

15 Moore was the colonel of the 52nd regiment, and in January 1803 its two battalions were divided at Chatham. The 2nd became the 96th regiment and the 1st continued as the 52nd but became light infantry. For this new role only the fittest men were selected.

16 Oman (1913) states that there were around 30 Royal Engineer officers and perhaps only 34 Royal Military Artificers in the Peninsula *c* 1810. There were also some Royal Staff Corps members.

17 Wellington 1838, 601.

18 Porter 1889, 169.

19 The historic background to the formation of the Chatham establishment and the service of the Royal Engineers in the Peninsular war is described in Thompson 2009.

20 TNA WO 55/965.

21 1818 Standing Orders of the Royal Engineers Establishment.

22 TNA WO 55/965.

23 TNA WO 55/965.

24 TNA WO 55/965.

25 TNA WO 55/965.

26 TNA WO 55/768.

Chapter 9

1 It was less easy for a recruit to desert from an island, and Chatham was considered too close to London, where deserters could lose themselves in the general populace.

2 TNA WO 55/767 has correspondence with Lewis Wyatt.

3 TNA MFQ 1/1315.

4 Dupin 1822b, 115.

5 The original barracks were like separate houses and had individual messes.

6 TNA MR 815 Board of Ordnance survey 1806 shows stabling for 530 horses on land west of the Duke of Cumberland's bastion that included stabling for sick horses and gunner driver barracks.

7 TNA WO 55/767.

8 TNA WO 55/767. This could refer to the concealed gun chambers at the barrier ditch, but seems unlikely. The term 'great ditch' is applicable to the Lower Lines.

9 TNA WO 55/767. Prisoners of war continued to be held on prison hulks in the river.

10 TNA WO 55/3071.

11 TNA WO 49/247.

12 TNA WO 55/767.

13 Soldiers could supplement their rations by growing food.

14 TNA PC 1/3580.

15 Hasted 1798, 192.

16 BL Add MS 11643 provides a good plan.

17 Hasted 1798, 192.

18 Jefferys 1801. There were earlier and destructive fires, such as in 1774, which was put out by using small beer from the nearby Best brewery.

19 A further major fire occurred in 1820, again doing much damage to largely timber-built houses. In 1845 the roles were reversed when the Joiners Shop at the dockyard caught fire at 2 am. The garrison troops, dockyard labour force, townspeople and fire engines raced to the scene to extinguish it.

20 Census figures from *Parliamentary Papers* **53**. NB the revision of Chatham boundaries introduces a discrepancy over the 1801 figure stated in the text.

21 TNA WO 55/767.

Chapter 10

1 At this period the *United Service Journal* provides a record of which regiments were at the various stations of the British army. For 1840, 26 regiments on foreign service were using Chatham as their home depot, 24 regiments were in India, 1 in the West Indies, 4 in New South Wales (Australia) and 1 in Van Diemens Land (Tasmania).

2 Brompton barracks were occupied by troops of the East India Company awaiting transfer to India.

3 MacMullen 1846, 20.

4 A canteen was operated for profit by a canteen master who had paid the Barracks Department a fee for the privilege .

5 MacMullen 1846, 22–3.

6 MacMullen 1846, 24.

7 MacMullen 1846, 27–8.

8 MacMullen 1846, 28–9.

9 *Allen's Indian Mail* 13 August 1846, 513.

10 The only major new building outside the dockyard was the Melville naval hospital (since demolished) that opened in 1828.

11 There was no naval hospital at Chatham before 1828, as hulks would have served that purpose. In 1828 Melville hospital was built close to the main gate of the dockyard and was entirely separate from the hospitals serving army and Ordnance Board troops. It was replaced in 1905 by a new naval hospital and was demolished in the 1960s.

12 This figure excluded any sailors present in the dockyard and the civilian employees of that site. In 1841, 3 prison hulks (*Fortitude*, *Euryalus* and *Wye*) contained a further 59 wardens and their families and 957 civilian prisoners.

13 TNA WO44/565.

14 Stratton 1851, 278–9.

15 Stratton 1851, 279.

16 Stratton's report recorded that due to overcrowding at their own barracks, 150 marines were sleeping at the Brompton barracks. There men suffered no fatalities, and the Brompton barracks had only two cholera cases.

17 TNA WO 55/2920.

18 Stratton 1851, 255.

19 Dupin 1822a, 96–7, 99–104.

20 Cement became a major industry in the Medway area during the 19th century.

21 Pasley's observatory was removed by later improvements at the Brompton barracks. TNA WO 78/3179 is the design for a new observatory on the Inner Lines at Chatham 1879–83.

22 Founded 1741.

23 TNA WO 55/2458 is a plan showing 'works thrown up in the progress of field instruction and crater of a mine' near the Duke of Cumberland's bastion.

24 TNA WO 55/771.

25 Reid 1838, 8.

26 Lithograph by Major-General Sir Joshua Jebb in the RE Museum and Library.

27 This area also contained the small hamlet of Tom All Alones, which pre-dated the Chatham Lines and was associated with a recluse who had no knowledge that his home would one day be part of such a great garrison.

28 *See also* BL 10368.e.5(12) (1837), 10368.e.4(17) (1839), 10368.e.4(19) (1841).

29 TNA WO 44/124.

30 Reid 1838, 8–9.

31 *Illustrated London News* 28 July 1849, 63.

32 *Annual Register* 1850, 76–7.

33 Many of these are held by the RE Museum and Library.

34 *Papers on subjects connected with the duties of the Corps of Royal Engineers* **4**, 1855.

35 Penrice 1845, 167.

36 Figures from Tucker (2000).

37 Stratton 1851, 261–2.

38 Stratton 1851, 259.

39 Stratton 1851, 260–1.

40 *Tait's Edinburgh Magazine* **1**, 1834, 711.

Chapter 11

1 *The Parliamentary Debates from 1803 to the present time* **23**, from a debate on the Ordnance Supplementary Estimates. Calcraft was Secretary to the Treasury.

2 Despite this clear recommendation, these barracks continued in use until the 1960s.

3 *Third report from the select committee on the army before Sebastopol*, 1855.

4 *Army sanitary administration and its reform under the late Lord Herbert*, June 1862.

5 *British and Foreign Medical Review* **15**, 1839, 211.

6 This reflects the high number of Irish in the British army.

7 *Accounts and papers of the House of Commons*, 1858, section XII: Medical and Surgical History of the British Army which served in Turkey and the Crimea during the war against Russia in the years 1854–55–56.

8 This also included a lunatic asylum.

9 The Chatham hulks are discussed in Gulvin 2010.

10 Dupin 1818, 413–14.

11 TNA WO 54/516 lists six floating magazines at Upnor.

12 The new magazine was known at Upnor as the Torpedo Sheds. The two magazines were joined together by the construction of an empty case store in 1893.

13 The explosion was heard at Chatham dockyard where windows and doors were forced open.

14 Later demolished to make way for the fort of *c* 1860.

15 Hans Busk directed attention to this in his 1859 publication *The Navies of the World* (p 181) as part of a campaign to prevent the Royal Navy falling behind.

16 TNA ADM 1/5838.

17 Only one new slip was eventually provided – No. 8 Slip.

18 TNA ADM 214/48 contains a report on how all land for dockyards at Chatham was acquired and describes the nature of the marshes now reclaimed.

19 TNA ADM 195/7.

20 Two of three of these large structures, the Boiler Shop and No. 8 Machine Shop, survive. The third example known as the PROM EW building was the same size as the Boiler Shop but was demolished in the 1990s after a public inquiry.

21 It was construction of the naval barracks after 1898 that destroyed the St Mary's hornwork that terminated the Lower Lines.

Chapter 12

1 *Report of the commissioners appointed to consider the best mode of re-organising the system for training officers for the scientific corps together with an account of foreign and other military education*, 1857.

2 The training of the Royal Engineers and their contribution to civil engineering and architecture for dockyards, prisons, railways and other projects are discussed in Weiler 1987.

3 A narrow gauge railway was used from before 1879 to move material around the site for use in major fieldworks. Remains of it are visible where it once crossed the Lower Lines.

4 A design for the sand-modelling shed and other instructional buildings, dated 1878, is held at the English Heritage Archive in Swindon .

5 This was the successor to the Committee at the Tower of London that was established by royal warrant in 1782 so that four eminent engineers could assist the Chief Engineer of the Ordnance Board.

6 Head 1869, 108.

7 Head 1869, 74.

8   Head refers to 806 guns firing 15 million rounds in the attack on Sevastapol.

9   Many of the photographs have been used in this publication.

10 See reports in *The Times* 1 and 3 March 1862.

11 The Drummond light was used in the siege exercises of September 1867 – see *The Times* 2 September 1867.

12 Rare physical evidence of two experimental searchlight emplacements as variations on the see-saw principle dating from the 1890s has been revealed as part of the Lower Lines park.

13 TNA WO 78/4415.

14 Gerald Napier (2005) describes how the Weinling family were persuaded to move to Chatham as they had the specialist skills for balloon manufacture.

15 *The Times* (23 December 1875) reported experimentation at Chatham Lines with a parakite capable of lifting a man aloft for observation purposes.

16 *The Times* 22 January 1861.

17 *The Times* 23 January 1861.

18 *Report of the Parliamentary Commission into Military Education* 1869, 47.

19 The *Royal Engineers Journal* is the successor publication.

20 Several drawings for this house and similar are held at the English Heritage Archive in Swindon.

21 *Illustrated London News* 18 June 1864.

22 *Illustrated London News* 18 June 1864.

23 Steam sappers or traction engines were also used to move the siege guns.

24 RE Museum and Library, SME Chatham Siege Operations and Mining Practice 1877.

25 Brown 1952, chapter 1.

Chapter 13

1   No such blocks now survive, but compare the roof form in Fig 13.2 with that in Fig 4.3, or with the one 1757 block that still remains.

2   Douglas Galton was also responsible for the Herbert Hospital at Woolwich.

3   The drawings for these quarters are held at the EH Archive in Swindon, and the 42 rooms appear to indicate that these quarters were occupied by the married men from St Mary's casemates.

4   The museum was to move one more time to the former electrical school where it remains.

5   *Red, White, and Blue; Sketches of Military Life* vol **1**, 1862, 126.

6   TNA WO 78/3049.

7   TNA WO 32/6079.

8   The cost of the Institute is stated to be £5,000, to which the War Department contributed £2,000. Florence Nightingale gave £75 and the officers of Fort Pitt hospital £100. The rest was raised by contributions from the public and the soldiers.

9   *Red, White and Blue; Sketches of Military Life*, vol **3**, 1862, 67.

10 TNA WO 32/6212.

11 Reports in *The Times* on 18 and 31 October 1856 of the military sports days at Chatham suggested that this was a new experiment. The *United Services Magazine* **82**, 1856, 464, reported the day more lightheartedly, including the 'Veterans Scramble', a race of 100 yards for the injured of the Crimean War that attracted 6 entrants, some on crutches. The 'Lilliputian Handicap' was a race for the drummer boys and buglers.

12 *United Services Magazine* **171**, 1869, p 129, recorded that it was laid out under a supervising committee of officers that took the advice of a Mr Menzies, who was the Deputy Surveyor for Windsor Park.

13 *Our Plague Spot* 1859.

14 4,500 sq m is c 60% of the area of an international football pitch.

15 It also contained 24 dwellings and various outbuildings.

16 The Chatham lock hospital is described in *The Lancet* 19 February 1870.

17 Report to the Association for Promoting the Extension of the Contagious Diseases Act, 1868, p 35.

18 The rifle ranges at Chatham on St Mary's island had been lost to the dockyard extension.

19 The first Act was in 1864, followed by others in 1867 and 1869, when 17 named locations had been brought within the terms of the legislation.

20 *The Times* 1 May 1857.

21 Colonel Elers Napier in an account of his military service (1856, 255) gave a gruesome description of a flogging at Chatham where the use of a left-handed drummer resulted in more laceration than usual to the unfortunate victim. Traditionally, it was the drummers who applied the lash.

22 *The Penny Illustrated Paper* 8 October 1864.

23 House of Commons Papers **11**, Reports from committees 1857–58 – Select Committee on the exemption from rates of public establishments, 27. One of the committee was Sir Frederick Smith, the MP for Chatham and a former Director of the Royal Engineer Establishment.

24 Stratton 1851, 261–2.

25 *The Otago Witness* 28 October 1882.

Chapter 14

1   TNA WO 78/2933 has plans and photographs.

2   This replaced two smaller structures, one of which was constructed before 1851.

3   Shell filling continued to take place at Upnor in the 1906 shell-filling sheds, making use of the 1904 filled shell store.

4   Defence Committee meeting 22 March 1882, Memorandum on the proposed demolition of a portion of the Chatham Lines.

5   Borstal was established as a prison in 1870 and appears to have been a new construction for convicts working on the ring forts. It was a more convenient location than the prison at Chatham whose convicts worked on the dockyard. Around 1902 Borstal became an experimental establishment for juvenile offenders, and its name was subsequently applied to many of the prisons.

6   Pers comm Victor Smith, who also supplied plans.

7   TNA WO 33/942.

8   TNA WO 147/60.

9   TNA WO 30/43.

10 TNA WO 33/575.

11 TNA WO 78/4415 is an 1899 drawing of the Brennan torpedo factory.

12 Behind St George's chapel there is a monument to the French prisoners of war from the Napoleonic period who died whilst incarcerated on the hulks. They were first buried in St Mary's marsh, but their remains were exhumed and moved to this spot when the dockyard extension was built.

13 TNA ADM 214/48.

14 The most prominent surviving buildings are the clock and laundry towers.

15 There were 28 Royal Engineer Tunnelling Companies (25 British, 3 Australian, 3 Canadian and 1 from New Zealand). In 1916 up to 24, 000 men were working underground.

16 Barton *et al* (2004) provide a fascinating account of their contribution, and Sebastian Faulks's novel *Birdsong* (1993) gives a harrowing fictional account of war underground.

17 Royal Engineers also made a considerable contribution to the fighting at Gallipoli through mining.

18 Evidence for the foundations of large huts found on Black Lion Field, Gillingham, may relate to this incident.

19 TNA WO 78/4400.

20 This land is now the military sports ground, and episodes of subsidence are attributable to the collapse of the chambers of the dugout that were held up by timbers.

Chapter 15

1 An earlier proposal was to name the barracks after Major General R C Maxwell who had commanded the Thames and Medway defences in 1914. He is recognised in the name Maxwell Road.

2 These are a variation upon the Sandhurst block design for barracks adopted as a standard type in the late 1930s.

3 This land no longer contained the magazine as it had been used for naval detention barracks in conjunction with HMS *Pembroke*.

4 Though not now routinely accessible, this complex survives with a high degree of integrity, including signage, graffiti and a casualty dressing station.

5 The air-raid shelter arrangements for this hospital are not yet understood.

6 The Nore command bunker did not become known as HMS *Wildfire* until after the Second World War, when it assumed a Cold War function in the nuclear age. The Subterranea Britannica website holds a well-illustrated report on the bunker, which is now derelict and not accessible.

7 Medway Archives Rochester_City_Council 1227_1974/MP_WW_06.

8 TNA WO 166/3655.

9 TNA WO 199/627.

10 This road was named after the royal prince who trained as a Royal Engineer at Chatham in the late 19th century.

11 This use is presented at the fort as a reconstructed incident room available for use by school parties.

12 Some bombs fell on the Brompton barracks, in the dockyard and around the Medway towns.

13 Dickson 1901, 8.

14 There was a further military cemetery behind the Brook Theatre at Chatham in the shadow of Belvedere battery of Fort Amherst. This was reportedly cleared of burials in the late 20th century and is now a car park.

15 Gordon was an alumnus of the SME and met his death at Khartoum in 1884.

16 *Allen's Indian Mail* 30 December 1846, 100.

17 Dickson 1901, 15.

18 The *North British Review* **1**, March 1869, 4. Sobraon was the decisive battle of the 1846 First Anglo-Sikh war in India. Chilianwala was a 3-day battle in 1849 as part of the Second Sikh War and generally regarded as a Sikh victory. Meeane (Miani) was the British victory in 1843 by which Sindh was added to British India.

GLOSSARY

AA anti-aircraft as in gun.

abbatis an obstacle formed by felling whole trees and placed on the outer edge of the ditch of a field fortification.

barbette breastwork of a battery sufficiently low so that guns can fire over the top of it without the need for embrasures.

bastion a projection out from the general line of a fortress in order that the defenders can achieve flanking fire on the ground to the front.

battalion a military unit, of between 600 and 1,500 soldiers today, made up of several companies and with battalions grouped to form regiments or brigades.

battery a place where artillery (guns) are mounted.

berm a strip of flat ground between the base of the rampart and the top edge of the ditch.

billeting the quartering of military troops at public expense, most commonly in inns but sometimes upon private households.

blockhouse a small fortification serving as a post for a small garrison.

breastwork another term for a parapet.

camouflets an underground explosion, often in a countermine, designed to not break the ground at the surface.

canteen an establishment within barracks where soldiers could buy alcohol or food from a supplier who had purchased from the military authority the right to sell such items.

caponier either a covered communication allowing protected access across a ditch to an outwork or a casemated projection into a ditch.

carronade a large calibre, short-range cannon – much used by the navy and named after the Carron ironworks as its original place of manufacture.

cartridge the container, often a material bag, for black powder loaded into a gun barrel behind the projectile before it is fired.

casemate a bombproof vaulted structure normally provided within the ramparts to accommodate a gun and/or to provide troop accommodation.

cavalier a work in the interior of a fort that is raised in height so as to fire over the main parapet without interfering with the fire of the latter.

chevaux de frise an improvised obstacle formed out of a wooden frame with many long projecting iron spikes or spears/sword blades.

citadel a fortification protecting a town, or the strongest part of a fortification, often serving as a last place of refuge should the outer defences be overrun.

communication a designed means by which access could be gained from one place to another. In the Chatham context it was used to describe passage over the River Medway by means of a pre-positioned pontoon bridge.

countermine an underground work designed as part of a fortification to allow the detection and interception of siege tunnels or mines.

counterscarp the external or outermost slope or revetment of a ditch.

coup de main literally, a 'blow of the hand', used to describe a swift attack that relies on speed and surprise to achieve its objective in a single episode.

couvre porte literally, a 'covered gate', describing a defended gate through a fortification, which was a point of weakness in need of additional defences.

covered way a continuous communication on the outer edge of the ditch that was protected from enemy fire by a parapet (*see* glacis).

curtain a length of rampart forming part of a fortification, often between two bastions.

DEL Defence Electric Light – the early term for a searchlight.

demi-bastion literally, a 'half bastion', describing right- and left-hand versions and commonly found in pairs to make a hornwork, as in the Lower Lines.

dragon's teeth pyramidal concrete obstacles,

square in plan, placed in groups during World War II to impede tanks and mechanised infantry.

dugout an underground cavity excavated for the protection of troops from shellfire with a roof usually supported on timber props. Much used in World War I.

embrasure an opening through a rampart or a wall to enable a gun to be fired.

enfilade fire coming from the flanks.

entrenchment (or intrenchment) a type of fortification formed by digging trenches.

escalade an assault on a fortress using scaling ladders that were carried by the attackers to surmount the ramparts and ditches.

evolutions a term for military exercises, either for an individual's use of a musket or for the movement of a body of soldiers.

fascine a bundle of brushwood often used in improvised field or siege works.

fausse braie a low subsidiary rampart built forward of, parallel with and below the main rampart of a fortification.

field of fire the land to the front of a fortification that came within range of its guns and which was deliberately kept open as ground that an attacker would have to cross.

fire barn another term used in place of magazine to describe a storage facility for explosives or combustibles.

firestep a low platform running behind and parallel with a parapet, the use of which enabled infantry fire.

fraise wooden stakes projecting horizontally into a ditch from the front of a rampart (*see* palisade).

gabion normally a wickerwork basket filled with earth and used in fieldworks and/or siege works to create protection for troops. Latterly they were made of metal.

glacis the area outside the ditch of a fortification shaped as a gentle slope running away from the covered way and kept clear of obstructions. It created a clear view for the defenders, but prevented an easy sight of the ditch and rampart by an attacker.

gorge the area to the rear of a fortification (either open or closed), such as the open back of a bastion.

Great Lines the land outside the fortifications, the former field of fire.

Gunwharf the term applied to the Ordnance Board's facility, incorporating wharfage, for the manufacture and storage of arms.

hornwork a detached work beyond the main ditch, differentiated by its shape from a ravelin. Normally consists of two demi-bastions linked by a length of curtain.

howitzer a short-barrelled cannon used for high-angle fire.

invalid a soldier injured in the course of his duties or made unfit by disease and sent for assessment to an Invalid Depot, either for discharge or retention on limited home service.

laboratory the building where explosive charges were prepared, eg cartridges, shells or grenades filled with explosive mixture.

lines the collective name given to continuous lengths of rampart and ditch intended to fortify a specific location (sometimes referred to as an entrenchment). Can also be used to describe a system of separate fortified positions intended to achieve the same end, as in the Lines of Torres Vedras.

lock hospital a hospital where women detained under the Contagious Diseases Act could be forcibly held and treated for STDs.

loop holed describes a structure with slits or openings through which guns might be fired.

machicolation a projection from the top of a wall with openings in it so that fire could be brought directly down on attackers at the base of the wall.

magazine a structure within a fortification or an ordnance depot, used for the safe storage of explosive material, ie powder for weapons. A distinction can be drawn between the main storage magazines and 'expense' magazines located close to the guns, from which powder would be taken for instant use.

mantlet a protective screen used to protect diggers from gunfire at the head of a sap.

Martello tower a brick-built gun tower built *c* 1805 as part of a chain of gun positions defending the invasion beaches of the south coast.

merlon the solid part of a parapet between two embrasures.

militia a form of reserve force for the army based on county regiments that did limited peacetime training but could be embodied for home service in times of war.

mine an excavation (often a tunnel) dug under a fortification for the purpose of breaching it by undermining or by the use of explosives. The term more recently describes an explosive device laid in a minefield.

miners the men responsible for mining, who were sometimes civilian miners drafted in for military works.

mortar a short form of cannon used for throwing a shell or bomb.

ordnance military materials including weapons of all sizes, ammunition and powder, but frequently meaning artillery. Relates to the branch of an army responsible for procuring, storing and issuing military material.

palisade an obstacle in ditches made of close-set vertical pointed wooden stakes (*see* fraise).

parallels the siege trenches dug by an attacker to approach a fortification under some measure of protection. These run parallel to the main line of the fortification.

parapet the wall of earth or masonry for the protection of the troops situated on the foremost edge of the rampart.

picquet (or picket) the soldiers placed forward of a position to warn against an enemy advance.

pontoon a barge-like purpose-built boat for transporting troops and guns across water; several could be linked together to form a pontoon bridge.

QF quick fire – applied from the late 19th century to types of gun and forms of ammunition with a rapid rate of fire.

rampart the earthworks forming the main part of a fortress, on which the troops and guns are positioned, normally made of earth excavated from the ditch.

ravelin a detached work, normally triangular, built in front of the main line of fortification as an additional defence and usually occurring between bastions.

RBL rifled breech loader – applied to later 19th-century artillery that had a rifled barrel but with the loading of the projectile and the charge in the breech of the gun.

redan a projection from a fortification out towards the field of fire, usually V-shaped and with two sides.

redoubt a small work of fortification capable of independent defence, ie not attached to a main line of fortification but often within such.

revetment the means by which the rampart or the ditch sides are retained, normally by a wall of brick or masonry.

RML rifled muzzle loader – as for RBL, but for artillery which is loaded from the muzzle, ie rammed down the length of the barrel.

sallyport a passage through a rampart to provide access to the ditch so that the defenders could make a counterattack or sortie.

sap a trench used to provide a safe approach to a fortification for its assault – hence the term sapper used as the nickname for a Royal Engineer soldier.

sap roller a large wicker cylinder similar to a gabion but filled with stones or logs and used to protect those digging saps.

scarp the outer slope or revetment of a rampart or the inner slope of a ditch.

sconce a small protective fortification, often in the form of a mound for artillery.

shell an artillery projectile containing an explosive that increases its lethality on impact. Shells are normally fused to control the explosion.

shifting house a structure associated with a magazine or ordnance depot where, for example, barrels of powder could be opened, the contents examined as to condition and then re-packed.

spigot mortar a weapon of World War II much used by the Home Guard to fire a finned bomb a distance of 75–200 yards. Also known as a Blacker Bombard.

spur an arrow-shaped projection from the front of a curtain wall.

tattoo the signal by drum or bugle at night to inform troops to go to their quarters.

tenaille a small low work situated in a ditch of a fort between bastions.

tête de pont a fortified position defending the end of a bridge nearest to the enemy (a bridgehead).

torpedo initially used to describe a fixed underwater charge that could be remotely detonated to destroy shipping (submarine mines). It came to be used to describe a self-propelled explosive device fired at other vessels from a ship or from the shore.

traverse an earthwork designed to prevent enfilade fire along part of a fortification, such as on a rampart or at an entrance. At ordnance depot earthworks, a traverse around buildings was designed to control blast in the event of an accident.

trou de loup an anti-infantry obstacle in advance of a ditch consisting of a deep sloping pit with a sharpened stake in the bottom.

victualling yard the Victualling Board was responsible for provisioning the Royal Navy, and their premises for this role was the victualling yard.

REFERENCES

Adams, S 1990 'New Light on the "Reformation" of Sir John Hawkins: the Ellesmere naval survey of January 1584'. *English Historical Review* **105**, 96–111

Barker, L 2002 *Cockham Wood Fort, Hoo St Werburgh, Kent*. English Heritage Archaeological Investigation Reports AI/20/2002

Barton, P, Doyle, P and Vandewalle, J 2004 *Beneath Flanders Fields: The Tunnellers' War, 1914–18*. Staplehurst: Spellmount

Bray, W (ed) 1863 *Diary and correspondence of John Evelyn, F.R.S. vol 3*. London: Henry G Bohn

Brown W B 1952 *History of the Corps of Royal Engineers, vol 4*. London: Longmans

Burnham, R and McGuigan, R 2010 *The British Army Against Napoleon: Facts, Lists and Trivia, 1805–1815*. Barnsley: Frontline Books

Busk, H 1859 *The Navies of the World*. London: Routledge, Warnes and Routledge

Cobbett, W 1829 *Advice to Young Men, and (incidentally) to Young Women in the Middle and Higher Ranks of Life*. London: Mills, Jowett and Mills

Cormack, A and Jones, A (eds) 2001 *The Journal of Corporal Todd 1745–1762*. London: Sutton Publishing for Army Records Society

Cruden, R P 1843 *The History of the Town of Gravesend in the County of Kent and of the Port of London*. London: William Pickering

Defoe, D 1762 *A Tour Thro' the Whole Island of Great Britain, vol 1*. London: D Browne

Defoe, D 1824 *A Tour Thro' the Whole Island of Great Britain*. London: G Strahan

Dickson, W K 1901 *The Life of Major-General Sir Robert Murdoch Smith, K.C.M.G., Royal Engineers*. Edinburgh and London: William Blackwood & Sons

Douglas, J 1793 *Nenia Britannica*. London

Dupin, C 1818 'Brief account of the first journey in England, in 1816'. *New Monthly Magazine* **10**, 405–14

Dupin, C 1822a *View of the History and Actual State of the Military Force of Great Britain, vol 2*. London: John Murray

Dupin, C 1822b *A Tour Through the Naval and Military Establishments of Great Britain in the years 1816–17–18–19 and 1820*. London: Sir Richard Phillips and Co.

Faulks, S 1993 *Birdsong*. London: Hutchinson

Finch, W C 1929 *The Medway, River and Valley*. London, C W Daniel Co.

George, H B 1899 *Napoleon's Invasion of Russia*. London: T Fisher Unwin

Grose, F 1785 *A Classical Dictionary of the Vulgar Tongue*. London

Gulvin, K R 2010 *The Medway Prison Hulks*. Chatham: L-13

Hasted, E 1798 *The History and Topographical Survey of the County of Kent vol 4* Canterbury: Simmons and Kirkby

Haythornthwaite, P J 1994 *The Armies of Wellington*. London: Brockhampton Press

Head, F 1869 *The Royal Engineer*. London: John Murray

Jefferys, W 1801 *An account of the fire at Chatham which happened on the 30 June 1800, the money collected for the relief of the sufferers, the distribution of the same etc*. Chatham

Longmate, N 1991 *Island Fortress: The Defence of Great Britain 1603–1945*. London: Hutchinson

MacDougall, P 1999 *Chatham Past*. Chichester: Phillimore

MacDougall, P 2000 'The Abortive Plan for Northfleet Naval Dockyard during the Napoleonic Wars'. *Archaeologica Cantiana* **120**, 149–68

Maclaren, A 1862 *A Military System of Gymnastic Exercise for the use of Instructors*. London

MacMullen, J M 1846 *Camp and Barrack-Room; or, the British Army as it is*. London: Chapman and Hall

Morris, J 1983 *The Domesday Book: Kent*. Chichester: Phillimore

Napier, E H D E 1856 *The Linesman; or, Service in the Guards and in the Line during England's long place and little wars, vol 1*. London: George W Hyde

Napier, G 2005 *Follow the Sapper: An illustrated history of the Corps of Royal Engineers*. Chatham: Institution of Royal Engineers

Oman, C 1913 *Wellington's Army 1809–1814*. London: Edward Arnold

O'Meara, B E 1822 *Napoleon in Exile; or, a voice from St Helena, the opinions and reflections of Napoleon on the most important events of his life and government, in his own words, vol 1*, 2 edn. London: W Simpkins and R Marshall

Oppenheim, M (ed) 1914 *The Naval Tracts of Sir William Monson vol 5*. London: Navy Records Society

Page, W (ed) 1926 *The Victoria History of the County of Kent vol 2*. London: St Catherine Press

Pasley, C W 1810 *Essay on the Military Policy and Institutions of the British Empire*. London: Edmund Lloyd

Pasley, C W 1814–17 *Course of instruction; originally composed for the use of the Royal Engineer Establishment*. London

Pasley, C W 1822 *A Course of Elementary Fortification*. London: John Murray

Pasley, C W 1826 *Outline of a course of practical architecture compiled for the Royal Engineers*. Chatham: Royal Engineer Establishment

Pasley, C W 1838 as *Observations on limes, calcareous cements, mortars, stuccos and concrete*. London: J Weale

Pattison, P 2002 *Fort Clarence, Rochester, Kent*. English Heritage Archaeological Investigation Series 40/2002

Penrice, H N 1845 'Journal of the Practical Operations in Mining, carried on under the Glacis in front of the left face of the Ravelin, and the right face of the Duke of Cumberland's Bastion, Chatham Lines, during the months of October and November, 1844, under the direction of Lieutenant-Colonel Sir J.M.F. Smith, Royal Engineers, Director of the Establishment for Field Instruction'. *Papers on Subjects Connected with the Duties of the Corps of the Royal Engineers* **8**, 156–85

Porter, W 1889 *History of the Corps of Royal Engineers, vol 2*. London and New York: Longmans, Green and Co.

Reid, W 1838 'On Intrenchments as Supports in Battle, and on the Necessity of Completing the Military Organisation of the Royal Engineers'. *Papers on Subjects Connected with the Duties of the Corps of Royal Engineers* **2**, 1–18

Reitzel, W (ed) 1947 *The Autobiography of William Cobbett: The Progress of a Plough Boy to a seat in Parliament*. London: Faber

Saunders, A D 1985 *Upnor Castle, Kent*. London: English Heritage

Scott, L F and Hildesley, A 1920 *The Case of Requisition in re a Petition of Right of De Keyser's Royal Hotel Limited*. Oxford: Clarendon Press

Shrubsole, W and Denne, S 1772 *The History and Antiquities of Rochester and its Environs*. Rochester: T Fisher

Simes, T 1781 *A Military Guide for Young Officers*. London

Smithers, A J 1991 *Honourable Conquests – An account of the enduring work of the Royal Engineers throughout the Empire*. London: Leo Cooper

Stratton, T 1851 'History of the Epidemic Cholera in Chatham, Rochester, and Strood, in 1849'. *The Edinburgh Medical and Surgical Journal* **75**, 250–94

Thompson, M S 2009 'The Rise of the Scientific Soldier as seen through the Performance of the Corps of Royal Engineers during the early 19th century'. Unpublished PhD thesis, Univ Sunderland

Tucker, S C 2000 *Handbook of 19th century Naval Warfare*. Stroud: Sutton

Weiler, J M 1987 'Army Architects – the Royal Engineers and the Development of Building Technology in the Nineteenth Century'. Unpublished PhD thesis, Univ York

Wellington, Duke of 1838 *The Dispatches of Field Marshal the Duke of Wellington vol 8*. London: John Murray

INDEX